WOMEN

OF THE BIBLE

A Visual Guide *to* Their Lives, Loves, and Legacy

WOMEN
OF THE BIBLE

A Visual Guide *to* Their Lives, Loves, and Legacy

CAROL SMITH

ELLYN SANNA

RACHAEL PHILLIPS

Print ISBN 978-1-62029-183-2

Key writers for Women of the Bible were Carol Smith, Rachael Phillips, and Ellyn Sanna, with assistance from Jeff Walter and Paul Muckley.

Interior design: Mullerhaus Publishing Arts, Inc., www.Mullerhaus.net

Cover design by BrandNavigation

Published by Barbour Publishing, Inc., P.O. Box 719, Uhrichsville, Ohio 44683
www.barbourbooks.com

Our mission is to publish and distribute inspirational products offering exceptional value and biblical encouragement to the masses.

ecpa Member of the
Evangelical Christian
Publishers Association

Printed in the United States of America.

CONTENTS

Many of the women of the Bible seem like this pair at Jerusalem's Western Wall–veiled, aloof, somewhat mysterious. This book will help bring their lives to light.

Introduction

While the events described in the Bible occurred within a patriarchal social system, the women of the Bible have a strong presence and are remembered for significant, righteous, and courageous actions.

Because of this patriarchal nature of their culture, women do receive lesser ink in the Christian scriptures than do men. In fact, of the almost 1,500 names mentioned in the Bible, fewer than 200 are women's names. Why is this?

First of all, family genealogies were typically recorded based on the men in the family tree rather than the women. A woman was known as the wife of her husband or the mother of her son, as was the case with many tribal cultures. Men were also typically in leadership. Whether this meant political leadership or church leadership, the accounts recorded in the Bible involved more men than women because they were the records of turning-point events in the journeys of people and of the religious community.

As a balance, however, remember that this was a culture for which family was of more importance than any one individual. For each of the male champions described in the Bible, there was a woman (or several), even if unnamed, as part of the picture.

Keep in mind also that throughout history a Jewish mother has held a highly regarded place in the family. In fact, traditional Judaism maintains that a person is a Jew by birth only if his or her mother is a Jew.

Through childbirth Jewish women assured the future of their people.

Sources of Information

The Bible is not a wealthy source of information about the daily lives of ancient women because it was not written for the purpose of recording those kinds of details. The Old Testament documents the history of the Israelite nation, highlighting the public arena in which rulers, judges, politicians, and national champions affected history. The collected writings of the New Testament document the life and death of Jesus, the formation of the early church, letters of instruction, and an apocalyptic prophecy. Neither the Old nor the New Testament were written to record the everyday details of people's lives but to reveal God's plan of salvation for all humankind.

Thus, much of what is known about the everyday goings-on of ancient culture is gleaned from other writings, such as surviving contracts or agreements. But here caution must be used, for ancient contracts were only needed when something was done in an unusual way. To observe an ancient culture in light of only its exceptions would be the equivalent of a future generation finding a contract for an elderly person entering a care facility, then assuming that this was the only way twenty-first-century families dealt with the elderly across the board.

Yet gleaning from historical documents does help to flesh out the world in which these women loved, lived, hoped, and dreamed.

Keep in mind, however, that these were three-dimensional people who dealt with the relational, political, idiosyncratic, and inconsistent complexities of life, just as we do today.

These tablets record the sale of a slave girl for two white horses.

What You'll Find Here

This book attempts to describe the whole scope of life for women in Bible times—both the famous, whose stories we know, and the average, everyday women who have been lost to history.

In Section 1—Women in Bible Times, you'll see how these ancient women faced many of the same issues as those of the twenty-first century, from the seemingly inconsequential (such as hairstyle and makeup) to the more important (such as health, sex, and child rearing). Section 1 also describes the various laws that biblical women lived under.

Section 2—Daily Experiences of Bible Women, provides a composite portrait of an average woman and what she did to survive and thrive in her environment. Section 3—Women's Roles and Jobs, shows the wide range of women's work outside the home, while Section 4—Bible Women and Their Interactions with Men, offers an intriguing glimpse into the male-female relationships of ancient times.

The final two parts of this book are a catalog of actual biblical women. Section 5—The Named Women of the Bible, provides biographical and bibliographic information for every woman identified by name, while Section 6—The Unnamed *Women of the Bible*, describes many of those unnamed women—real and illustrative—who add such flavor to the scriptural account.

We hope you'll find *Women of the Bible* informative, interesting, and inspirational.

CAROL SMITH, RACHAEL PHILLIPS,
AND ELLYN SANNA

Created from one of Adam's ribs, Eve enjoys the earthly paradise of the Garden of Eden in this sixteenth-century painting by Jacopo Bassano.

Women in Bible Times

FROM THE BEGINNING

We've already noted that the Bible's record regarding women features many gaps. The story of biblical men is much fuller and richer than that of their female counterparts, but women are clearly an integral part of God's plan for humanity. Here are some things we know for sure:

- The Bible begins with the idea that both men and women are created in the image of God and that both are responsible for caring for the earth.

So God created man in his own image, in the image of God created he him; male and female created he them. And God blessed them, and God said unto them, Be fruitful, and multiply, and replenish the earth, and subdue it: and have dominion over the fish of the sea, and over the fowl of the air, and over every living thing that moveth upon the earth.

GENESIS 1:27–28 KJV

• In God's covenant with Israel, both men and women were held responsible for their actions.

If there be found among you, within any of thy gates which the LORD thy God giveth thee, man or woman, that hath wrought wickedness in the sight of the LORD thy God, in transgressing his covenant, and hath gone and served other gods, and worshipped them, either the sun, or moon, or any of the host of heaven, which I have not commanded; and it be told thee, and thou hast heard of it, and enquired diligently, and, behold, it be true, and the thing certain, that such abomination is wrought in Israel: Then shalt thou bring forth that man or that woman, which have committed that wicked thing, unto thy gates, even that man or that woman, and shalt stone them with stones, till they die.

DEUTERONOMY 17:2–5 KJV

• In both Jesus' ministry and in the early church, women played a prominent supporting role.

This fifteenth-century painting, The Holy Women, by Hans Memling, portrays Jesus' mother, Mary (in black) along with other women who followed and supported the Lord, grieving after His crucifixion.

[Jesus] went throughout every city and village, preaching and shewing the glad tidings of the kingdom of God: and the twelve were with him, and certain women, which had been healed of evil spirits and infirmities, Mary called Magdalene, out of whom went seven devils, and Joanna the wife of Chuza Herod's steward, and Susanna, and many others, which ministered unto him of their substance.

LUKE 8:1–3 KJV

Though the biblical laws reflect an era and a culture in which women did not have the same rights women enjoy today, the Bible also confirms that God called women into His service. He expected them to answer His call whatever their situation. Some were wealthy, others poor. Some resided in traditional settings, while others lived outside of the norm. Women of the Bible like Rahab, Sarah, Ruth, and Deborah faced life's circumstances and followed God through those circumstances, sometimes regardless of cultural expectations, just as women do today.

SAME WOMEN'S ISSUES?

Most lists of women's issues include familiar concerns: familial, career, victimization, contraception, politics, and health. How different are the issues facing women today from those that faced females of the ancient world?

Family/Children

As important as family and children are to most women today, their value was even greater to the women of early civilization. The goal at that time was populating the earth and building one's family. Women were raised with the understanding that bringing children into the family was their primary contribution. Their family defined them.

Career

Just to survive, premodern stay-at-home moms faced a balancing act between growing their own food, making their own clothes, caring for extended family, tending to farm animals, and trading for what they couldn't make themselves. Children were worked into that mix rather than the other way around. A woman's daily work chores, outside of caring for her children,

The choice wasn't between working and raising children. Women often had to do both at the same time.

could take up to ten hours a day with kids in tow the whole time. Some child care could be provided if there was an older woman (too old to do housework) living in the home. Older children could also provide some child care, but by the time sons and daughters were old enough to watch younger siblings, they were old enough either to participate in the chores or to be married and manage households of their own.

Victimization

While there may have been a great sense of equality between the genders in the earliest of civilizations, by the time humanity was organizing into power structures, the status of women was considered much lower than that of men. Therefore women were left open to more abuse and victimization, with far less recrimination against those who would take advantage of them. The biblical Ruth gleaned in the fields, going behind the men reaping the grain to pick up what was left. Boaz, who would later become her husband, felt the need to warn his workmen not to touch her. A single woman gathering grain would have been easy prey.

Ruth gleans grain while Boaz and his workers look on, in a nineteenth-century woodcut by Gustave Doré.

> So Boaz said to Ruth, "My daughter, listen to me. Don't go and glean in another field and don't go away from here. Stay here with my servant girls. Watch the field where the men are harvesting, and follow along after the girls. I have told the men not to touch you."
>
> RUTH 2:8–9 NIV

Contraception

While ancient women were typically more interested in becoming pregnant than in controlling pregnancies, they did employ a variety of methods for contraception. Nursing a new baby was, as today, often a way to make pregnancy less likely, though, again as today, it was not certain.

Women concocted substances to block the cervix or even to

cause infertility. Some of these—for instance, the Egyptian crocodile dung barrier—can seem bizarre to the modern mind. But in a world in which germs were not yet understood, these may have been ingenious solutions. Another form of vaginal suppository was made from honey and vinegar. The vinegar may have been somewhat effective as a precursor to modern spermicides. There were also suggested practices to inhibit pregnancy; for instance, women were told to squat after sex and sneeze multiple times. There were also concoctions and methods to induce abortions.

Though Deborah is a notable exception, women entered politics in Bible times primarily by their marriages to male leaders. Today, leaders such as Liberian president Ellen Johnson Sirleaf are often elected to office. Sirleaf is the first female to be elected head of an African state, in 2005.

Politics

Except for a few women such as Deborah (the Israelite judge, prophet, and military strategist) and some far-less-than-savory queens and queen mothers, Israelite women did not hold significant political leadership roles. We do, however, have record of women wielding influence in the political arena. Esther was the wife of a Persian king and petitioned him on behalf of her people. Pilate's wife warned him of a dream she had that seemed to influence him to wash his hands of Jesus during Jesus' trial. Bathsheba made requests affecting the kingdom and offered counsel to both her husband, King David, and her son, King Solomon.

And Bathsheba said, Well; I will speak for thee unto the king. Bathsheba therefore went unto king Solomon, to speak unto him for Adonijah. And the king rose up to meet her, and bowed himself unto her, and sat down on his throne, and caused a seat to be set for the king's mother; and she sat on his right hand. Then she said, I desire one small petition of thee; I pray thee, say me not nay. And the king said unto her, Ask on, my mother: for I will not say thee nay.

1 KINGS 2:18–20 KJV

Health

In the ancient world, sickness was often interpreted as God's judgment, and the mystic mixed with the medicinal. Still, there were physicians, even if in the form of healers or midwives, for women to seek out when they had concerns about their health. For the Israelites, the first institutionalized health care was administered by the tabernacle priests. It was to these men that a person would go for some diagnoses—for instance, of leprosy—and for confirmation of a cure or at least effective treatment. Leviticus records some of the responsibilities of the priests regarding health. Of course, as scientific study developed so did women's options for helpful advice and treatment.

THE SAME INTERESTS?

Women we read about in the Bible had unique abilities and interests all their own, yet in many ways they had more limited options than a modern woman has. Nevertheless, these women still shared and kept secrets, helped each other in distress, grieved with their communities, and hoped for their hearts' desires. Today we stereotypically think of women's interests as including relationships, particularly of the opposite gender, clothes, beauty care, and jewelry. What about the women of the Bible?

Relationships, Dating, and Men

Most of a single woman's relationships were among her family and extended family. She didn't go to school, so she didn't have school friends. She did go to the synagogue and might have made friends there. But most likely her closest friendships were with cousins and the children of her parents' closest friends and family.

She didn't date, though she was raised to hope toward marriage. Once married, unless a tragedy struck, she set about raising children and building relationships with the women of her new family and the synagogue she attended. Most often she would be married to someone within her own larger

Jacob, sent by his father Isaac to find a wife among relatives, meets his cousin Rachel watering sheep at a well. He falls in love, they kiss—and Jacob works a total of fourteen years for his uncle for the right to marry Rachel (Genesis 28–29).

clan. So while she would move to a different household, there was the chance that she would live nearby and could still stay in touch with her immediate family.

After a woman in an early civilization married, much of her well-being depended on her husband—who had the power to make her life miserable or wonderful.

Today, women vary widely in terms of how they choose to push back within their marriages to have a voice in decision making and lifestyle of the family. The Bible women would have also varied, but their options were much more limited.

Clothing

For most of the people whose lives are recorded in the pages of the Bible, clothing was simple. Of course, there were the royal and the wealthy, who had many pieces of clothing and accessories and opportunities to show those off. For the working class, however, clothing was simple and minimal. It seems the norm that their wardrobe would increase one cloak a year, as is described for Samuel when his mother visited him with his yearly new coat.

Clothing that was sewn rather than tied or pinned was not common until after the first century AD. Rather a woman's main garment would have a length of cloth wrapped around her body under one arm and tied or perhaps pinned together with a simple pin made of bone or, less often, metal. Her outfit could have also included a mantle or perhaps a sash.

Carved some eight hundred years before Jesus' birth, this ivory plaque shows a well-coiffed woman looking out from a window.

Neither the Old Testament nor the New Testament seems to require women to wear veils covering their faces except in a wedding ceremony. For the most part, that assumption is made because of the story of Tamar in Genesis 38. She put on a veil to impersonate a prostitute and then took off her veil when the ruse was over. Veil or not, however, women probably did wear a head covering, particularly when outside, as did men. Headbands, perhaps made from cloth or metal, held those headdresses in place.

The fabrics most available during Bible times were linen, made from flax or other plants, and wool, made from animal fleece. There was also some cloth made from camel hair or hemp.

Hair and Makeup

In the Bible, God calls His people to a distinctive faith that is revealed from their inner lives, not their outer appearances. The Old Testament prophets decried those who made themselves up on the outside but displeased God on the inside, and certainly Jesus confronted the leadership of His day about the same thing. That is not to say, however, that the women of the Bible were unaware of or opposed to wearing perfumes and makeup, as Ruth 3:3 and Esther 2:12 indicate. In Peter's admonition to wives, he reminds them their beauty should come from the inside rather than the outside, but he didn't say they shouldn't be outwardly beautiful as well.

As early as 4000 BC, cosmetics were used in Egypt in the form of eye paint and cheek blush as well as perfumes and oils for skin and hair. In some cases the eye paint was supposed to help with eyesight or in healing. Oils and

AVON CALLING

Samuel described a powerful king taking the people's daughters to be perfumers (see 1 Samuel 8:13). Evidently, even in this era of ancient Israel, some forms of what we consider cosmetology were already skilled vocations.

perfume functioned for hygiene (this was a world without the ease of bathing we have today) as well as for social enhancement and purification. Since women couldn't wash their hair as often as we do today, oils and perfumes were used. Ointments made from the oils also provided skin care in a dry climate that could be hard on a woman's skin.

Then Jehu went to Jezreel. When Jezebel heard about it, she painted her eyes, arranged her hair and looked out of a window.
2 KINGS 9:30 NIV

Jewelry

Part of a woman's adornment was her jewelry. In some cases jewelry was a tool of superstition—like an amulet for good luck—but that wasn't always the case. A woman's jewelry could include necklaces, bracelets, armlets, anklets, hairpins and hair ornaments, pins for securing tunics, earrings, nose rings, finger rings, belts, and pendants. Gemstones were not plentiful in Palestine, but they could be brought in by traveling merchants from Egypt or Mesopotamia. The

This jewelry—dating from about the 1400s BC— was excavated from the Gaza area, approximately 50 miles southwest of Jerusalem.

apostle Paul encouraged the women of the congregation to shy away from immodest or lavish clothing and hairstyles (see 1 Timothy 2:9–10). Christian women were called to keep all things in balance. Just as today, these women had to answer the question, "When it comes to outward appearances, how much is too much? At what point do we begin to be about our outward appearance rather than our God-honoring hearts?"

WOMEN IN THE CHRONOLOGY OF THE BIBLE

As we examine the women of the Bible, it helps to put them into a context. Here are some general historical eras into which these women fit. Rather than being organized by years, these groups are organized according to how the people of God were identified.

Hebrews. The people of God were referred to as the Hebrews during the days of the patriarchs: Abraham, Isaac, Jacob. From the creation account in Genesis to the story of Jacob's family and its move to Egypt, the Hebrews were believing in God's promise, passed down through Abraham, of a land that would be given to them. The female story line of this part of Bible history includes the lives of Eve, Sarah, Lot's wife and daughters, Hagar, Rebekah, Keturah, Rachel, Leah, Bilhah, Zilpah, Dinah, and Potiphar's wife.

Israelites. When Jacob's family members relocated to Egypt to escape a famine, they settled there long enough to grow into a nation. Because Jacob's name was changed to Israel, his descendants were referred to as the Israelites. This era of the nation lasted from the Exodus from Egypt through the period of the Judges into the monarchies of Saul, David, and Solomon. The story of the Israelites includes women such as Miriam, Zipporah, Delilah, Deborah, Ruth and Naomi, Abigail, and Bathsheba.

Jews. After the Israelite kingdom divided, the ten tribes in the north were known as Israel and the southern territories of Judah and Benjamin were referred to as simply Judah. The people of the southern kingdom may have been referred to as Jews at that point (short for Judah), but it was not a term that implied the whole of the twelve tribes of Israel. Eventually the northern kingdom was defeated and assimilated by Assyria and the southern kingdom by Babylon. For a time some of the citizens of Judah were exiled in Babylonia, which later was defeated by Persia. When the exiles were allowed to return to Judah, they were all that was left of the Israelite nation. From then on, the nation as a whole was referred to as *the Jews*. The women of note associated with this era include Queen Jezebel and Queen Esther of Persia.

Christians. The New Testament expounds on the life of Jesus and the initial years of the early Christian church. The women of the early church were a mix of Jewish and Gentile, though of course there was a strong Jewish influence since the leaders of the early church were Jewish men. These first Christian women mentioned in the New Testament include Mary Magdalene and Lydia, a woman who sold purple cloth.

This statue of the Greek goddess Artemis, dating to the first century AD, might represent the clothing and appearance of an urban woman of the time.

Urban women vs. country women

Most of the women you read about in the Bible resided in small towns and on farms. In fact, 90 percent of women in Bible times lived in the country, where families raised or grew whatever they needed. The rural woman carried a large and essential workload and thus probably had a greater say in the way the household was managed.

Of those who lived in the cities, we hear about many in Jerusalem because that is where so many accounts in the Bible are played out. A city woman had fewer roles to fulfill, more conveniences, a market to trade in, and less farmland to develop. Her husband probably had an occupation separate from home, such as soldier, craftsman, or bureaucrat.

In the city, the families were not self-sufficient. They worked for pay and traded for what they needed. The woman's role was minimized, then, as the family depended on the income of her husband. Since she shared less of a responsibility for her family's survival, she also probably had less of a voice.

At the height of Israel's monarchy, there were both kinds of women, as was true of New Testament times. After the Jews returned from exile in Babylon, however, Jerusalem was no longer a large city. For the rest of the Old Testament and those years between the last prophet and the New Testament, there was not as big of a disparity between rural and city dwellers.

WOMEN'S RIGHTS IN BIBLE TIMES

As compared with the rights of women in the modern world, the rights of Bible women were very limited, yet perhaps not as stereotypically as they have been portrayed in the last few decades.

The Old Testament reflects more of the patriarchal structure. Wives and daughters had little right to make decisions about their own lives. Men could divorce objectionable wives (see Deuteronomy 24:1), but no similar rights for a woman are listed. In fact, according to Old Testament law, if a woman was raped, she was treated with some suspicion. In some cases she was faced with either death or entering into a marriage with her rapist.

There were *some* guidelines given to provide humane treatment of women. A father could legally sell his daughter into slavery, particularly to pay off debts, but he was forbidden to force her into prostitution. There were laws to protect widows as well, as they were a part of the disenfranchised for whom God called His people to provide.

Keep in mind that a woman's freedom was as existent as her husband allowed it to be. Women could make vows in the temple and in business dealings (and be held responsible for those vows) so long as they were not overruled by their husbands. There are a few examples in the Bible of women seeking recourse according to the law. Tamar was guaranteed a husband from her deceased husband's family—according to Israelite law. When the men in that family did not do what the situation required of them, she resorted to trickery, but in the end her actions were vindicated because, according to the laws, she had the right to provide her husband an heir (see Genesis 38:6–26). Another example is Zelophehad's daughters who, upon their sonless father's death, petitioned and were granted the right to inherit their family's property. Because of their bravery, God established a new law for the Israelites: If there is no son, any daughters can inherit their father's land (see Numbers 27:1–11).

Given that it was a male-dominated world, a woman's flexibility and freedom to develop and express herself depended on what kind of man she was under the protection of. Did he encourage her? Or did he simply use her? If that man approved of her action and gave her the okay, then she could move through life with the kind of authority and skill described in Proverbs 31:10–31, earning praise from her husband for all she did.

But even in the days of the Old Testament, in the eyes of God women were afforded, just as

A woman of Pompeii, a Roman region, holds a wax tablet and stylus in this fresco from around 50 AD. Her hairnet, made of golden threads, was fashionable in the period of Emperor Nero.

men, the right to be considered His children. In this way, a woman wasn't "grandfathered in" by her husband's relationship with God. There were no gender requirements for God's family. She could participate in worship and sacrifices, consult prophets, and take vows (for instance, the Nazirite vow that was most famously taken by Samson). The condition of her heart was not gender-related.

The New Testament was still patriarchal, and certainly Rome was a male-led society, but in that culture there was more freedom for women in some ways. Some women who had money, privilege, or power were able to secure a divorce from their husbands. They bought, sold, and inherited property. They sometimes obtained freedom from slavery. Some women, like Lydia, had their own business.

New Testament women had rights within their communities of faith as well. Jesus dealt directly with women on many occasions. Paul, while often reputed to minimize women's rights, talked about women as co-laborers. Priscilla and Nympha had churches in their homes. Priscilla taught Apollos, one of the great orators of the first-century church. Multiple women were listed in the New Testament letters as Christian workers.

Women of the New Testament must have felt quite liberated within the Christian community, where women and men worshipped together. Women's voices could be heard in the same places and conversations that had been gender-specific in Judaism.

Isis, the Egyptian goddess of motherhood, magic, and fertility, is shown holding her son Horus in this ancient bronze idol.

GLOBAL CONTEXT

Throughout the history of Israel, the nation existed among other cultures that held differing values and customs. At times the women described in the Bible were forced to assimilate to some extent into those cultures. Abraham asked his wife, Sarah, to pretend to be merely his sister when they traveled through the land of Gerar, and thus she lived for a time in the household of King Abimelech. Esther lived as an exile in Persia, entered a contest to become queen, and for a time was an incognito Israelite queen of Persia.

Many of the women mentioned in scripture were from a culture other than the Israelites. Ruth was a Moabite woman. Rahab was from Jericho. Jael, who killed the Canaanite commander Sisera, was the wife of a Kenite.

Whether the women you read about in scripture lived in another culture, traveled through another country, came from another culture, or simply lived among foreigners in their own town, they faced the same things we face in terms of holding on to our own values in the midst of cultural differences.

The great difference between the people of Israel and most of the cultures they encountered was Israel's monotheism—a religion and spiritual practice that worshipped only one God. This set the Israelites apart because most ancient cultures, and some even into the first century, worshipped a variety of deities. Throughout the Israelites' history they were tempted to incorporate these other deities into their own worship practices. This is a theme woven throughout the Old Testament. The divided hearts of the people were revealed in the ease with which they were influenced by the gods and religious practices of the nations around them.

Egypt

Egypt was Canaan's neighbor to the west. Throughout scripture women traveled to Egypt. Sarah went there with Abraham because they faced a famine in their homeland. Jacob took his whole family—sons, daughters, wives, and children—to Egypt for the same reason. Even in the days of Jesus, Mary and Joseph escaped to Egypt when warned of danger from Herod. That means Mary raised Jesus in His earliest years in Egypt.

Egypt played an even larger role in the life of Israel when Jacob's family settled there and grew into a nation, and it was from Egypt that the Israelites escaped in the Exodus.

A bust of the Egyptian queen, Nefertiti, from the 1300s BC.

The religions of both Egypt and the Israelites included a creation story and a belief in an afterlife. The Egyptian story of creation involved several gods who grew out of the creation process as opposed to the Hebrew version of creation in which one God preceded and instigated creation. The most important Egyptian deity was Re or Ra, the sun god.

Both Egyptian and Hebrew cultures had a strong connection between their politics and their religion. In the case of the Hebrews, God was seen as the leader of the nation. For Egyptians, however, their king or *pharaoh* was considered a representation of Egyptian gods on earth and the owner of all the land.

Egyptian women typically had more rights than Hebrew women. They could and did own property, buy and sell, borrow and lend, sue and be sued, make a will and inherit property. Yet, Egyptian widows, like their Hebrew counterparts, were in a precarious position.

While for Hebrews marriages were typically arranged by parents, in Egypt marriage was accomplished when a woman brought her belongings and moved in with a man. There was no legal registration required. For Hebrew women there were generally no options for divorce. It was the man's choice. For Egyptian brides, however, divorce was accomplished by simply moving out. Either party could initiate the divorce. Though there was no legal registration for marriage, there was a divorce certificate in both cultures. In both, the woman needed a written statement from her ex-husband so that a man she might marry in the future could be sure that his bride was free to make the commitment.

Canaanite People

When the Israelites traveled through the wilderness back to Palestine, they passed through and settled among the people who were already living there.

The territories they passed through on their way included the lands of the Edomites, Amalekites, Ishmaelites, Midianites, Moabites, and the Ammonites. Each of these people groups were identified by their common ancestor, at least in terms of the original settlers of the territories. Through the years people had come and gone and became associated with the region though they were not descendants of the progenitor.

Having passed through these territories, the majority of the Israelites settled west of the Jordan in the area settled by people groups who were collectively referred to as the Canaanites.

This clay figurine of Asherah was made about a thousand years before Jesus' birth. It was worshipped as a "house deity."

While there were some distinctions to the religions of these groups, they also had many similarities. While they worshipped multiple deities, the two preeminent objects of worship were El, worshipped as the "father of man," and El's alleged son Baal, a fertility god mentioned often in the Old Testament. Asherah was a goddess associated with El and Baal. Also related to fertility, Asherah was symbolized by figurines with exaggerated sexual characteristics. For some of the Canaanite people groups, worship involved religious prostitution and sexual fertility rites that included great excess in drunkenness and sexuality.

In comparison, Israel differed greatly from this. The monotheism of Israel, including the Ten Commandments, required lives of restraint and purity. The two styles of religion were in conflict. God commanded the Israelites, men and women, to keep themselves apart from the Canaanites, but that would have been a difficult task. They shared the same land area, their dialects had similarities, and the Canaanites had skills and materials that the Israelites needed, so trade was inevitable. In the Canaanite territories in which sexual promiscuity was rampant, the Israelite men were tempted not only to get involved with the orgiastic worship practices but also to take the Canaanite women for wives, a practice that caused dissension throughout the Old Testament. Esau married Canaanite women, specifically Hittite women, who grieved Esau's parents, Isaac and Rebekah (see Genesis 26:34–35).

When the remnant of Jews returned to Jerusalem after their

exile in Babylon, they faced the dilemma of so many having taken wives from the surrounding countries. These wives and children were sent away (see Ezra 9–10).

Because life expectancy was higher for men than women (particularly with the deaths that occurred during childbirth) it would have been tempting for an Israelite man to look to take a wife from surrounding people groups, particularly since the laws would keep his property in his own family rather than in his wife's.

Perhaps the multiple warnings against these marriages and the religious havoc that could be wreaked by them teach us something about the Israelite home. While the culture is most often described as stereotypically patriarchal, evidently these foreign wives wielded much religious influence. If not, the warnings would be unnecessary. This speaks to the fact that wives and mothers wielded great influence within the home.

The story of Naomi, Ruth, and Orpah reveals the relationships between a culture and its deities. Naomi and her family had moved to the land of Moab, a culture whose primary God was Chemosh and whose religious practices at times included child sacrifice. When Naomi's husband and sons died, she decided to return to Israel. When Ruth insisted on accompanying her mother-in-law, Ruth gave her well-known entreaty that Naomi's people would be her people and Naomi's God would be her god. The decision to relocate in this ancient land was a religious decision as much as a cultural and physical one.

Ruth clings to her mother-in-law Naomi, while sister-in-law Orpah sadly returns to her homeland of Moab. This 1795 painting is by William Blake.

Conquering Powers

Both Assyria and Babylonia utilized deportation as a strategy to obliterate and assimilate the cultures they conquered. This means they brought exiles from nations like Israel and Judah into Assyria and sent Assyrians to take their place. In this way the cultural identity and heritage were often watered down to the point that they were no longer recognizable.

Whether a woman was deported, or left behind, she was truly victim to the conquering power. Families were torn apart. So it goes with war.

Jesus talks with the woman of Samaria, in an 1870 engraving by Gustave Doré.

The northern kingdom, Israel, eventually disappeared completely under Assyrian rule. The area was then known as Samaria. Even in the days of Jesus, the people of Judea looked down on these Samaritans who were now part children of Abraham and part other cultures, leading the Jews to a deep-seated prejudice against the people who used to be their countrymen. Besides the cultural differences, there was a difference in beliefs,

with the Samaritans believing only in the Law of Moses (first five books of the Bible) as scripture and that the high holy place where all Jews should worship to be Mt. Gerizim, in Samaria, rather than Jerusalem in Judah.

From the time of the return from exile, even into the days of Jesus, conflicts existed between the Jews and the Samaritans. You can see them in Jesus' dialogue with the Samaritan woman at the well. She asked why He, a Jew, was talking to her, a Samaritan. She also referenced the well as Jacob's well, a Samaritan holy place (see John 4:9).

As you would expect with two people groups in such conflict, marriages between the two were all but forbidden. Resentment was fed by practices such as extreme isolation from each other and the fact that Jews treated Samaritans like they would Gentiles, barring them from the temple and its inner worship.

Gentiles and Jews

In the first-century church, the women of the Bible were more culturally varied than ever before. The church, for instance, was made up of both Jews and non-Jews, finally establishing that the non-Jews did not need to convert to Judaism in order to follow Jesus.

Since the Christian church grew out of Judaism, its first leadership was made up of Jews, in particular Jewish men. After a whole history based on separating themselves from the cultures around them, these people now accepted the task of embracing other cultures and dialoguing with them.

For the women in the early church, the first century was a time of amazing change. Jesus had gone about His ministry in a way that valued women and gave them a voice, but that voice was still a distinctively Jewish voice. While women were not allowed in the inner courts of the temple in which men were, Jewish women were allowed farther into the temple than non-Jews or Gentiles were. So in the midst of a faith in which the position of women was elevated, Paul wrote that in Jesus there was no male or female, they were also expected to grant the same elevation to those whom they had always considered "less than," at least in a spiritual sense (see Galatians 3:28).

By the time Paul had begun his missionary journeys and the church was spreading throughout Rome, Asia, and even Europe, women and men, Jews and Gentiles were laboring together to live out and spread the message of Jesus.

Christians vs. non-Christians

Since the first century, the Christian church has been working to find

In this model of Herod's temple in Jerusalem, the Court of Women is the enclosed area in the lower right of the compound.

a balance between being in the world and not of it. Christians have faced the same struggle that the ancients faced—how to maintain the value they felt God had called them to while interacting with other people groups and cultures around them.

Catherine Booth (1829–90), cofounder of the Salvation Army, felt strongly that women should publicly share God's Word—and became one of the most popular preachers of her time.

The women of the Bible reach out to us still providing an example. Women who supported Jesus' ministry and Paul's ministry, the ones who hosted communities of faith in their homes, remind us to be a part of communities. Women like Lydia, a seller of purple cloth; Dorcas, who sewed for widows in her community; and Priscilla, who worked with her husband as a tent maker, remind us that becoming a skilled craftsperson and walking with dignity and faith among the marketplace have their merits.

In the New Testament church, women received the same spiritual gifts as men. Passages like Ephesians 4 and 1 Corinthians 12 do not assign gender to the gifts of the Spirit, even those of teaching and evangelism. Joel's promise of prophecy quoted by Peter claims that God's Spirit will pour out on all people, men and women (see Acts 2:17). These people, these women, fulfilled their roles as God's children in whatever ways their culture allowed them to. Today, their examples still stand for us to follow, spreading the truth and living the abundant life.

RELIGIOUS/BIBLICAL RULES RELATED TO WOMEN

The Israelites lived by a code, the most basic form of which was the Ten Commandments. The fleshed-out version of those laws spanned the first five books of the Bible— Genesis through Deuteronomy— which were referred to as the Law of Moses or the Pentateuch.

But for the Israelite or first-century Jew, the law was even narrower than that. Religious leaders had taken the laws of Moses and defined their specific applications.

For instance, if a commandment said to honor the Sabbath, what *exactly* did that mean? One answer is, it meant not to work. What exactly constitutes work? Is a woman walking to the well to get water considered work? How many steps would she have to take before it was officially considered work?

Breaking the laws down into that level of specifics made for a grueling amount of sub-laws. This was the life of the Israelite woman. She had a rich heritage of faith, but in many ways that faith had been boiled down to an intricate web of dos and don'ts. While in the New Testament times Judea was under Roman rule, the religious legal system of the Jews was still allowed to function. That meant that breaking one of the Jewish laws was punishable, just as breaking one of the Roman laws was punishable. This is why Jesus was in conflict with the religious leadership of His day, clashing with the prevailing interpretations of the law—for instance, He healed on the Sabbath, which the Pharisees deemed as work.

The Old Testament Laws of Moses

When you read the laws included in the Old Testament, they can seem at times random or unwieldy. Bodily discharges, moldy houses, skin diseases, women's menstrual periods. . .not what you expect to find in the pages of the Bible. Of course there were sanitation benefits to these laws as the Israelites moved camp over and over again during their nomadic existence.

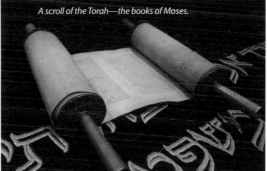

A scroll of the Torah—the books of Moses.

There are several themes that run throughout the Old Testament laws. One is the holy versus the unholy. To honor God's holiness, the people were to keep themselves holy. That rule of thumb worked itself out in terms of being clean rather than unclean and being pure rather than impure. From an ancient understanding of bodily functions, the people were to stay away from anything they considered unclean, impure, or diseased; thus there were laws to clarify what constituted something that was unclean or diseased.

Rachel sits on her father's household idols, saying she can't rise in Laban's presence because "the custom of women is upon me" (Genesis 31:35 KJV). The painting is by French artist Gabriel Jacques Saint-Aubin (1724–80).

Another theme was regarding the nature of blood. Because the life of a creature is in its blood, the people were to abstain from eating blood at all costs (see Leviticus 17:10–14). Even still today, this admonition governs kosher meat, which is drained of all blood in a way that nonkosher meat is not.

Another vital theme in the Israelite understanding of God's laws was the difference between life and death. Whatever was going toward death was to be shunned. The most impure thing for an Israelite to touch was a corpse. This clarifies why there are so many laws regarding diseases such as leprosy. These conditions were going toward death rather than life.

MENSTRUATION

Understanding the prohibitions for the Israelites regarding blood, it is no surprise that a woman's menstrual cycle required specific practices. Women in Bible times had monthly menstrual cycles just as most women do today. But these ancients had no running water, no ability to bathe daily, and no disposable sanitary napkins or tampons. They had only cloths or rags that had to be washed and reused. According to the Law of Moses, when a woman experienced her menstrual cycle, she was considered unclean, thus she needed to isolate herself for seven days. Throughout history the starting point of her period of seclusion fluctuated between the first day of her menstruation and the last, depending on which was easier to determine.

Not only was the woman considered unclean while menstruating, but whatever she touched was considered unclean as well. Her husband was to abstain from sexual relations or he would also be considered unclean and would require seven days purification (see Leviticus 15:19, 24).

> " 'When a woman has her regular flow of blood, the impurity of her monthly period will last seven days, and anyone who touches her will be unclean till evening.
> " 'Anything she lies on during her period will be unclean, and anything she sits on will be unclean. Whoever touches her bed must wash his clothes and bathe with water, and he will be unclean till evening. Whoever touches anything she sits on must wash his clothes and bathe with water, and he will be unclean till evening. Whether it is the bed or anything she was sitting on, when anyone touches it, he will be unclean till evening.' "

LEVITICUS 15:19–23 NIV

While it may have happened often, we do have one example of a biblical woman who used the ruse of her period to manipulate someone. When Rachel left the home of her father, Laban, she took the house idols. Laban followed Rachel and Jacob and stopped them to search for the idols. When he searched Rachel's tent she apologized for not standing in his presence, claiming that it was because of her period. She was, of course, sitting on the idols, and her ruse kept her father from finding the stolen goods (see Genesis 31:19–35).

Women did often try to keep menstruation a secret. This is not to say that they didn't want to participate in the purification rituals, but that they wanted this to be a private matter. Their husbands were not to touch them during their periods, however. In order for her husband's standoffishness not to be a giveaway, then, they would need to refrain from touching in public most of the time.

CHILDBIRTH

After giving birth, a woman was considered unclean. She had to be separated from the community for seven days as she would if she had been having her period. These seven days may have been related to the afterbirth, treating it like the flow of her period. If the woman had a boy, she was considered impure for forty days including that initial seven. If she had a girl, eighty days of purification were required, again including the initial seven.

These two white doves, used in a modern wedding ceremony, would have been an appropriate offering for Mary and Joseph, consecrating Jesus at the temple.

When her time of purification for a son or daughter was over, she was to offer a sacrifice consisting of a burnt offering (lamb) and a sin offering (pigeon or dove). A very poor woman could substitute one bird for a lamb, thus presenting one bird for the burnt offering and another for the sin offering (see Leviticus 12:2–8). Joseph and Mary are a good example of this purification rite, as they take Jesus to the temple, to present Him as their first-born, and make a sacrifice according to the Law (see Luke 2:22–24; Exodus 13:2, 12; Leviticus 12:8).

It's not that the act of having a child is considered sinful, but that the flow of blood and other discharges associated with birth caused uncleanness.

And the Lord spake unto Moses, saying, Speak unto the children of Israel, saying, If a woman have conceived seed, and born a man child: then she shall be unclean seven days; according to the days of the separation for her infirmity shall she be unclean. And in the eighth day the flesh of his foreskin shall be circumcised. And she shall then continue in the blood of her purifying three and thirty days; she shall touch no hallowed thing, nor come into the sanctuary, until the days of her purifying be fulfilled.

LEVITICUS 12:1–4 KJV

OTHER DISCHARGES

As serious as the Israelite law treated a woman's monthly period, there was an even greater concern over an unusually long period or female discharge (see Leviticus 15:25–30).

The same purification is required as with a normal menstruation, but the woman has to go through the same sacrificial ceremony as the man with an abnormal discharge (see Leviticus 15:13–15).

The laws concerning abnormal discharges shed light on the story of the woman who couldn't stop bleeding who quietly sought healing from Jesus (see Luke 8:43–45). She walked through a crowd to get to Jesus, probably trying to keep her unclean condition a secret, but Jesus knew she had touched Him and experienced healing.

While this seems a delicate topic to include in the Bible, keep in mind that these were a nomadic people just organizing as a nation. This was their first system of some kind of national health-care awareness. Were they to let a contagious condition into the camp without any checks placed on it, it could have spread like wildfire and destroyed a whole tribe. The simplest way to identify anything unusual would be to observe what comes out of the body and what grows on the body. Thus these irregular emissions and atypical skin conditions were telltale signs that the priests needed to check on.

" 'When she is cleansed from her discharge, she must count off seven days, and after that she will be ceremonially clean. On the eighth day she must take two doves or two young pigeons and bring them to the priest at the entrance to the Tent of Meeting. The priest is to sacrifice one for a sin offering and the other for a burnt offering. In this way he will make atonement for her before the LORD for the uncleanness of her discharge.' "
LEVITICUS 15:28–30 NIV

The woman with the "issue of blood" (Mark 5:25) stoops to touch the edge of Jesus' robe, in this fresco from the early fourth century.

DIVORCE AND REMARRIAGE

Marriage was serious business in those days. Divorce, the end result of more than half of today's marriages, was far rarer then. Jewish tradition discourages divorce, requiring a hefty payment as a deterrent. After the Jews' release from Babylonian captivity, around the fifth century BC, divorce did become more common, but it was nothing like today. And the cards were definitely not stacked in a woman's favor. Under Mosaic Law, divorce could typically be initiated only by the man. Rabbis differed over the permissible

ONE CAVEAT TO REMARRIAGE

If a man divorced his wife and she remarried and her *second* husband either divorced her or died, the first husband was not to remarry her. This kind of arrangement would be displeasing to God (see Deuteronomy 24:4).

grounds, with some saying it should be reserved for only severe moral transgressions such as adultery, while others allowed it for practically anything a woman might do to make her man unhappy. While a woman could not initiate divorce proceedings, she could in some cases go to court and force her husband to divorce her.

A divorce could come as easily as the man's statement that "She is not my wife, and I am not her husband" (Hosea 2:2 NIV). Later, a woman would be divorced when her husband wrote out a paper, called a *get*, stating the two were no longer married, she was now available to other men, she was no longer bound by the laws of adultery, and her legal rights as an unmarried woman were now returned to her.

Reasons a woman could find herself divorced included discovery that the bride was not a virgin; infidelity by the wife, or even suspicion that she had been unfaithful; her refusal to have sexual relations with him; his unhappiness with her cooking or the way she operated the household; his belief that she had abandoned her faith; or general disrespect or insubordination toward him or his family. Joseph, betrothed to Jesus' mother, Mary, was described as a righteous man who did not want to disgrace Mary (once he found out that she was pregnant). Until an angel appeared to him in a dream, Joseph intended to divorce Mary quietly (see Matthew 1:18–21).

After the Jews' return from exile in Babylon, there was a widespread movement—led by the prophet Ezra—for Hebrew men to divorce their foreign wives, so the Jewish faith would not be contaminated by people who worshipped other gods. In the early days of the Christian church, only a mixed marriage—or unequal yoking, as Paul put it—of a Christian to a pagan was viewed as an acceptable reason. Later, couples were allowed to separate but not to marry again. At one point, there were grumbles of leniency from conservative quarters when the church began allowing widows to remarry, though the apostle Paul, in 1 Corinthians 7:8–9, had urged widows, "if they cannot control themselves," to marry, "for it is better to marry than to burn with passion."

Jesus upheld the sanctity of marriage, challenging the Pharisees on the Mosaic Law regarding divorce. Matthew, Mark, and Luke all report Jesus' views on divorce law. That law was written because the people's hearts had grown hard, He said, but God in the beginning created woman and man for each other and they were to become as one flesh, with no one ever tearing them apart. Jesus shocked the disciples when He gave women equal rights regarding such issues. He said that a man who cheats on his wife is no different from a woman who does so; and that a man who divorces his wife and then marries again has committed adultery against his first wife. Jesus also spoke of people who would choose not to marry because of the kingdom of heaven—or because of their commitment to God.

GENDER EQUALITY

Although the ancient world was rife with gender inequality, both men and women were held equally accountable in the eyes of God for their spiritual lives. The penalty for idolatry was the same regardless of gender (see Deuteronomy 17). When the people stood in the presence of God, all—men, women, children, and slaves—were held to the same standard of purity (see Deuteronomy 29:10–13). While the laws governed human society, even in this oldest recorded law God related to each of His children directly. Here are some other laws in which men and women were called into equal accountability.

- Exodus 21:15, 17. Men and women alike who murdered or cursed either their father or mother would be executed.
- Exodus 21:20–21, 26. If either a male or female slave was victimized, the laws against the aggressor were the same.
- Exodus 21:28–31. The owner of an ox that had injured a person—male or female—would receive the same penalty.

SEX

The sexual discharges of Israelite women were considered more contaminating than those of men.

For both genders, sexual intercourse demanded one day of impurity. This is not to say that sex was considered dirty. Procreation was essential to the building of the nation. It may be more likely that the holiness of the fluid that produced life made the participants unholy.

It is true, however, that when the nation was to prepare itself by some kind of purification, its people often abstained from sexual relations. David once clarified for the priest that his soldiers could partake of the consecrated—holier—bread because they had kept themselves from women as a matter of course in preparing to go to battle (see 1 Samuel 21:4–5).

Again, this is not to say that sex was considered unholy. The abstinence in such cases was more a sacrifice, a fasting, in order to connect with God in a special way before a special event.

SUSPICION OF ADULTERY

Numbers 5:11–31 describes a test that could be given to a woman simply because she had a suspicious husband. If a man was jealous and suspected his wife

of infidelity, he was to take her to the priest. There he would make an offering in light of his jealousy. Then she would be required to drink a combination of holy water and dust from the tabernacle floor. The results of this test were judged according to how the woman's body reacted to this drink. If she had not been unfaithful, then the water was to have no effect. On the other hand, if she had indeed been unfaithful, her abdomen would swell and she would miscarry and possibly become infertile. The woman had to agree—saying, "So be it" (Numbers 5:22 NIV)—before she drank.

Long before suspicious husbands and wives started hiring private investigators to catch their spouses in adultery, God set up a system for testing a woman's faithfulness to her husband in Numbers 5.

To modern ears this test can sound rather barbaric, and at risk of proving the wrong thing. But just the existence of the test would have accomplished several things.

First, it gave a husband somewhere to go with his jealousy besides domestic conflict. There was an action plan in place that brought the priest into the picture rather than letting the husband feel free to act on his suspicions whether founded or not. It also gave the wife something to prompt a response. If she believed that she could be struck with infertility, she might choose to admit her behavior. If she was innocent of the charges, the fact that she willingly took the test could put her husband's suspicions to rest.

As with much of ancient law, there was not a reciprocal test for the woman who suspected her husband. In fact, the laws about adultery existed to protect bloodlines. If a man was unfaithful to his wife, so long as he wasn't unfaithful with another man's wife, this didn't affect his bloodline. If his wife was unfaithful, however, he couldn't be sure whether the children she brought forth were his own.

ADULTERY

In many of the laws of the Old Testament there was an inequity between men and women. Men could initiate divorce but women couldn't. Men could own property, but in the original laws, women couldn't. Regarding sexual

Indiscretion, however, both the indiscreet married woman and the man were to be held accountable (see Deuteronomy 22:22).

English queen Anne Boleyn (reigned 1533–36), the second wife of Henry VIII, was executed after being charged with adultery.

In the original law, they were to be put to death. According to history, the Israelites did lighten this penalty. Later, the woman was immediately divorced from her husband but was not allowed to marry her lover. The woman cut loose in this way had the same plight as a widow without children, but without the status of a widow, protected by so many laws. It was not a far leap for these women to depend on prostitution to survive.

Keeping these laws in mind sheds light on the New Testament situation in which an adulterous woman was brought to Jesus for judgment (see John 8). The Pharisees sidestepped the actual law by claiming that the woman should be put to death, with no mention of the man. Jesus invited the sinless to throw the first stone at the woman if that was her fate. While Jesus could have confronted these religious leaders on their misuse of the guidelines in Deuteronomy, He used the situation instead to put *all* sin on an even footing.

PROPERTY

In the original Law of Moses, there was no provision for women to own property. A woman existed under the guardianship of her father, husband, or son. It was the men who owned the property. Later in the journey, however, a man named Zelophehad died leaving no sons but five daughters: Mahlah, Noah, Hoglah, Milcah, and Tirzah. These five women approached Moses, requesting they be given the land of their father so that his name would not die out. After prayer, Moses gave the property to these women, changing Israelite law. If there was no son in a family, women could inherit property (see Numbers 27:1–11).

This change in the law highlights several realities. First, it is a reminder that while we view history in a snapshot, frozen in time, these people were becoming. They were gaining understanding and figuring out how to proceed just as we today give thought to what isn't working and look for equitable solutions.

The daughter of George VI might have had good reason to be grateful for the precedent set by the daughters of Zelophehad. On the death of her father (like Zelophehad, George had no sons) Elizabeth (seen here with President George W. Bush) became queen of Great Britain and the largest landowner in the world.

Women weave a carpet from colored goat's wool, near the West Bank city of Hebron.

Zelophehad's daughters also remind us that the priority for these people, their guiding principle, was the land God had promised to their ancestor Abraham. This was their inheritance from God, and their priority was on caring for that inheritance. In this case, the women represented the best reasoning—the continuing of a family bloodline in terms of landownership. The priority was not keeping women from owning land, it was maintaining family lines.

CLOTHING

The Old Testament contains some laws regarding clothing. Deuteronomy 22:5 prohibits a woman from wearing a man's clothing, or vice versa. It's interesting to note that the clothing worn by men and women was much more similar in the ancient world than today. Back then, at least among the common people, there was not really "casual" wear versus "formal" wear. In terms of outerwear, both men and women wore loose fabrics tied or attached with clips of some kind. The bigger difference was in the inner garment, which for a man was similar to a skirt covering only his lower torso and upper legs, while for a woman it covered her whole torso and was typically tied or clipped over one shoulder.

Another prohibition was weaving wool with linen (see Deuteronomy 22:11). The principle behind this law is unknown. It might have been a symbol of the separation that would be required of the people as they entered Canaan, or it may have had ramifications that the modern world is simply unaware of. It would, however, have been a guideline for the Israelite women who would have been primarily responsible for making fabric to be used by their families.

VOWS

An important part of the spiritual life of the Israelites, were vows—commitments to God beyond what the law required. The people made vows, often accompanied by a specific sacrifice that signified a special kind of consecration they were entering into before God. Women could make a vow just as men, but they had to be in agreement with their guardians. If a daughter or wife made a vow that a father or husband disagreed with, the vow was nullified (see Numbers 30).

In some ways this provided protection for the woman. If she had made a rash promise, one that she regretted or that would cost her too much in order to honor it, her husband could release her from that vow. A widow or divorced woman was bound to her vow even if it was spoken rashly.

Even in these ancient days when an Israelite woman had little to no civil rights, spiritually she still had her own connection with God. True, her vow could be nullified, but the fact that she could make it, of her own choice before God, reveals that her experience as a child of God was fully hers.

NEW TESTAMENT LAWS THAT AFFECT WOMEN

With the life, death, and resurrection of Jesus, a new kind of spiritual path emerged. From the perspective of the Christian church, the *people of God* were defined differently. In the Old Testament the Jewish nation was presented as God's chosen people, though faith was still available to all. With the coming of Jesus as Messiah, *people of God*, for Christians at least, came to mean those who followed God by putting their faith in Jesus.

While faith has always been open to all people, this was even more evident with the first-century decision that people did not have to become Jews to become Christians. This meant that people were no longer required to eat certain things (or not) because of their faith. They didn't need to follow Jewish customs, nor did they need to offer sacrifices. Jesus had offered Himself as the once-for-all sacrifice.

Yet Jesus had been clear that He did not come to abolish the law, but to fulfill it. There needed to be a new interpretation, a new call to the spirit of the law rather than simply the letter of it—merely the dos and don'ts.

This clarification and application is what a lot of the teaching of the New Testament is all about. It opens with the Gospels, which provide a window into snapshots of Jesus' ministry and life. The books that follow, then, for the most part, tell the story of that first-century church figuring out what it means to follow Jesus.

JESUS' TREATMENT OF WOMEN

Jesus was quite revolutionary in His treatment of women:

- He had female students (see Luke 10:38–39).
- He accepted women as friends and ministry supporters (see Luke 8:1–3).
- He ignored ritual impurity laws to help a woman of faith (see Mark 5:25–34).
- He talked to foreign women (see John 4:7–10).

Jesus' interaction with the Samaritan woman at the well was a popular subject for classical artists. This painting by Bernardo Strozzi dates to the early seventeenth century.

- He applied the same guidelines of responsibility to the husband as to the wife in a divorce (see Mark 10:11–12).
- After Jesus' resurrection, in a culture that rejected women as witnesses, women were asked to help share the good news (see Matthew 28:5–7; Luke 24:5–11).

Jesus treated women with respect. He honored them as people whom God loved, rather than assign them a level of worth as defined by the culture around them. Even while insisting He was not trying to do away with the Old Testament law, He seemingly ignored the opportunities that law may have afforded Him as a Jewish man to hold Himself above the women He came in contact with. He chose instead to honor the heart of the law.

Jesus had women as friends. In Bethany, siblings—Mary and Martha—shared their home with Jesus on several occasions. According to the Gospels, these people seem to have been more than merely acquaintances of Jesus. Mary neglected her hospitality duties (very important duties in this culture) to sit and visit with Jesus. Martha, seemingly the busier of the two, brought her grievances about Mary to Jesus' attention to get Him

to advocate for her with her sister. When their brother Lazarus died, both sisters were familiar enough with Jesus that they each expressed their displeasure to Him that He had not come sooner to help them (see John 11:21, 32). These interactions paint a picture of real relationships, almost sisterly-brotherly, between Jesus and the women.

The recently resurrected Jesus tells Mary Magdalene, "Touch me not" (John 20:17KJV), in this sixteenth-century painting by Hans Holbein the Younger. Mary was the first follower of Jesus to see Him after the resurrection.

Much has been made in modern fiction writing about the relationship Jesus had with Mary Magdalene, a woman who had been healed by Jesus and then joined His band of followers. She was present at Jesus' crucifixion, observed His burial, and witnessed the events related to His resurrection. The Bible doesn't give us enough details about Mary's life to warrant the speculation made about their relationship, but it does tell us enough to know that Jesus allowed Himself to have close, respectful relationships with the women He was around.

Jesus also allowed women to support His ministry. Accompanying Jesus and His disciples around Galilee, women, two of whom were Joanna and Susanna, supported Him out of their own substance (see Luke 8). Interestingly, Joanna's husband worked as a manager for Herod's household.

Jesus conversed with women—directly, intelligently, even lightheartedly. When the woman with excessive bleeding touched Him, hoping to secretly gain healing, He turned and spoke with her directly. When the Canaanite woman came to Him, asking for healing for her daughter, Jesus verbally sparred with her in a seemingly jocular way before granting her request (see Matthew 15:22 28). Jesus was not only respectful and civil to women of His own ethnicity but also of the surrounding nations. There is no better example of this than His conversation with the Samaritan woman at the well, a woman He could have shunned based on her gender, her nationality, or her lifestyle.

RELIGIOUS RULES REGARDING WOMEN IN THE EARLY CHURCH

Following the Gospels, the book of Acts gives us a picture of specific women who stepped up to serve in the first-century formative years of the church. The epistles that follow were letters to either people or local congregations, and written to answer specific questions or simply to educate or train. Here we find most of the teachings *about* women in general.

PAUL AND WOMEN

Much of the teachings about women in the church, particularly the ones that seem harsh or pejorative, come from letters traditionally attributed to Paul. For this reason, among some groups Paul has the reputation of not championing women in the first century. It is important to look at Paul's mention *of* women as well as his words *about* women in specific first-century situations, while keeping in mind that Paul worked with women as colleagues as the church was being established and the gospel was being spread among so many different cultures.

The apostle Paul writes a letter in this painting attributed to either Nicholas Tournier or Valentin du Boulogne, apparently from the early seventeenth century. Though some of his views on the sexes are controversial today, Paul clearly had strong personal and working relationships with many women of his time.

Just after Jesus' ascension, His group of followers was left to figure out how to proceed, given the instructions that Jesus had left with them. Mary (Jesus' mother) and the other women who had supported Jesus' ministry were among that group (see Acts 1:14).

Some of the fruits of Paul's labors were female converts to the faith. One such convert was Lydia, a businesswoman dealing in purple cloth, who offered her home to Paul and the apostles. It was there that Paul and Silas met with the other apostles after being miraculously freed from prison (see Acts 16:13–15, 40).

In his letter to the congregation in Rome, Paul mentions several women who had served the church and ministered to him personally: Phoebe, Priscilla, Mary, Tryphena, Tryphosa, and Persis (see Romans 16:1–16).

In Philippians, Paul made a request of two women—Euodias and Syntyche—who evidently were in disagreement over something. He describes these women as having worked alongside him for the sake of the gospel (see Philippians 4:2–3).

Among the other women whose homes were the venue for first-century Christian churches, Nymphas is mentioned (see Colossians 4:15).

Paul refers to Apphia as his sister in his letter to Philemon (see Philemon 1:1–2).

While there may always be disagreement in the modern church about how exactly to apply Paul's words about women, women played a valuable, even essential role in the beginnings of the Christian church.

NEW TESTAMENT WORDS ABOUT WOMEN: KEEPING THEM IN CONTEXT

In looking at the key passages in the New Testament that seem to address women's behavior in the first-century church, it's important to note a verse that is often quoted as a guiding principle regarding women:

> There is neither Jew nor Greek, there is neither bond nor free, there is neither male nor female: for ye are all one in Christ Jesus.
> GALATIANS 3:28 KJV

While this is an important verse in the Bible, one that speaks freedom to all, it is essential to examine this verse (which appears in bold below) within its own context:

> For ye are all the children of God by faith in Christ Jesus. For as many of you as have been baptized into Christ have put on Christ. **There is neither Jew nor Greek, there is neither bond nor free, there is neither male nor female: for ye are all one in Christ Jesus.** And if ye be Christ's, then are ye Abraham's seed, and heirs according to the promise.
> GALATIANS 3:26–29 KJV

In context, Galatians 3:28 appears in a discussion not about *women* and their function in the church, but about *all* people within the salvation of God.

Following is a look at some of the key scriptures in the New Testament letters that address women's roles in the first-century church. There are many opinions still as to how to apply Paul's teachings for our modern culture. This is a sometimes-difficult thing to discern for all who study and interpret the scripture—determining when a directive is related to a specific first-century situation or whether it is a command that stands outside of time and culture.

Christianity is perhaps the most diverse religion of all—with women and men of "all nations, and kindreds, and people, and tongues" (Revelation 7:9 KJV).

Now I praise you, brethren, that ye remember me in all things, and keep the ordinances, as I delivered them to you. But I would have you know, that the head of every man is Christ; and the head of the woman is the man; and the head of Christ is God. Every man praying or prophesying, having his head covered, dishonoureth his head. But every woman that prayeth or prophesieth with her head uncovered dishonoureth her head: for that is even all one as if she were shaven. For if the woman be not covered, let her also be shorn: but if it be a shame for a woman to be shorn or shaven, let her be covered. For a man indeed ought not to cover his head, forasmuch as he is the image and glory of God: but the woman is the glory of the man. For the man is not of the woman: but the woman of the man. Neither was the man created for the woman; but the woman for the man. For this cause ought the woman to have power on her head because of the angels. Nevertheless neither is the man without the woman, neither the woman without the man, in the Lord. For as the woman is of the man, even so is the man also by the woman; but all things of God. Judge in yourselves: is it comely that a woman pray unto God uncovered? Doth not even nature itself teach you, that, if a man have long hair, it is a shame unto him? But if a woman have long hair, it is a glory to her: for her hair is given her for a covering. But if any man seem to be contentious, we have no such custom, neither the churches of God.

1 Corinthians 11:2–16 KJV

1 Corinthians 11:2–16

Here the first thing to keep in mind is that Paul is addressing an issue or answering a question that we are not privy to. This is the first letter we have to the Corinthians, but it refers to an earlier letter (see 1 Corinthians 5:9–11). So readers are stepping into the middle of a conversation already begun.

We do know the church in Corinth was a diverse congregation that reflected the demographics of the city in which it was based. Since leaving the area after starting the congregation, Paul had sent Timothy to guide the church and remind the congregation of Paul's teachings. Part of this letter from Paul is to correct the people because they had misunderstood something he wrote to them earlier.

We also need to keep the cultural climate in mind. During Paul's day, it was customary for a woman to wear a head covering, a practice widespread among women throughout the ancient Near East as a sign of honor, dignity, security, and respect.

While the question of whether or not a woman should have her head covered or have a particular length hairstyle may not seem important today, from this passage it seems to have been a sensitive matter for the early church. It was a question

The apostle Paul's letters to the Corinthians addressed a troubled church surrounded by pagan practices. These are the ruins of a temple to the Olympian god Apollo.

of whether a woman was behaving appropriately within that culture's expectations. An apt comparison might be that these people were just as shocked at a woman's uncovered head as the modern culture is when a woman shaves off all her hair. We don't have morality attached to a woman's hairstyle in the same way these first-century people would, but a shaved head is certainly not a look we expect.

In the wide array of interpretations of this passage, us that how we choose to live in our external selves does seem to correlate in some way to the welfare and posture of our internal selves.

> For God is not the author of confusion, but of peace, as in all churches of the saints. Let your women keep silence in the churches: for it is not permitted unto them to speak; but they are commanded to be under obedience as also saith the law. And if they will learn any thing, let them ask their husbands at home: for it is a shame for women to speak in the church. *1 Corinthians 14:33–35 KJV*

some accept the order that seems to be represented here, that males have an authority females do not have and that somehow this difference connects to God's order in creation. Others strongly disagree that we can rest firmly on such an assumption given the other assertions Paul makes. Notice that he acknowledges here that women pray and prophesy. He also acknowledges that men and women cannot operate independently of each other. He was calling both genders to appropriate behavior, however, as it was defined at this point in history.

Most Bible scholars seem to agree that Paul's admonition here to the Corinthian church reflects a pattern of looking to the way God has guided in the past (because creation is referred to here) to discern lifestyle decisions in the present. Paul's words also remind

1 Corinthians 14:33–35

Paul's instruction for women to keep silent is a hotly debated scripture since it seems to minimize women's contributions in church. These verses are particularly puzzling in light of Paul's other comments about the work women do in the church, at this time often hosting congregations in their homes and thus taking on a form of leadership.

Interpreters have hypothesized about this seeming contradiction— maybe he was addressing different women; or maybe he was discussing the behavior of women at home in the head-covering passage in 1 Corinthians 11 and their behavior in public places here in chapter 14; or maybe he simply changed his attitude. These are merely hypotheses, however, because we aren't given the details to conclusively support these scenarios.

This marble statue, dating to late in the first century, shows the "braided hair" of young Roman women of the day.

I will therefore that men pray every where, lifting up holy hands, without wrath and doubting. In like manner also, that women adorn themselves in modest apparel, with shamefacedness and sobriety; not with broided hair, or gold, or pearls, or costly array; but (which becometh women professing godliness) with good works. Let the woman learn in silence with all subjection. But I suffer not a woman to teach, nor to usurp authority over the man, but to be in silence. For Adam was first formed, then Eve. And Adam was not deceived, but the woman being deceived was in the transgression. Notwithstanding she shall be saved in childbearing, if they continue in faith and charity and holiness with sobriety.

1 Timothy 2:8–15 KJV

At the core of his comments, Paul is discussing the order with which a worship gathering should be carried out. Keep in mind that the context of this passage is a discussion on spiritual gifts and how those gifts should be used within the community worship service. If a woman is using her gifts in such a way that it brings confusion or dissension, then that can serve as a caution flag that she may need to reconsider whether God wants her to use her gifts in that way.

1 Timothy 2:8–15

Paul's letter to Timothy was a pastoral letter. He was advising Timothy in Timothy's role as leader of the church at Ephesus. Within this admonishment from Paul is a statement about women dressing and making themselves up modestly. From Paul's perspective, this seemed to mean without a lot of fanciness or fuss. This admonition faces modern readers with the decision of how to apply this first-century definition of modesty today—is there a modern equivalent or do the instructions stand today as written?

But perhaps more troubling is Paul's admonition again for women to be silent and submissive and not to take authority over a man. Paul references Eve's deception in the account of creation. Certainly if there is a passage that seems to paint women in a less-than-flattering light, it is this one.

The same questions discussed earlier must be grappled with here: Was Paul addressing a specific need for this congregation, perhaps troublesome women, or was he presenting a timeless truth that should be followed throughout the generations?

Another question is whether this is a command for women not to teach at all, or for women not to teach without the approval of those in charge. This would be a relevant perspective given that Paul is writing in support of the leaders of the congregation.

It does seem obvious from this passage that the norm for this congregation is participative women; otherwise Paul would not have had a reason to address the issue at all.

EQUALITY IN ACCOUNTABILITY

Ananias and Sapphira are good examples of the fact that women were held accountable for their Christian conduct as much as men were. At the time, church members often gave all of their belongings to the church and lived in community. Although not required, it was a commitment they were welcome to make. This couple sold some property and brought *part* of the selling price to the apostles. In itself, keeping part of the money was not an issue, but what was *definitely* an issue was Ananias and Sapphira's pretense that they were bringing the whole amount to give to the church. When questioned separately by Peter, both lied and both died immediately. Had women been seen as "less than," Sapphira may have been held less accountable. After all, her husband was ultimately responsible for the business deal. But the reality was that her deception mattered just as much to the community as her husband's did (see Acts 5).

NEW TESTAMENT WORDS ABOUT WIVES

While not quite as controversial, there are also New Testament scriptures pertaining to women specifically in their role as wives.

Ananias lies dead at the apostle Peter's feet, victim of his own dishonesty. His wife, Sapphira, will suffer the same fate about three hours later (Acts 5:1–11). This fifteenth-century painting is from the Brancacci Chapel in Florence.

Though the apostle Peter focused on Sarah's obedience to Abraham, many classic painters chose to depict her foolish decision to start a family through her servant girl Hagar. This seventeenth-century painting, by Pieter Lastman, shows Abraham ordering Hagar and her son, Ishmael, to leave the household.

1 Corinthians 7:1–40

This passage contains a lot of information regarding married women, from sex to divorce, to unbelieving spouses, to the advantages and disadvantages of singleness over marriage.

Ephesians 5:21–33

Here both husbands and wives are reminded of their responsibility before God to tend to the relationship and be appropriate partners. It is in this way that Paul teaches about Jesus and the church. The husband should mirror Jesus' commitment to the church, and the wife should mirror the devotion of Christians to their Lord. To understand only part of this—say, only the women's role in the relationship—is to miss Paul's greater lesson regarding Jesus and His bride, the church. These teachings are echoed in Colossians 3:18–19.

1 Peter 3:1–7

Peter's teaching echoes Paul in terms of women defining their faith by their inner rather than their outer selves. Peter references Sarah as an obedient wife to Abraham. He also calls the husband into accountability as to how he treats his wife, a fellow heir of God's grace.

Titus 2:3–5

Paul's pastoral letter to Titus seeks to address Titus's specific situation. He adds here an admonition to the older women to mentor the younger women.

A WOMAN'S LIFE IN THE NEW TESTAMENT

The women of Roman-ruled Judea were varied in background and culture. The world was quite a different place from the one their early Israelite ancestors navigated. The same Roman Empire that ruled Judea also ruled, in part, Asia, Europe, and Africa. That meant that travel and trade were quite fluid among these areas.

Bust of Cleopatra VII, queen of Egypt. She died about thirty years before the birth of Jesus.

The Roman government was a male-driven entity. There were countries just outside of Rome's control that had strong female leadership—such as Egypt's Cleopatra—but within the Roman political structure, women were seen as inferior.

Not only did New Testament women face a new layer of chauvinism in Roman government, but there also was yet another hierarchy to be oppressed under. Rome gave preference to Roman citizens. Anyone could become a Roman citizen—anyone who had enough money, that is. In this way, Rome incorporated the wealthiest people of the cultures it occupied and thus received support from the most powerful of these communities. Paul the apostle was a Roman citizen, born into a family who had evidently already bought their citizenship. This came into play in Acts 22 when he was imprisoned and about to be beaten—until he clarified his citizenship status.

Palestine, where most of the Judeans lived, would have been considered an outlying area of the Roman Empire. It was still an agrarian society even then. As was typical of the Roman government, Judea was allowed to maintain its own justice system to a certain extent, but it was also occupied by

Roman soldiers in order to maintain control. The people were taxed heavily and were required by law to give the Roman soldiers anything they asked. Throughout the first half of the century, while Jesus was traveling and ministering, there was growing civil unrest that eventually led to a conflict beginning in AD 66 and ending with the destruction of Jerusalem in AD 70.

There was a great difference for first-century Judean women between those who were Roman citizens and those who were not. If a woman was a Roman citizen, she was to marry only a man who also was a Roman citizen. If that woman lived under the protection of her male guardian (typically her father, husband, or son), she received the privileges of landownership and functioned as the operations manager of the household, which gave her a significant level of authority. There were even wealthy female Roman citizens who functioned as the head of their own households.

For rich, citizen women, their only purpose was to birth an heir to the family's fortune. Since the household had the wealth to pay for conveniences, this woman was not as essential to the survival of the family as a lower-class noncitizen farmer's wife.

A servant girl waits on her Roman mistress, in a stone relief on display at the Getty Museum in Los Angeles.

Slave Women

While there was a fluctuating middle class made up of merchants and tradesmen, there was a great disparity between the upper-crust Roman citizens and the lower-class Judean citizens. Many of this latter class of people were either slaves or freed slaves. If a woman was a slave, she belonged to her master as property. She was expected to do whatever a man of the household asked, including sexual favors. If she bore a child, that child then belonged to her owner. The law provided for marriage only between free individuals, so a slave could marry only privately and informally. There were no legal rights attached to the partnership.

After the age of thirty, a slave woman could be freed (sometimes buying her own freedom), though at times she stayed in the same household as an employee doing the same tasks she had done as a slave. In that case it was only her status that changed. If she did not continue in her household, then she made her way like her counterparts, poor women of the working class who had not been enslaved. These women often worked as vendors selling food, wares, perfumes, or clothing, or hired themselves out as wet nurses for wealthier families.

Free Women

The largest majority of noncitizen women in Judea worked in agriculture, though some worked their own land and others worked as tenants on someone else's land. The small farms were always under risk of takeover. Rome taxed the farmers heavily, so they were often at risk of losing their livelihood.

As with any culture, even today, the primary difference between these classes of women was simply the amount of power they had. Certainly their wealth made a difference—the cloth their clothes were made with was finer, they had more servants—but that difference was mostly evidenced by the power they could wield within their community even over other women.

HOW WOMEN RELATED TO EACH OTHER

The world that most Bible women faced could be a world of community if for no other reason than it took more than one or two people to survive. There would have been exceptions—slaves or wives who were sold or given in marriage to a man who lived an isolated nomadic life, for instance. But for the most part, extended families tended to live together in the same compound or to share the same land. This community brought with it a price—just because these people were family doesn't mean they always got along. Also, with the nature of arranged marriages, a woman could marry into a group of not only strangers but also people she disliked. Perhaps most difficult, there could be competition, particularly between wives of the same husband.

Nevertheless, in comparison with the modern Western world of air-conditioned homes, single-family dwellings, and a mobile culture, the ancient world of the agrarian societies held less potential for isolation. In terms of how women related to women, we don't have a lot of historical documentation. Most of the record keepers in early history were men and were more concerned with key events than everyday women's relationships. Nevertheless, one of the strengths of the female gender is usually relationships. Here are some examples from the women of the Bible.

Mothers and Daughters

The most basic of female relationships is mothers and daughters. In early civilizations, from a girl's birth, her mother knew she would one day leave and become a part of another family, often by the age of thirteen.

Arranged marriages were typically within the same tribe or even clan. If marriages stayed within the tribe, then so would the land. This gave some hope that a daughter could stay in touch with her family of origin, but the expanse of the regions and the ancient modes of travel and communication meant that a daughter would most likely make a life of her own away from her mother.

Here are some biblical examples of mothers and daughters:

- Mother **Jochebed** and her daughter **Miriam** conspired to keep Jochebed's baby, Moses, safe from a slaughter imposed by the Egyptian king (see Exodus 2).

With the head of John the Baptist on a platter, Herodias contemplates her life without the meddling prophet. This 1843 painting is by Paul Delaroche.

- Part of the ruling family of Herod's in first-century Judea, **Herodias** and **her daughter** worked together in a murderous scheme. Herodias resented the presence and the message of John the Baptist, particularly in the areas that confronted her own lifestyle. Her daughter's dancing so pleased Herod Antipas, he promised to grant her any request. Herodias then encouraged her child to ask for the head of John the Baptist on a platter. Thus the great prophet's life was ended (see Matthew 14).
- One **mother pleaded for the life of her daughter.** The woman was a Canaanite rather than a Jew; yet Jesus healed the woman's child (see Matthew 15; Mark 7).

While these biblical examples may not reflect the typical mother-and-daughter relationships of the ancient world, there are nonetheless some similarities to these significant relationships today, especially in terms of how mothers and daughters advocate for each other, accomplish tasks together, and influence the men around them.

Wives of the Same Husband

While monogamy was the norm, there were biblical examples of multiple wives for a husband. Some of the more well known were Leah and Rachel (sisters who were wives of Jacob) and Hannah and Peninnah (wives of Elkanah). In both these homes, the women were pitted against each other both for the husband's attention and in terms of who produced children more quickly and easily (see Polygamy later on in this section).

Jacob scolds his father-in-law, Laban, for giving him Leah for a wife rather than her younger sister, Rachel. In the end, Jacob got both women as wives—but loved Rachel more, causing much friction in the home. This 1627 painting is by Hendrick Terbrugghen.

Working Relationships

Rachel and Leah's situation is also a good example of a man's having

At Sarah's insistence, Abraham reluctantly orders Hagar and her son, Ishmael, into the desert of Beersheba (Genesis 21:8–14).

category.) Rachel and Leah both offered their servants—Bilhah and Zilpah—to Jacob (see Genesis 30). Between his four wives, Jacob had twelve sons.

Sarah, wife of Abraham tried the same path. God promised that Sarah would bear Abraham a son even after she was past childbearing years. Sarah offered her servant Hagar to Abraham in an effort to speed God's promise along (see Genesis 16). Hagar did become pregnant and, though by custom of the day the child would be seen as Sarah's, Sarah couldn't hold back the resentment she felt for Hagar, a good picture of the strife that could enter a household of this type. Eventually Sarah did bear Abraham a son, Isaac, but the conflict created with the birth of these two boys was far-reaching.

not only more than one first wife, but also more than one second wife. As was typical in the ancient world, if a woman was barren, it was acceptable for her to offer her servant to her husband to bear him children. Such a servant became a kind of second wife. (Concubines also sometimes fit in this

Sisters

Sisters Mary and Martha were seemingly opposites according to the account of Jesus' visit to their home (see Luke 10). Martha has come to define the stereotypical detail-oriented (rather than relationship-oriented) sister, while Mary put aside preparing a big dinner to simply spend time with Jesus. Martha complained about Mary's behavior, but Jesus commended her instead.

OTHER WORKING RELATIONSHIPS

An Aramite soldier named Naaman was cured of leprosy because his wife's Israelite handmaiden told him about a prophet who could heal him. And Elisha did heal Naaman (see 2 Kings 5).

Jesus talks with sisters Mary and Martha in their home in Bethany. This 1655 painting is by the Dutch master Jan Vermeer.

Leah and Rachel, already mentioned as two wives of the same husband, were also sisters. Their father, Laban, required Jacob to work seven years in order to marry Rachel. In this way, Jacob was paying a bride-price. But on the wedding night, when the bride's face was concealed behind a veil and darkness had set in, Laban tricked Jacob and gave him Leah instead. Laban explained his deception by saying that it was not customary to allow the younger Rachel to marry before the older Leah (see Genesis 29). Jacob did not love Leah, however, and this trickery set up these

sisters for a lifetime together with elements of competition sewn into the fabric of their lives. Jacob was left working another seven years to pay another bride-price.

Lot's two daughters offer insight into several key elements of the lives of ancient women. When God decided to destroy Sodom and Gomorrah because of their sinfulness, Lot and his family were living there. His two daughters were engaged. When two angels came to warn Lot to take his family and leave the city, some townsmen came to overtake the angels sexually. In what stands as a truly horrifying moment, Lot offered the townsmen his virgin daughters as a bargaining chip because of the responsibility he felt as a Near Eastern host. The townsmen refused his offer, but by the next day Lot, his wife, and his daughters had escaped, and the cities, including the fiancés of the daughters, had been destroyed.

Having lost everything they had known, the girls concocted a plan to get pregnant by their own father. Every man they had known had just been killed and they were desperate that there was no one left with whom they could have children (see Genesis 19).

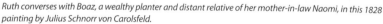

Ruth converses with Boaz, a wealthy planter and distant relative of her mother-in-law Naomi, in this 1828 painting by Julius Schnorr von Carolsfeld.

This story of two sisters pulls back the curtain on the dark side of an ancient woman's world—the desperate importance of bearing children and the fact that these sisters could not count on true protection from even their own family.

Extended Family and In-Laws

In the Old Testament, Israel was structured around the tribes or descendants of the twelve sons of Jacob. Each tribe, which was a broad extended family, occupied an assigned region of land.

Tribe members did not seek to move away from their designated territory. When they married, they wanted to marry someone else living within that land. Given the rudimentary nature of communication and travel and the fact that families were self-sufficient on their own land, it wasn't a situation in which everyone in the "county" knew each other. There were enough residents that people could marry distant relatives and still stay within their own region.

Ruth and Naomi represent an interesting exception to most of these rules. Naomi was a wife with a husband and two sons when she moved from Bethlehem to the land of Moab, a non-Israelite nation, to escape a famine. While the family was in Moab, Naomi's sons married women from Moab. Her husband, Elimelech, died and then her sons also died. This left Naomi a widow with two daughters-in-law who were also widowed. When Naomi decided to return to Bethlehem, she gave the other two women permission to return to their families and perhaps marry again and start new families. One of them, Orpah, did just that. But the other, Ruth, chose to return to her mother-in-law's hometown in Israel.

Ruth was granted this opportunity because once she married Naomi's son she was an essential link to carrying on the family name. With Ruth's husband's death, it became Naomi's family's responsibility to provide another husband for her so that Elimelech's family line could live on. (See Levirate Law farther in this section.) Ruth did indeed marry a man named Boaz, a distant relative of

Naomi's husband. She had a son who then carried on the family name. It was in this way that part of the bloodline through which King David, and even Jesus of Nazareth, was born was a woman from Moab, not only outside of the tribe of Judah but also outside of the nation of Israel.

Though a break from the norm, Ruth is still a good example of how family and political structures of Israel were built to support the survival of the tribes.

THE OTHER SIDE OF THE COIN

Other in-law situations in the Old Testament didn't turn out so well. Esau, twin brother to Jacob, married Canaanite women, specifically Hittites named Judith and Bashemath. These daughters-in-law were a grief to Esau's parents. When Esau realized how strongly his parents felt about the foreign wives, he married another woman, Mahalath, the daughter of Ishmael and granddaughter of Abraham.

Mary and Elizabeth are examples of extended family from different tribes. Elizabeth, of the tribe of Aaron, was a relative of Jesus' mother Mary of the tribe of Judah. It is unclear exactly how Mary and Elizabeth were related—maybe cousins, maybe aunt and niece.

But they do give us a picture of extended family, the members of which are aware of each other though they don't live in the same town and who support each other during significant events.

Pregnant relatives Mary and Elizabeth embrace in this Renaissance-era painting by Sebastiano del Piombo. The women would give birth to Jesus and John the Baptist, respectively.

Sisters in Christ

Where the Israelite women of the Old Testament served God by keeping themselves from the cultures around them, these New Testament women obeyed God by inserting themselves—and, thus, the gospel of Jesus—into the culture around them.

This provided new liberties and new challenges. The early church had no pattern to follow. Modern churches often fight over changing the way they have always done things; these first-century Christians, by contrast, were deciding for the first time how to serve and how to evangelize and what roles individuals should fill. They struggled with gossip, with busybodies, and with celebrating their newfound freedoms until their religious feasts became parties on their own. They were finding their boundaries as communities of faith, still searching for the balance of being in the world but not of the world system that existed apart from God's laws.

One of the unique challenges of the women of the New Testament Christian church was the transition from defining God's people as those who make up a nation to defining God's people as those who surrender in faith. The reality was that even in the Old Testament, God accepted anyone who believed.

There are non-Jews woven throughout the pages. Yet, this faith in Yahweh—one God—was a way of thinking that set this Israelite nation and all who joined it apart from the surrounding cultures.

In the New Testament, the challenge then was whether the customs that had defined the worship of Yahweh were still required for the worship to be true. Did a woman still need to prepare Passover? If a woman was not a Jew, did she need to learn all the Jewish feasts and make sacrifices at the temple? Did she need to attend the synagogue and pray three times a day? If she came from a Jewish background, on the other hand, could she freely accept women who dressed differently, had worshipped idols in the past, and still had family members who were not of the faith?

These were the questions women answered as they, along with the apostles and other new Christians, forged this new congregation, still based on the worship of Yahweh but no longer waiting for a Messiah to come—for His work was complete.

This ketubah, *or marriage contract, was drawn up by a Jewish couple in Italy in 1774.*

WOMEN AND MARRIAGE

God's intent for women and men to enter into marriage was made known in Genesis 2, which—after relating the creation of Adam and Eve—states that a man will leave his parents to become as one flesh with his wife. God, after all, had created woman because he had determined that it was not good for man to be alone. Adam described the woman as "bone of my bones and flesh of my flesh" (Genesis 2:23 NIV), indicating the interdependence that would characterize the marriage relationship.

In today's world, where there has been much discussion about what exactly can constitute marriage, it is interesting to note that, even in Bible times, there were a variety of views about what kinds of marriage relationships were appropriate (although they were all between women and men).

A woman was expected to marry at a young age—often as young as twelve years old, to a bridegroom ranging from age thirteen to many years older—and start a family. Doing so would achieve multiple purposes. It would enlarge and strengthen the overall community. It would create an alliance between two families, increasing the larger clan and tribe and further ensuring the future care of family members. In these days, families were tightly knit, with an obligation to work for the interest of the larger group and to help any needy relatives. The marriage also served to enlarge and ensure the inheritance of land and legacy of the woman's husband's family.

Concepts that are common today, such as romance and choosing one's mate, were not such a large part of the marital equation back then. More likely than not, a young woman's marriage in Bible times was based on reasons that were largely economic and/or political, and it was usually decided by the parents, with little or no input from the couple themselves.

Zipporah, one of seven daughters of a Midianite chief, was given by her father to Moses as a bride after Moses had rescued the daughters from shepherds and watered their flock (see Exodus 2). The bride did occasionally have the opportunity to weigh in on the proceedings once the arrangements were made. In one extreme case, Saul's daughter Michal went so far as to let it be known that she loved David, whom her father had grown to fear and despise.

Of course, wealth and power had their privileges, just as they do

Mildred Reardon was a Hollywood star of the 1920s. The publicity machine dubbed her, "the Girl with the Brown Eyes." Proof perhaps that a woman's beautiful eyes could be more attractive and seductive than other attributes.

today. Esther's story is a classic rags-to-riches tale of how a beautiful Jewish orphan girl grew up not only to become King Ahasuerus's queen but also to help deliver the Jewish people from persecution in Persia.

Just as is the case today, a woman's physical beauty was a major attribute, seen as a key contributor to a man's happiness. Beautiful eyes were especially appreciated. A man was advised not to marry a woman he had not first seen. Marriage between a man and woman who were of similar height or complexion was not encouraged in the Talmud, the central rabbinical text of Jewish law.

In the Family, in the Faith

There were plenty of laws, codes, rules, and other expectations about whom one could and could not marry. Because of the desire to keep marriages within a clan, marriages with foreigners were frowned upon, although they did happen. A notable exception to the rule was Samson's Philistine wife, whom Samson had sought permission from his parents to marry. Other women found themselves marrying Hebrew men after being captured in war. Marriage within the Hebrew faith was strongly encouraged, however, in the interests of keeping the religion pure and avoiding the

chance that pagan gods and practices would be introduced into the culture. This line of thought extended to the New Testament, with the apostle Paul notably speaking out against Christians marrying non-Christians.

A first cousin was considered the ideal spouse. Beyond that, there were commands against certain familial relationships, and these grew stricter over time. The stories of Abraham, Sarah, and Abimelech (see Genesis 20) and of Amnon and Tamar (see 2 Samuel 13) indicate that it was acceptable for a man to marry his half sister on his father's side, though it was later forbidden (see Leviticus 20:17). The simultaneous marriage of two sisters, Rachel and Leah, to Jacob was explicitly prohibited in later years (see Leviticus 18:18). Moses' parents were an aunt and her nephew (see Exodus 6:20). Mosaic Law, as stated in Leviticus, prohib-

The various manifestations of the god Baal were a constant problem for those trying to keep the Jewish faith pure. This statue of Ba'al was unearthed in Syria in 1934 and is now housed at the Louvre in Paris.

Ludwig Herzog valued his family tree so highly he commissioned a painting of it in 1585. A known family tree in Hebrew times helped prevent unsuitable marriages and could also convey considerable status.

ited marriages between a man and his mother, stepmother, mother-in-law, father's sister, mother's sister, paternal uncle's wife, half sister, stepsister, brother's wife, living wife's sister, daughter-in-law, stepdaughter, granddaughter, or daughter of stepson or stepdaughter.

Early marriages in some early societies, including Egypt, may have been based on matrilineal descent. Later, however, it is clear from Hebrew genealogies that descent was traced through the males of a family.

THE ARRANGEMENTS

A young girl in Bible times reached a marriageable age by about thirteen, or at puberty. When girls today are entering middle school and often considered too young to date, a girl in early civilizations was expected to be ready to live with a husband, bear children, and manage a household. But before all that happened, there were arrangements to be made.

A young woman typically would have little to no role in the selection of her future husband, though she could refuse to marry a man under certain circumstances. Instead, her parents would choose a husband for her and then make arrangements with the parents of that man. More than likely, the bridegroom would be someone from within the young woman's religious group and clan, perhaps even a first cousin, so she may have known her husband before marrying him—but not always, as in the case of Rebekah and Isaac.

It was considered the obligation of a young man's father to find a suitable mate for his son in order to carry the family into the next generation, and it was the obligation of the woman's father to marry his daughter into as positive a situation as he could negotiate. These kinds of arrangements were not required by biblical law— marriage was a civil institution, not a religious one—but they were customary in the Near East.

This young bride-to-be from Ramallah is wearing a dowry headdress. The wealth she is taking into her marriage is collected in coins, which are pierced and sewn into her headdress.

The mothers in this picture from Ethiopia don't look long out of girlhood themselves This was, and still is, common in many cultures.

It was not uncommon for the two families to negotiate over the business terms of the upcoming marriage. The father of the bride-to-be was compensated for the loss of his daughter by the payment of a fee called the *mohar* or "bride-price." This payment also served as a demonstration of the man's love for his intended bride. In some cases, the future groom might make the payment in trade instead of money, by working for his bride's family for a specified period of time.

Some scholars believe that the girl's father also paid a dowry to the couple or to the groom; if so, it is possible that the groom was not allowed to spend it, that it in effect was held in escrow and was returned to the bride in the event of a divorce or her husband's death. There is evidence that the payment to the groom was a custom that began in New Testament times.

It was customary for a bride to leave her own family upon marrying, and she and her children would be absorbed into her husband's family. There were, as always, exceptions, such as Leah and Rachel remaining with their father, Laban, after their successive marriages to Jacob—who worked seven years for Laban to pay the bride-price for each one, plus six more years after the second marriage.

THE

Engagement rings were not always a symbol of betrothal. In this portrait of Jane Small by Hans Holbein, the third finger of her left hand is conspicuously free of rings. In sixteenth-century Europe many men and women were painted with flowers, often red carnations, as the symbol of their commitment to marry.

BETROTHAL

Once the marriage had been negotiated, a woman was betrothed. Betrothal—the ancient equivalent of today's engagement, except it was considered nearly as binding as marriage itself—would follow, typically lasting about a year.

According to one ceremonial tradition, the young woman would receive a visit from the would-be bridegroom. In the presence of at least two witnesses, he would offer to her father a marriage proposal—a covenant or contract—that included his bride-price. If the father found this offering to be acceptable, his daughter would be offered a cup of wine. This was her moment of choice. If she drank the wine, it would indicate her acceptance of the terms, and the betrothal would become official. She would receive gifts from her betrothed to help her remember the commitment they had now made; this would be akin to today's engagement ring. The joyous news would be announced, often accompanied by the sounding of a trumpet. Then the bridegroom would depart.

A PERIOD OF WAITING

A betrothal period would ensue. This period lasted from several months to a year—unless it was

In this painting by John Everett Millais, Mariana aches from waiting for her man. In the poem by Tennyson, which inspired the painting, Mariana eventually convinces herself he isn't coming and wishes she was dead. The bride-to-be in biblical times must have had similar doubts and fears.

A BRIDAL METAPHOR

In Matthew 25, Jesus used the reality of the waiting bride to create a word picture about His own return. He described a bride and her bridesmaids who wait for the groom. Those who were prepared brought extra oil for their lamps so they could wait into the night.

a widow who was remarrying, in which case the period could be as short as a month. Although betrothal was treated very similarly to marriage, the prospective husband and wife, if they spent any time together at all, were always chaperoned. It was just as likely, though, that the bride would not see her future husband again until just before the wedding ceremony, even though her father would already be calling him "son-in-law." According to ancient custom, no date would be set for the wedding—leaving the bride to wait, and perhaps even to wonder whether he would ever return. While she might have doubts, she had been consecrated—promised, committed, set aside—and was to faithfully await his return, as her bridegroom went back to his father's house to prepare a *huppah*, a marriage chamber or honeymoon room. This would be where the bride and groom would ultimately consummate their commitment to each other.

THE CEREMONY

The bride's patience would be rewarded when her bridegroom came to get her, having completed the preparations for their new home. She would be waiting, decked out with her bridesmaids in their wedding finery, perfume, and jewelry, when he and his party arrived at her father's house, typically late in the evening, near midnight, in a torchlight procession. They would announce their impending arrival with a shofar, a ram's horn used as a trumpet, so she would know to be ready. Just as today, she would wear a wedding dress and a veil, though the fabric and fashion were still in the Middle Eastern style of dress. (The bride's veil played a particularly important role in the story of Leah's wedding to Jacob; see Genesis 29.)

Once the ceremony was under way, a blessing was given. Then the veiled bride would be carried by her groom and his friends under an ornate canopy, with much singing, dancing, and celebration along the way to what would be her new home. The songs sung in her honor would extol the virtues

A Yemeni Jew blows a shofar to proclaim the Sabbath. Shofars were usually made of horn and came in all shapes and sizes.

Then the bride and her groom would leave the party and be escorted to the marriage chamber—or huppah--for their honeymoon. Only then would the man remove his bride's veil, and they would consummate their marriage. She was expected to be a virgin, and the stained linen would be kept as proof of that. If she were found not to be a virgin, he could take the evidence to court so as to have the marriage invalidated. They would remain alone together for seven days before returning to the ongoing celebrations, which in some cases would continue for yet another week.

of the young woman on the eve of her wedding. The party would arrive at the house of the bridegroom, where the bride and her bridesmaids would spend the night in a specially prepared room.

The celebration continued the next day, with music, dancing, and games. The bride, wearing white and adorned in jewelry and other ceremonial garb, would be accompanied by her bridesmaids, also attired in white. After an elaborate feast with fine food and wine, the wedding party would throw seeds at the couple's feet. Sometimes a pomegranate was crushed, a symbol of a new beginning.

TWELVE STEPS IN AN ANCIENT JEWISH WEDDING

Selection of the bride
Price of the bride
Betrothal (*ketubah*)
Consent of the bride
The cup of the covenant
Gifts for the bride
Purification of the bride (*mikvah*)
Departure of the bridegroom
Consecration of the bride
Return of the bridegroom
The marriage chamber (huppah)
The marriage supper

For a year after marriage, the groom was exempt from military service so that the newlyweds could get their marriage off to a good start and begin building a home.

THE BRIDE AS A SYMBOL OF THE CHURCH

It is clear that marriage was important not only culturally and socially in biblical times, but also from a religious perspective. Jesus attended weddings, and in fact His first recorded miracle occurred at a wedding. Beyond that, the Bible compares the relationship between Jesus and the Church, or Christians, to that of a betrothal and impending wedding. Jesus on more than one occasion likened the arrival of the kingdom of heaven to a wedding feast, with Himself as the bridegroom. Jesus said that no one but the Father would know when He would return to claim His bride (see Matthew 24:36). This was the same response of any Jewish groom. His father had to approve his preparations. So if he was asked when he would go for his bride, he had to answer that only his father knew. Jesus also used the relationship between Himself and the Church to illustrate commitment between husbands and wives—a comparison reiterated by Paul (see Ephesians 5:31–32).

A Subservient—but Essential —Role

Of course, as with other elements of society in these ancient times, women were relegated to a lesser role. While there has been much debate over the meaning of God's reference to Eve as Adam's "helper" in Genesis, it is clear that women were expected to be subservient to their husbands. In fact, the common Hebrew word for the verb *laqach*, "to take in marriage," is related to the verb "possess," and the noun for husband, *gĕbîr*, is similarly related to *gābir*, the noun for "master or lord." That said, a woman in Bible times was not really so much identified as a female as she was by her position in the family—wife, mother, daughter, sister—and by the functions she performed around the house and in the community: cook, textile worker, baker, teacher, worshipper, etc.

Although a woman (like her children) was considered the property of her husband, she was valuable property and was therefore well cared for. Her husband was expected to keep her fed, clothed, housed, and sexually satisfied. A good and virtuous woman, in the eyes of the rabbis, was one of the greatest blessings a man could have, while

This 1849 American illustration shows the stages of a woman's life, during which she will be a child, daughter, sister, wife, mother, aunt, grandmother, perhaps a widow, great grandmother...a working woman doesn't seem to have been an option in those days.

a quarrelsome one was viewed as worse than death.

While the husband was the provider, protector, and decision maker, the wife managed the household and had a say in family matters, sharing almost equally in decisions such as the naming of the couple's children. She had her own room within the house, and in some cases her own separate house. Her status was certainly higher than that of a servant or slave, as she directed those, and she could not be sold, though she could be divorced or disowned. In a sense, it was her responsibility

to ensure that things went as smoothly as possible, while staying out of the way.

Proverbs provides a number of adjectives to describe how a woman was expected to acquit herself. Among her attributes, she was to be soft-spoken, disciplined, intelligent, kindhearted, discreet, agreeable, noble, strong, hardworking, fiscally responsible, enterprising, dignified, wise, faithful, God-fearing, and generous to the needy.

In wealthier households and among royalty, the wife's range of authority sometimes extended beyond the family and into

At the Wyoming state capitol in Cheyenne, Esther Hobart Morris is honored for her efforts in earning women a right to vote.

against Judah's idolatry (see 2 Kings 22). Abigail, a beautiful and intelligent woman married to a wealthy but mean man named Nabal, acted quickly to make up for her husband's offense against David and later became David's wife (see 1 Samuel 25).

Paul made it clear that both husband and wife bore marital responsibilities to each other in terms of sharing their bodies, and that neither should deprive the other except during brief times, by mutual consent, when they were devoting themselves to prayer. Otherwise, they might put themselves in a position of being tempted by Satan (see 1 Corinthians 7:3–5).

society and government. By New Testament times, women in general were gaining more influence within the walls of the home and without, in some cases serving as partners with their husbands. One example of such a relationship is Priscilla and Aquila, a husband and wife who not only made tents together but also were partners in ministry. Deborah was not only a wife but also a judge and prophet to the Israelites (see Judges 4–5). The prophet Huldah, wife of Shallum, boldly spoke out

Levirate Marriage: For Her Protection

There were various laws designed to protect women, including the concept of levirate marriage. The practice, followed by Israelites, Canaanites, Assyrians, and Hittites, required a close male relative, usually the deceased's brother, to marry the dead husband's widow (see Deuteronomy 25:5). If there had been no children in that marriage, the first child born from the new couple would be considered the dead man's son, carrying his name and inheriting his property. Even if there were already children, a relative was expected to marry the widow so that she would have a protector, financially and otherwise.

This London statue reminds us that women didn't always need protecting. Queen Boudicca was an implacable British opponent of the Roman invaders. But it's hard to be a warrior and a nurturer. If women were to have babies and raise families then men had to take on the role of protector.

In those days, women were seen as always needing protectors. From childhood to marriage, a woman would be under the authority and protection of her father. After marriage, she would be the responsibility of her husband. In the event of her husband's death, subsequent marriages would keep her protected. The marriage of Ruth to Boaz is a well-known example of levirate or "kinsman" marriage.

The Sadducees tried to use the levirate marriage law to trick Jesus. They posed a theoretical case in which a woman married one of seven brothers, subsequently marrying another as each died, until she had been married to all seven. The Sadducees' question was this: Whose wife would the woman be in the resurrection? (This was an interesting question for the Sadducees to be asking, because they did not believe in the resurrection.) Jesus responded that they did not know the scripture because in heaven people would not be married but would instead be like the angels (see Matthew 22).

Polygamy

Polygamy was accepted in ancient times, with finances being the only real limit to the number of wives a man could have. Hebrew laws are generally interpreted as favoring one wife per man, however, and most marriages were monogamous—if not for legal reasons, then financial. There are many examples of polygamous relationships in the Bible, but most of them seem to have been among men of wealth

Joseph Fielding Smith, sixth president of the Church of Jesus Christ of Latter-day Saints, married six times and had forty-three children.

and royalty such as King David, King Solomon—who is said to have had 700 wives and 300 concubines—and Gideon.

A woman's inability to bear children was considered a reason for a man to take a second wife—or at least a concubine or a slave girl by which to continue his bloodline. It was this thinking that led Sarah, at that point barren, to give her handmaid Hagar to her husband, Abraham, for the purpose of bearing a child. Whatever benefits might have been accrued by multiple wives were surely balanced by problems. From the women's standpoint, jealousy was sure to arise between competitors, even more so when one woman's child was favored over another's.

Monogamy became even more the rule in New Testament times, though there were still prominent exceptions, such as Herod, who had nine or ten wives.

CHILDBIRTH AND MOTHERHOOD

God commanded people to populate the earth (see Genesis 1:28). A woman's ability to conceive and carry a child was essential to that process. Besides that, the survival of a family in the ancient world depended on its ability to live off the land by hunting and farming—so the more family members, the better. In the most practical sense, children were additional workers as well as the potential for carrying on the family name and providing for the older family members when they were unable to hunt and farm any longer.

Up until relatively recently and even in America children were important contributors to a family's finances. These girls are harvesting sugar beets on a Colorado farm in 1915.

In a spiritual sense, childbirth mattered as well. The nation believed its inheritance from God was the land of Canaan. If a husband and wife were childless, who would maintain their ownership of the land God had apportioned to them? This was of supreme importance. In fact, it was of such a cultural priority that the custom of levirate marriage was established.

From the standpoint of Jewish identity, the mother was the determining factor. According to traditional Judaism, a Jew is defined as someone whose mother is a Jew—regardless of who the father is—or one who has gone through a formal conversion to Judaism. Many people find it puzzling that one's Jewish status is determined by his or her matrilineal descent, when just about everything else in the society is based on the father's bloodline. In fact, it is unclear just why this is, as the scriptures do not specify that matrilineal descent be followed. Several passages, however, do give the indication that the offspring of a Jewish woman and a Gentile man is a Jew, while others seem to say that the offspring of a Gentile woman and a Jewish man is *not* a Jew.

JEWISH OR NOT?

As the Jews returned to Israel from Babylonian captivity, a man named Shechaniah told the prophet Ezra that they had sinned by taking foreign wives. The men who had done so then made a covenant to put away their non-Jewish wives and the children produced by such unions (see Ezra 10:2–3)—which would not have been an option had the children been considered Jewish.

Fertility (and the Lack Thereof)

Outside the Israelite culture—which worshipped only one deity, Yahweh—fertility gods abounded, as did the fertility rites performed to please those gods. Some of these rites included temple prostitutes. For the Israelite woman, according to the first two of the Ten Commandments, many of these practices were not an option. For the

Becoming pregnant by her husband was a major indicator of success and fulfillment for a woman in biblical times. The more times she achieved this, the better a wife she was thought to be. Of course some very good wives never achieved this state.

Like Hannah, Rachel was initially barren and shared her husband Jacob with another wife. In this unusual case, that other wife was her sister, Leah, who was fertile but struggled with the fact that Jacob loved Rachel more than he loved her. Leah bore Jacob four sons, hoping this would increase his love for her.

woman who had trouble getting pregnant, it would have required a lot of faith to not give in to the pagan practices in desperate hope.

There were customs among the Israelites to help a woman's chances in becoming pregnant. One of the most important was prayer. The situation of Hannah, a woman who had been unable to conceive, was only aggravated by the fact that she was one of two wives of Elkanah. While Elkanah loved Hannah the most, his other wife, who had borne children, taunted Hannah to the point of tears, leaving her unable to eat. After she poured out her soul to God and promised that were she to have a son, she would commit him to the tabernacle for service, Hannah did finally become pregnant (see 1 Samuel 1).

SURROGATE MOTHERS

The practice of surrogate motherhood is fairly common in modern society, but it's nothing new. In Bible times, it was sometimes necessary to preserve a woman's dignity, as well as her marriage. To be a childless married woman was to invite the pity or even scorn of one's community. A large family, especially one with many sons, was seen as a great blessing, carrying on the family name and adding to the family's wealth. If a married woman was unable to conceive, she could allow a maidservant or a concubine to be impregnated by her husband, and the child would be considered the wife's. If the wife was barren and there was no maidservant or concubine, she might well find herself divorced.

The story of Rachel and Leah reveals several approaches for an ancient Israelite woman to take in order to provide an heir for her husband. One involved the common belief that the ingestion of mandrakes stimulated female fertility. Rachel struck a bargain with Leah in order to obtain the mandrakes Leah's son had picked. The other approach involved the culturally accepted practice of offering a servant to bear children in the stead of a woman who had not been able to conceive. Rachel offered her servant Bilhah to Jacob for this purpose. After Bilhah bore two sons, Rachel did finally become pregnant.

The daughters of Lot, living with their father in a cave after the destruction of Sodom and Gomorrah, were desperate to become pregnant to "preserve [the] seed" (Genesis 19:34 KJV)—continue the bloodline—of their father. With no other men around, the women resorted to an extreme measure: getting their father drunk and lying with him. Both daughters succeeded in becoming pregnant and bearing children by Lot.

Childbirth and Child Care

As is the case today, the birth of a baby in biblical times was a big event. And though medical care has changed dramatically, the emotional experiences are very much the same now as they were thousands of years ago.

THE PREGNANCY TEST

In Bible times, there was no quick-and-easy over-the-counter home pregnancy test. There was, however, a rudimentary pregnancy test that involved pouring a woman's urine onto foliage. If the woman was pregnant, the plants would increase in growth much like they would if given a fertilizer. Other tests involved the woman drinking a concoction, sometimes mixed with a mother's nursing milk. If the woman got sick from the mixture, this was considered a sign of pregnancy.

PREGNANCY AND CHILDBIRTH

Today the problem of infertility can bring a woman great pain, and this was even more so in Bible times, when a woman's fertility was directly linked to her worth in society. This priority on bearing children meant that a woman would go to great lengths to get pregnant. Keep in mind that from the ancient world to the first century, the typical life span was much shorter than it is today, with the women's life expectancy, due to the rigors of childbirth, averaging about ten years shorter than men's. Unfortunately, with an infant mortality rate as high as 50 percent, a woman had to get pregnant almost twice as many times in order to have the amount of children desired. Also keep in mind that while early people understood pregnancy, they didn't understand completely the biology of conception. Since it was the woman who got pregnant, if a woman didn't get pregnant, it was assumed that the problem lay with her rather than with her husband.

If any healthy baby was seen as a blessing from God, how much more amazing must twins have been—or triplets or quads?

There aren't a lot of biblical references that shed light on the journey of a pregnant woman in the ancient world. Most references to a baby's birth merely say that a woman got pregnant and then she had a child, with not much description in between. Yet we do know something more of Rebekah's pregnancy. She was pregnant with twins, and the twins, both male, were so active in her womb that she prayed for an explanation from God (see Genesis 25:21–23).

While there was much mystery in this era of history surrounding the science of childbirth, we have no reason to believe that what the woman experienced was any different in terms of inconvenience and discomfort. What was different was the limited options available to her for the treatment of the physical maladies that can go along with pregnancy—nausea, exhaustion, aching joints and muscles, etc. For these

JOY IN THE WOMB

The New Testament offers some interesting details regarding the pregnancy of Elizabeth, a relative of Mary, Jesus' mother. After many years with no children, Elizabeth became pregnant and went into seclusion for five months. (Her son was John the Baptist, who later heralded the coming of Jesus as Messiah.) In Elizabeth's sixth month, a pregnant Mary came to visit. Upon hearing Mary's greeting, Elizabeth's baby leaped inside of her, and she was filled with God's spirit and spoke a spontaneous prophecy over Mary and her child (see Luke 1).

Some of the Apocryphal Gospels have a midwife called Salome assisting with the birth of Jesus.

women of ancient times there were far fewer remedies and less knowledge to assist them when something went awry.

Midwives

In Bible times, midwives were commonplace, almost functioning like the nurse practitioners of today. They gave medical advice on a variety of medical concerns, but their identifying role was assisting in childbirth.

Priority was given in the ancient world to the firstborn child in a family, particularly a son. Tamar was pregnant with two boys, though the midwife couldn't have been sure of that fact. One of the babies reached his hand outside of Tamar's womb, which would have marked him as the firstborn, but he pulled his hand back inside the womb. In quick order, while the baby's hand was outside, the midwife tied a red cord around the

Moses only lived to be found by Pharaoh's daughter because of the courage of two Hebrew midwives who loved God more than they feared Pharaoh.

infant's wrist. Thus, when the boys were finally born, it was clear who would receive the benefits and responsibilities associated with the firstborn (see Genesis 38:27–30).

Shiphrah and Puah were Israelite midwives living among their people in Egypt. When the king gave the order to have all baby boys killed at birth, these two women connived to thwart the decree. Because of their efforts, many baby boys, including Moses, survived what could have been a state-mandated massacre (see Exodus 1:15–20).

CHILDBIRTH-RELATED JOBS FOR WOMEN

In addition to serving as midwives, women also hired out as wet-nurses and nannies. Wealthy women often hired women from the lower classes to provide child care. When Pharaoh's daughter found Moses hidden in the basket floating in the Nile, she hired a Hebrew woman (not realizing it was his own mother) to nurse him. It was only after he was weaned that the princess adopted him.

Labor

Genesis 30:3 indirectly describes the practice of the woman in labor, sitting on the knees of another woman. In this way, the pregnant woman was held upright and could be assisted in her balance, but there was room for the baby to drop into the hands of the midwife. Later a woman sat on two rocks positioned so there was space between them for the baby to drop. Even later, delivery stools (see Exodus 1:16) served the same purpose: to provide support for the mother with a way for the baby to be delivered. These stools were made with handgrips, a

This illustration from a sixteenth-century instruction book for midwives shows a woman on a birthing stool. The actual event might have been a little less elegant.

THE ABANDONED BABY

Ezekiel's prophecy against the wickedness in Jerusalem starts out with the image of an infant girl who has been tossed aside onto a garbage heap. The infant is described without her cord cut, without her being washed or rubbed with salt or wrapped in cloths—the typical methods of caring for a newborn. The salt was believed to firm up the skin and to provide some sanitation. In Ezekiel's word picture, this baby, left uncared for, was found, cleaned up, and adopted. This was a plausible scenario for the life of an unwanted child who might then be found by someone and adopted into a family (see Ezekiel 16:1–14).

back to lean against and a crescent-shaped hole in the seat.

When Rachel offered her servant to her husband, Jacob, to bear him children in her stead, Rachel said the servant, Bilhah, would bear those children upon Rachel's knees. This probably referred to Rachel providing the assist. Once in hard labor, Bilhah would sit on Rachel's lap, with Rachel holding on to her to provide balance and support, and the baby could be born between Rachel's knees. In this particular case, the practice would have given Rachel a bond with the baby (who culturally would have been considered Rachel's) that she would not have had otherwise.

BOY OR GIRL?

Given the largely patriarchal nature of societies in Bible times, it is no surprise that baby boys were much preferred to baby girls. One reason for this is that males controlled the wealth, and their marriages caused their own families to grow, since in most cases the future bride would move into her husband's home.

As Rachel was dying after the difficult childbirth of her second son, she named the boy Benoni, which means "son of my sorrow." Her husband, Jacob, however, subsequently named him Benjamin, which means "son of my right hand" (Genesis 35:16–20 KJV). In this case, Rachel's name for her son may be an example of a calling name.

Naming Children

The names given to children, in particular the names recorded in the Bible, often have special significance. A child was typically given a name by the mother just after birth. Leah named her firstborn Reuben; Hannah named her son Samuel.

As today, sometimes these names held family significance, but often in the Bible we are told the spiritual significance of a name. One woman went into labor when she found out about the death of her husband and her father-in-law after a battle with a tragic end for Israel. The woman died after childbirth, but first she named her son Ichabod—which meant "Where is the glory?"—because God's glory had departed His people (see 1 Samuel 4).

Without a school system, all moms were home-educators.

> *Honour thy father and thy mother: that thy days may be long upon the land which the LORD thy God giveth thee.*
>
> EXODUS 20:12 KJV

Child Care and Discipline

Mom had chief responsibility for care of small children, a task absorbed into all her other tasks.

This meant that in a culture with no school system, mothers were the primary educators. They were responsible for the socialization of children as well as their health, welfare, and cultural and academic education.

According to the Ten Commandments, the Israelite culture saw both parents in authority over their offspring (unlike other ancient Near Eastern cultures). Children were to honor *both* parents. This extended to grown children as well as to small children. Parents could haul a stubborn and rebellious son before the city's elders for such a sin as disobedience, gluttony, and drunkenness, and the men would stone him (see Deuteronomy 21:18–21). We have not found evidence that this actually happened, but it was in the law. At any rate, this shared responsibility between the Israelite parents probably means that a mother

CIRCUMCISION, REDEMPTION, AND PURIFICATION

When a male baby was eight days old, the infant was circumcised—the foreskin removed from his penis. This practice was upheld by more cultures than the Israelite culture, but specifically for these people it was attached to God's promise to Abraham. God told Abraham that one of the things that would set his descendants apart was this custom of infant circumcision.

While the timing of circumcision was commanded in Genesis 17:12 and again in Leviticus 12:3 as well as other verses, we now know that the eighth day of a typical infant is an optimum time for the procedure because of the blood's optimum ability to clot on the eighth day. Jesus was circumcised when He was eight days old, also the day when a Jewish child was typically given his name.

Other ceremonies also followed childbirth. *Redemption* was the presentation of a firstborn son to God one month after his birth (Numbers 18:15–16); the parents made an offering to "buy back" the child from God, thus acknowledging that the child belonged to God, the one who had given him life. *Purification* of the mother was a process that took place well over a month for the birth of a baby boy, and more than two months in the case of a baby girl; until this period had passed, the mother was considered ceremonially unclean and was prohibited from entering the temple. After her time of separation had ended, the mother and father were to make a burnt offering of a lamb and a sin offering of a dove or pigeon—or two doves or pigeons if they could not afford a lamb, as was the case with Mary and Joseph after Jesus' birth.

"THE CHANGE"

Menopause is not discussed much in the Bible except in terms of a woman's infertility. "It ceased to be with Sarah after the manner of women" (Genesis 18:11 KJV) describes a postmenopausal Sarah. This was, of course, before God blessed her with a miracle in the form of her son Isaac. Similarly, the angel tells Mary: "And, behold, thy cousin Elisabeth, she hath also conceived a son in her old age" (Luke 1:36 KJV).

Since women were considered unclean during their period and required a time of separation afterward, menopause had some spiritual rewards. Of course, in a time when many women didn't live to reach the age of thirty, menopause was somewhat rare. But those who reached that point had more potential for the ministry. Interestingly, in the New Testament, women found themselves with unprecedented influence within the growing young Christian church, valued for their spiritual fruitfulness rather than just their biological ability to reproduce.

Anna, seen here in an English church window, was present when Jesus was presented at the temple. She had dedicated her later years to worshipping, fasting, and praying. "And she coming in that instant gave thanks likewise unto the Lord, and spake of him to all them that looked for redemption in Jerusalem" (Luke 2:38 KJV).

had some influence over her children's marital arrangements and thus also had input into matters involving inheritances, land, and property.

Homemaking and Special Skills

Proverbs concludes with a portrait of what might seem like an idealized woman. She is wise, strong, skilled, hardworking, and compassionate. She loves God and is generous to those in need. She is a devoted wife and loving mother. She thrives at agriculture, food processing and preparation, apparel, real estate, home décor, trading, and even upholstery. And child care, of course.

Proverbs 31:13–19 (KJV) outlines her industriousness:

"She seeketh wool, and flax, and worketh willingly with her hands. She is like the merchants' ships; she bringeth her food from afar. She riseth also while it is yet night, and giveth meat to her household, and a portion to her maidens. She considereth a field, and buyeth it: with the fruit of her hands she planteth a vineyard. She girdeth her loins with strength, and strengtheneth her arms. She perceiveth that her merchandise is good: her candle goeth not out by night. She layeth her hands to the spindle, and her hands hold the distaff."

While it's very likely that the woman described here is a composite, the fact remains that, from humanity's earliest recorded days, women have kept the home fires burning. A woman in Bible times carried a lot of responsibility. A typical day in her life did include a wide range of duties related to running the household: fetching water from a well or cistern, grinding grain into flour, feeding and clothing the family, caring for children, and tending the animals.

Working Outside the Home

In addition to running the household, many if not most women in biblical times did their share of outside work, in the Old Testament as well as the New. These jobs covered a wide range of professions, quite often based on skills that originated in the home. If a woman was particularly skilled or industrious at a certain household task, she could potentially offer the fruits of her labors in the marketplace, helping to support herself and her family.

Where did women acquire these skills? It obviously wasn't from college or trade school. Educational opportunities in those ancient times were limited, and for women they were practically nonexistent outside instruction at the synagogue and in the home. Women learned, quite simply, by

The young girl in this painting by American artist Mary Cassatt seems more interested in the painter—but she probably soon learned needlework from her mother.

doing, out of necessity. Young girls learned many jobs by watching their mothers and eventually helping out around the house, in the fields, or wherever else they might be needed.

POWER WITHIN THE HOME

Women may have held a lower status than men in the community, but they wielded power within the home, both as mothers and as wives. They were the primary caretakers of the children, and as such were responsible for their discipline and much of their early education and training. This included religious instruction for both their daughters and their sons, at least until the boys reached the age when they could attend school, an option that was not available for girls. In-home instruction focused largely on stories from scripture and Hebrew history.

Samuel, who grew up to become a judge and one of the first and greatest prophets of Israel, is an excellent illustration of how the influence of a God-fearing mother can have lasting positive results. Initially barren, Hannah had prayed constantly for a son, promising the Lord that if He would grant her prayer, she would dedicate the boy to the Lord's service. When her prayers were finally answered, she kept her word. Hannah's son Samuel was trained by a priest and grew up to rule Israel throughout his life, a time of great peace for the nation.

HOSPITALITY

For the Israelites, the household extended to outsiders when the situation

Elijah restores the widow's son because of her hospitality and faith.

arose. Mosaic Law commanded them to be hospitable to aliens living in the land, treating them and loving them as one of their own (see Leviticus 19:33–34).

As the manager of the household, a woman of Bible times performed much of the work associated with inviting a stranger into the house: baking the bread, which was an overt symbol of hospitality and honor; cooking meat and vegetables; providing a place to sleep. When Abraham, in welcoming strangers into his home at Hebron, offered them a body- and soul-nourishing respite from the midday heat, Sarah assisted by preparing the bread (see Genesis 18). The widow of Zarephath took a major leap of faith in honoring Elijah's request to make him a cake of bread when her provisions were meager, at best (see 1 Kings 17).

SPECIAL SKILLS

The Bible contains no prohibitions against women working outside the home. In fact, the woman described in Proverbs 31, who not only ran a household but also was busy in the marketplace, is described as "virtuous."

While outside work was not necessary for women of royalty or others of extreme wealth—who commonly hired women for child care and household functions— some consider it to have been the rule rather than the exception for the women of the era.

Many women who did not have to work outside the home followed the same path as Elizabeth Fry, the English prison reformer, and dedicated themselves to the welfare of others.

TOO MANY COOKS?

If there were multiple wives, concubines, or slaves, they all lived in the same house and shared the household chores. While this distributed the workload, it also could bring considerable domestic strife.

Biblical Examples

Lydia, Paul's first European convert to Christianity, was a savvy businesswoman who became a community leader. Lydia's specialty was purple cloth, which was colored with a dye made from fluid obtained from a particular marine mollusk. Because of the complex process involved, purple cloth was costly and therefore worn only by royalty and nobility—and so, with such clientele, Lydia was most likely well-to-do herself. She was also skilled in hospitality, welcoming the apostle Paul and his companions into her home and serving them (see Acts 16).

Priscilla operated a tent-making business with her Jewish Christian husband, Aquila. The seemingly inseparable couple, who are mentioned in Acts, Romans, 1 Corinthians, and 2 Timothy, became early missionaries and beloved friends of Paul, and they traveled widely throughout the Mediterranean region, preaching the Gospel.

Dorcas, also known as Tabitha, was a prime example of how a woman could use her skills in ministry for the glory of the Lord. She was a disciple who made robes and other clothing for the poor people in the city of Joppa. The impact on her community was so great that when she died, her fellow disciples sent for Peter, who was in nearby Lydda. Peter came to the upstairs room where Dorcas's body had been placed, prayed over her, and then told her to get up, which she did. This miracle caused many people to become believers in the Lord (see Acts 9:36–42).

LIKE A FEMALE PRESIDENT

As far as work outside the home goes, possibly no woman in the Bible rose to such heights as Deborah. As the fourth judge of Israel, and the only woman to hold the position, she was essentially in charge of the entire nation. This married prophet, to whom Israelites came to resolve their disputes, also proved herself a capable military strategist and leader, advising and accompanying the general Barak in battle against Sisera. The resulting victory by the Israelite army ended twenty years of oppression at the hands of the Canaanites (see Judges 4–5).

SURVIVAL SKILLS

One might say that the ultimate skill is survival, and in that area the results are mixed—for Bible women, men, and children, but particularly for women. Many of the things we take for granted today were nonexistent back then: like hospitals and highways, shopping malls, refrigerators and microwaves and air-conditioning, to name a few. People in this era lived a much slower-paced life, and they (for the most part) lived a much shorter life. The average life span in Bible times is said to have been forty years or even less, in spite of some well-known examples of people who lived far beyond that. Constant threats were posed by things like famine, disease, plague, violence, the desert heat, bad weather, and possibly even supernatural forces.

The odds were further stacked against women, who had the added burdens of childbirth, a lesser social standing, and assorted other indignities. In the midst of some amazing adversities, these tough women wielded their wits and womanly wiles to survive, best as they knew how.

One thing to remember about a woman of Bible times is that, while she lived in a very different time, some of her challenges were similar to the ones today's woman faces. The emotions she went through when she had a child or—God forbid—lost one were no different from what the same event provokes today.

This Syrian Bedouin woman, photographed at the World's Columbian Exposition in 1893, faced many of the same challenges as her biblical counterparts two millennia earlier.

Mary, Mary Magdalene, and Joseph of Arimathea begin preparing the body of Christ before placing him in the tomb. The painting is by nineteenth-century Russian artist Wassilij Grigorjewitsch Perow .

Rather than remembering these ancient women as superhuman, or two-dimensional stereotypes, we should remember them as living, breathing, thinking, feeling, flesh-and-blood people like ourselves.

DEATH, MOURNING, AND BURIAL

Since the Fall in the Garden of Eden, when God told man he would ultimately return to the dust from which he came, death has been an unavoidable part of life. Death and dying permeate the Bible, and, naturally, women are included in this cycle. There are numerous biblical accounts of women's deaths and their aftermaths, as well as of women mourning the deaths of others and participating in their burial.

The Bible is, at its core, *about* death—both physical and spiritual—and the opportunity to transcend it. The defining moment in Christianity comes when two women visit the empty tomb of Jesus. Women in Bible times would have been constantly confronted with the realities of death, much as people are today, and they played key roles in the preparations and rituals surrounding it.

The overall mortality rate was high, a result of disease,

malnutrition, plague, violence, and generally unsafe living conditions. For women, the rate was even higher, largely because of the perils of childbirth (children's death rate was extremely high as well). Because of such ever-present hazards, it may have seemed that if a biblical woman wasn't dying or on the verge, she was mourning the death of a child or other loved one, or a friend or neighbor.

A Major Void to Fill

The death of a woman was a severe blow to her family. If she was married with children, the family found itself without its household manager: provider of food, clothing, child care, in-home instruction, and so much more. With young children in the picture, the father would probably have to make adjustments in his schedule or, more likely, the household itself to accommodate the loss. Extended families often lived together, in which case other relatives might be able to help with the household duties. There might be servants or slaves who could take up the slack. And the man might ultimately choose to remarry, as much for the household help that a wife would provide as for any romantic ideals.

Beliefs Surrounding Death

A culture's—or a family's—treatment of the dead was, and is, a direct reflection of its beliefs regarding an afterlife, or lack thereof. Ancient times were a veritable stew of belief systems populated by countless gods. Accordingly, ceremonies surrounding the mourning and burial of a person could range widely. The treatment of a dead person also depended to some extent on his or her financial and social status while living.

The ancient Hebrews did not always believe in an afterlife. In early Old Testament times many Hebrews believed in a dark, shadowy underworld known as Sheol where the dead went to reside. It has been compared to Hades or hell, though it was not a place of torment so much as place of separation from God, a severe punishment in itself. To some, however, Sheol meant merely the grave.

During and after the Jews' exile and subsequent return to Jerusalem, their beliefs about what happens after death began to shift. Many questioned whether a loving God would in fact allow Sheol to be the end of everything. The prophet Daniel wrote that the dead would awake, some

Death became a part of human life when Adam and Eve were expelled from Eden.

to everlasting life and others to eternal shame and contempt (see Daniel 12:2). By the time of the New Testament, opinion was divided among the Jews' ruling class, with Pharisees believing in a resurrection and Sadducees not.

Many people, especially in Old Testament times, viewed an individual's death as direct punishment from God for his or her sins, and there are biblical accounts of both women and men being struck down. Lot's wife was transformed into a pillar of salt, a presumably fatal condition, after disobeying God's warning not to look back on the evil cities of Sodom and Gomorrah (see Genesis 19).

Sin and death have been inextricably linked since the Garden of Eden, with Jesus' death on the cross—and subsequent resurrection—the route by which humans can avoid eternal spiritual death once their bodies surrender their physical life.

Preparing the Body

Preparing a body for burial was a job for women, usually members of the deceased's family. Soon after a person had died, the women went to work: washing the body, cutting the hair, trimming the nails, ultimately perfuming the corpse with oils and spices. The women then wrapped the body in special linen clothing. As is the custom today, the eyes of the deceased were closed. It was common for the women to recite scriptures and pray while preparing the body.

In most cases the corpse was not embalmed, which increased the need for an immediate burial. Embalming was common outside Israel, however—most notably in Egypt, where people painstakingly preserved and wrapped corpses—mummifying them—for their journey into the afterlife. When Jacob died in Egypt, his son Joseph had him embalmed, a process that took forty days, before returning him to Canaan for burial (see Genesis 50).

BITTERSWEET PERFUME

Myrrh, an aromatic resin acquired from the sap of certain scrubby shrubs or little trees in the Near East, was frequently used in expensive perfumes, especially for royalty. More significant, the Egyptians used it for embalming. It has been speculated that the myrrh presented to the Christ Child by the magi was a foreshadowing of His impending sacrificial death.

Many Jewish communities formed a Chevra Chadisha, or a burial society. It was their unpaid duty to care for the deceased of their faith. This ancient building in Prague was the home of one such society.

A Great Show of Mourning

Once a body had been prepared, it was carried to the burial site on a bier, or wooden stretcher, amid great grieving and lamentation.

The dead person's family and friends wept and wailed. They tore their mourning clothes, traditionally coarse sackcloth made of camel or goat hair, and rolled in ashes or put them on their heads. They often tore their hair, and men often tore their beards.

Sometimes there was a funeral feast at the tomb, but burial was traditionally followed by a period of fasting. Mourning typically went on for seven days, but sometimes longer. Joseph was mourned for seventy days, Moses for thirty. The family of the deceased would remain at home after the services and refrain from cooking, washing, or doing other household work, with friends and relatives providing for their needs, a custom not unlike the support families and communities of faith still offer today. The mourning period for a father or mother could last up to a year.

Through it all, the mourners sought to honor and reflect on the life of the person being laid to rest, much as they do today.

One Biblical Burial

John 11 relates the death and resurrection of Lazarus, the brother of Mary (the woman who'd anointed Jesus' feet with perfume) and Martha. Despite hearing that Lazarus was sick, Jesus had remained two days in Jerusalem. When He arrived in Bethany, the siblings' home, Lazarus had been in the tomb for four days, and both sisters told Jesus the same thing: If He had been there earlier, their brother would not have died. We find in this account some details of burial. Lazarus's tomb was a cave, as

This painting depicts women praying at the tomb of Mary. Over the years this has become considerably more than a cave closed with a rock.

was typical of this period. The cave was closed by rolling a stone across the entrance, much like the tomb that Jesus was eventually buried in. When Jesus requested they remove that stone, Martha objected based on the truth of a four-day-old corpse in this dry climate—the decomposing body would have an unpleasant odor.

PROFESSIONAL MOURNERS

Some women in ancient Israel were professional mourners, hired to weep loudly at funerals, stirring up other people's emotions. Jeremiah referred to these women when he prophesied about Judah's pending fall to the Babylonians, saying that God had issued a call for them to "take up a wailing" (Jeremiah 9:18 KJV) over the people.

The Burial of Sarah, *by Gustave Dore.*

Why Burial Was Necessary

Under ancient Hebrew law, bodies were to be buried, returning them to the dust from which they came. Placing a great emphasis on proper burial, the Israelites saw it as their sacred duty to the dead, and numerous scriptural references stress its importance.

The first recorded biblical instance of interment is in Genesis 23. When Sarah died at age 127, Abraham wept and mourned for her. Then he went to the Hittites, from whom he bought some land—specifically a cave—where he could bury his wife. This site, in the ancient city of Hebron, is known as the Cave of the Patriarchs and today is a holy site for Jews; Sarah, Abraham, Isaac, Rebekah, Jacob, and Leah were all interred there (see Genesis 49).

Jacob buried his wife Rachel, who died upon giving birth to her son Benjamin, in the mountains outside Bethlehem and marked her tomb with a pillar (see Genesis 35). The site also is a much-visited holy site for Jews, especially women unable to give birth.

Jewish law required that the dead must be buried within twenty-four hours of death. This was partly because the hot desert climate would hasten the decomposition of the body, but also for reasons of ritual purity and to keep animals from eating the corpse.

It was considered a curse and dishonor not to bury someone. The evil Jezebel was eaten by dogs that left no remains except her skull, feet, and hands (see 2 Kings 9). Rizpah kept vigil over her slain sons' bodies for five months to ensure that wild animals did not devour them (see 2 Samuel 21). Cremation, or burning the body, was forbidden—it was

MAKING SHROUDS

Sisterhoods or women's auxiliaries made shrouds, which were used to cover bodies, for those who had died in their community.

viewed as desecration, associated with pagans, and reserved as a punishment for extreme criminals, evil rulers, heretics, and others who were loathed.

The blocked up Huldah Gates in Jerusalem's Old City walls may have been named after the First Temple prophetess who is said to be buried nearby.

MARY MAGDALENE
SAW IT ALL

Mary Magdalene was at the forefront of a group
of women who followed Jesus throughout the
end of his earthly ministry. She was there at His
crucifixion and death, helped prepare His body
for burial, and witnessed His resurrection.

Mary Magdalene, from a painting by Angelo Bronzini.

Family Tradition

When the prophetess Huldah informed King Josiah that God would bring disaster on the land of Judah because of its sin and corruption, she reassured the righteous king that he would not have to witness the destruction but would be gathered to his fathers and be buried in peace (see 2 Kings 22). This was a reference to the Hebrew tradition of family tombs. It was customary to bury a person in the family tomb, just outside the village in which he or she had lived.

Family tombs, typically caves or openings carved out of rock, were used for multiple burials through the generations and could hold hundreds of bodies. Often there were rock benches that temporarily held the bodies of the deceased.

MOURNING WOMEN AT THE CRUCIFIXION

In Luke 23, as Jesus was being led away to be crucified, the crowd that followed included a group of Jewish women who mourned and wailed for Him. Jesus addressed them, telling them to weep not for Him but for themselves and their children because of the pending destruction of Jerusalem and the temple.

Laying the Loved One to Rest

After a body had been entombed, family members would keep a watchful eye on the site for three days, examining the body to ensure that the person was actually dead. This task was usually performed by the women, who would continue to treat the body with oils and perfumes.

MOTHERS WHO MOURNED

Hebrews 11:35 says, "Women received their dead raised to life again" (NKJV). One such incident involved the widow at Zarephath who provided Elijah with bread. After her son stopped breathing, she asked Elijah if he had come from God to remind her of her sin and kill her son. Elijah cried over the body of the boy, who returned to life (see 1 Kings 17). In 2 Kings 4, after her kindness to the prophet Elisha, a Shunammite woman was rewarded with the birth of a son. Later the boy complained of a pain in his head and subsequently died. The woman went to Elisha, who lay on the boy and prayed, and he raised the boy back to life.

Drawing water from a well—a common experience for biblical women—Rebekah meets Abraham's servant Eliezer, who is seeking a wife for Isaac. The seventeenth-century painting is by Bartolomé Esteban Murillo.

Daily Experiences of Bible Women

INTRODUCTION

During the centuries covered in the biblical accounts—from the early days after creation to the latter days of the first century—the day-to-day life of a woman would have changed significantly. As with any facet of life, there has been progress over time, though the speed of that progress would vary based on location, culture, and religion.

A challenge in understanding the daily lives of the women you read about in scripture is remembering that these were real people with real passions, hopes, concerns, challenges, and skills, not just two-dimensional characters based on the artwork we viewed in Sunday school.

There is no doubt that the women described in the pages of the Bible were anything but two-dimensional. Rahab and Deborah took risks in an age when doing so bore a far greater cost than today. Sarah and Hannah believed God's promises were true in an era without the written words of scripture that we depend on today to determine God's direction.

An important step in seeing from the perspective of these ancient matriarchs is to understand not just the broad scope of their lives, but also the daily details they contended with. It's true that their lives moved at a slower pace, at least in terms of technology. But they also faced a level of inconvenience virtually unimaginable in the modern Western culture. It could take them hours to accomplish what a modern woman does with the push of a button. Their strength in the midst of a life that required brawn and brains to simply survive can inspire us. Their femaleness in the midst of that kind of culture—finding husbands, raising children, preparing meals, sewing, and shopping—can connect us to them as we strive to understand their lives.

The Scope of History

In terms of a time line, throughout history people were progressing: from the simplicity of the early hunters and gatherers into settlers, with rooted civilizations giving rise to ever more sophisticated societies. As this progression took place, so did the roles of, and expectations toward, women. By the time Christianity began to flourish in the middle of the first century AD, women were taking an increasingly active daily role in society, both within and outside the church.

Besides chronology, however, it's important to remember that throughout much of that same history, class differences existed, with the upper end including not only the rich but also the royal. As today, the haves had access to more technology, better supplies, and a different kind of advantages than the have-nots. Rather than focus on the extreme ends of that sociological spectrum, this section will deal primarily with women of the middle class of their society. They were aware of those who were more and less fortunate, but they represent the balance between.

There was also a difference between the women living in cities and those in rural areas. The city dwellers enjoyed the fact that their social systems were more organized, and they were often

The differences between wealth and poverty—as seen in modern Manila—were evident in Bible times, too.

near trade routes, so they had a greater variety of goods. These elements together afforded them more advantages. As today, those in rural areas were farther from the cutting edges of technology and convenience.

In many ways the extremes of any of these comparisons reflected the future and past. As technologies developed (from wood to clay to metal tools, for instance), the wealthy and those in the bustling metropolitan areas of the time met their future first. Then, as today, the new way of doing things spread. By focusing on the middle of the range, we can paint a picture of

the kind of life that compares with what most of us face today, not having everything we want, but always knowing there is someone less fortunate.

Sources of Information

In the "day in the life" section that follows, we will look at what we know—and what we can safely assume— about women's daily routines and commitments in biblical times, offering scriptural references as well as outside scholarly research to support these depictions.

Because of the oral-history nature of the ancient world, mysteries do remain. The best

A COMPOSITE PORTRAIT

What we know about the women in the Bible comes from stories, snapshots really, of significant events in the life of the Israelite nation. Take a quick walk through that history to remember the women you've read about in the Bible and the lives they faced. From Eve to Mrs. Noah to Abraham's wife, Sarah, we follow a branch of a family tree. From Sarah to Rebekah to Leah and Rachel, we observe three generations of family dynamics with domestic disturbances galore. Through the years in Egypt, the nation of Israel emerges with Miriam in the forefront as prophetess and sister of Moses. Once settled in Canaan, Deborah appears among the champions and military leaders of this small nation. Through the exile of Judah (what is left of the Israelite kingdom) we see Esther, a Jewish woman caught in foreign intrigue of sorts. Then, into the New Testament we observe Jesus' mother, Mary; John's mother, Elizabeth; the women who supported Jesus' ministry; and the women who supported the early Christian church. Think of all these women, the challenges they faced, the accomplishments they participated in. Their history is the history of the Bible. Understanding their daily lives, even in the most general terms, allows us to honor their participation in God's redemption throughout history.

efforts of anthropologists, archaeologists, historians, linguists, art and literature experts, sociologists, theologians, and other authorities shed some light, however, on the lives of women in early civilizations. What follows is a general picture, but remember, there were exceptions to every rule, along with ample room for interpretation. So as you read the Bible, give these women room to surprise you. As God did amazing things in their lives, they rose to the challenges they faced.

SEASONS IN A LIFE

Biblical women faced similar seasons in life that women face today. They first experienced the world as young girls, grew into women, raised families, sometimes saw children married and even grandchildren, dealt with aging bodies, and cared for older family members.

What differs is this: The chronology of the seasons of their lives was more compact because life expectancy was much shorter. Lifestyles were more primitive and strenuous; for instance, most of the women you read about in the Old Testament—Rebekah, Rachel, Zipporah—went to a well for water and carried that water back home, rather than simply turning on a faucet or pulling a water bottle out of the refrigerator. Health care was certainly more primitive as well. The women of the Old Testament preceded Hippocrates, considered the father of modern medicine. All this said, the women found in the pages of most of the Bible probably averaged out to around thirty years of age—at best.

This more compact chronology meant that a larger portion of a woman's life was spent in the child-rearing phase. As women today,

however, a Bible woman often found herself caught between generations as she cared for extended family while building a family of her own.

This Armenian family were doing well to have five generations together in 1901, but the young mother would have had many more responsibilities than simply raising her own child.

Most often, a Bible woman's seasons were marked by the men in her life. She first lived under the guardianship of her father and then, she hoped, her husband. If she outlived her husband, then she would hope to be cared for by her sons. This guardianship didn't mean that these women were helpless, or that they had no voice in their families, but it was the reality of their culture and greatly affected their choices.

ADDING UP THE YEARS

Descriptions of short life expectancies in biblical times might seem to run counter to scripture that references women's long and fruitful lives. Sarah, for example, lived to be 127 years old, and Anna was listed as eighty-four years old. While there is no account of female longevity rivaling the 969 years lived by the patriarch Methuselah, it is possible that there were other women who made it into triple digits in birthdays. But these are exceptions. The beginning of written history brought records that document a significantly lower average, attributable to a high infant mortality rate, the limitations of health care, and other factors.

Girlhood

While we stereotypically think of girls in the Bible as "property" or "second-class citizens," the truth is that all children were considered blessings from God (see Psalm 127:3–5) and that the whole family was essential to survival. In fact, part of the reason a bride-price was paid for a woman was to compensate the family for the loss they would suffer in her absence.

When a baby girl was born into a family, she was swaddled, wrapped in a blanket, and then wrapped again with strips of cloth. She went wherever her family, and particularly her mother, went—out to the fields, to the market, to the synagogue, to visit extended family, or to a feast or festival. She was breast-fed for two to three years and usually was in very close contact with not only her parents and siblings but also the larger extended family.

At preschool age, she played with toys, more rudimentary than those in contemporary cultures, but similar—rattles, dolls, whistles. When the prophet Isaiah used the image of a young girl to describe God's treatment of Jerusalem, he said she was nursed, comforted, carried in her mother's arms, and bounced upon her mother's knees (see Isaiah 66:12–13).

By the time she had grown from an infant into a child, a girl in Bible times was participating in the family activities she had been observing since birth. This was not a culture

These young Afghan sisters demonstrate the bonds of interdependance required for family security in difficult conditions.

that required her to stay inside or remain veiled. In her free time, she could roam as freely as her parents allowed. While she may have wanted to go out to the fields or trade shops with her father or brothers, she more likely stayed with her mother at home, learning to handle household responsibilities like wood gathering, food preparation and storage, weaving, fabric making, and handling and transporting water While these were tasks typically relegated to females, they were essential to the survival of the family.

In thinking about children in early cultures, it's important to separate our thinking from the contemporary view, one in which childhood is considered an entity unto itself. In the ancient world, these children existed as potential adults, property workers, fabric makers. They learned skills not as a play-school activity, but in order to contribute to the existence of their family, people, and bloodline.

School Age

If a young girl had brothers, she watched them begin school around age six. She did not go to school herself, but that doesn't mean she received no education. Her mother educated her at home. Through the teaching of her mom, hearing oral tradition passed down by family members, listening to the teaching at the synagogue, and her participation in religious festivals, she learned the history of her people—a history she would hope to one day teach her own children (see Deuteronomy 4:9–10).

As today, a girl in ancient Israel had chores, though probably a heavier load of chores than her contemporary counterparts. She would have been expected to babysit any younger siblings. An unusual

NEVER MARRIED

In modern Western culture a woman who marries late, or not at all, typically still moves out from the home of her parents. She most often has a career, chooses whom she dates, and even travels with friends on vacation.

Not so in the ancient world. In that culture, a woman needed to be under the umbrella of a man for protection, provision, and stature in the community. If a woman didn't marry, she stayed under the care of her family of origin, trusting her father to provide for her. While women did learn certain trades, this did not provide the same kind of independence as is common today when women are expected, just as men, to make money, live under their own roofs, and provide for themselves.

circumstance but a typical example of this would be Moses' sister, who stood by the Nile River to watch the basket and the baby hidden there (see Exodus 2). A young girl would also begin to take over some of her mother's chores. Since her earliest years, she had been watching her mother—and then helping her—make cloth, cook food, and manage the family's water supply.

A young girl works with her mother, selling handicrafts in the west African nation of Mauritania.

As she grew older, a girl began to handle those chores on her own. (Keep in mind that girls often married around the age of thirteen, so by then they needed to be able to manage the same household chores their mothers had.)

When a girl in an early civilization had some free time, however, she did have toys to play with. She also played games (and probably fought) with her siblings. Archeologists have uncovered a variety of pastimes including dolls and dollhouses, board games, dice games, and ball games. Just as today children mimic the adult behavior around them with miniature kitchens, these ancient girls played with miniature pottery dishes and pots, as well as dolls with jointed arms and legs and miniature furniture to accompany them.

While a young girl in Bible times did not attend school, she did attend the local synagogue (sitting with the women, separately from the men) and celebrated religious holidays with her family and extended family.

Betrothal and Marriage

In biblical times, marriage was not an option. A woman was *expected* to marry. In fact, in such a patriarchal society, her standing in the community depended upon it—and childbirth was expected to follow within a reasonable period after the wedding. Because this was so ingrained in the culture, a typical young girl would look forward to the day when she would become betrothed, or engaged; be married; and raise a family. (For more details, see "Women and Marriage" in Section 1: Women in Bible Times.)

Raising children, then and now, is an activity best done with plenty of support.

CARING FOR CHILDREN

While boys did go to school at the synagogue at the age of six, they were still under the tutelage of their mother until the age of thirteen, when they were considered men. This meant that in her day-to-day life, a mother not only managed a home in a primitive time that required much manual labor, she also was her children's teacher. The bulk of this amount of labor highlights the advantages of extended families existing together. Although in contemporary times a young mother often feels isolated, this would have seldom been the case for these women. Extended families often lived together in compound-like arrangements. In this way, there would be a division of labor among the women of the larger clan.

Housekeeping Duties

In some ways, a day in the life of a woman in Bible times reflects the same kind of components as a woman in the modern world. A woman today typically handles food—getting it, storing it, preparing it, serving it, and disposing of it. She clothes her family by knowing sizes, shopping for clothes or the materials for making clothes. She deals with the furnishings of the home, procuring them, arranging them, and cleaning them. She cares for her husband and for children and for pets. She sometimes works outside of the home and still finds time to be a neighbor and friend, a part of the community. In the midst of it all, she works to find better ways to accomplish her tasks so that she can somehow get it all done.

For the women of Bible times, these same tasks took place. There is, however, a much more complicated process for each task. Here's what it would have looked like for her:

FOOD MANAGEMENT

Today, women make grocery lists, plan menus, and prepare meals. We eat several meals and often snacks during the day, so getting and preparing that food are daily activities. It was the same for the women of the Bible. While people often ate two main meals a day rather than the three that the modern world is accustomed to, these meals required some preparation.

In the most ancient of times, the men hunted while the women gathered. A woman, with children in tow, would search for berries, nuts, roots, and herbs with which to feed her family. She had no encyclopedias to identify which plants were toxic, and so she had to rely on her common sense and what she was taught by her own mother and other women older than herself.

In later eras, a woman could cultivate her own foods, tending to a small garden. Tilling and

A village oven built by the charitable organization American Colony in East Jerusalem. Such ovens would have been baking bread for centuries in the region.

planting by hand, she would have tended her garden daily during growing season. Since there was no refrigeration, she had to keep track not only of the foods she had stored, but also how long they would stay fresh so nothing went to waste. She may have raised, among other things, beans, onions, and melons. She may have also had access to vineyards as well as olive and fig trees. If so, she was also responsible for keeping up with the harvesting of the fruits as well as the processing of them, making wine, pressing for oil, and drying for storage.

AT THE WELL

Another daily task was dealing with water for drinking, cooking, and bathing. If a woman was fortunate, she lived near a spring or a man-made cistern, but if not, she probably walked each day to a well, often in the cool of the evening (see Genesis 24:11).

While she was at the well, she could visit with the other people—women and men—gathered there. Abraham's servant found Isaac's wife, Rebekah, at the well in Nahor. Isaac's son Jacob met and fell in love with his wife, Rachel, by a well. Moses met his wife, Zipporah, at the well in Midian. And there is Jesus' memorable encounter with the Samaritan woman at the well.

Dealing with the water was hard work. After walking to the well and lowering her pot, pitcher, or goatskin by a string or rope, she then walked back home carrying her load. Think about how heavy a grocery bag is that contains a gallon of milk or several two-liter bottles of drinks. Imagine walking to the store and carrying all the liquid your family would use for half the day—all uses, not just drinking—with you on your return trip.

This Philipino family are gathered around the village well. Note that only the females carry the water.

BAKING AND COOKING

Bread, the most basic of foods in biblical times, was a vital part of every meal. Therefore, bread making could be a daily concern for a woman. It was up to her to either grow or buy the grain, then to grind it into flour using some type of mortar and pestle or, later, millstones. She baked it into bread in small ovens fed by burning straw, dried grasses, and charcoal, which she and the children had to gather on a regular basis. Before she cooked the bread, however, she most often saved a portion of the dough to be used as leaven, mixed in with the next day's flour and oil.

Her family's main meal was prepared in clay pots over a flame, even in the heat of summer. While she didn't always have meat, she did serve vegetables, fruit, and milk or yogurt. Lamb was sometimes roasted, but often what little meat the family had was boiled. Fish, which she would have served

often, was cooked over a fire, smoked, or salted and preserved, much as we think of salty sardines or other canned fish today. Stews made of such ingredients as lentils or mutton were a good way for a woman to stretch her resources in feeding the family.

So, in terms of food management, part of a woman's day was spent making a fire, making bread, cooking food, and preserving food as she could by salting and drying it.

MILK AND HONEY

A woman also could hope to spend part of her morning milking a goat or sheep. She could then use that milk to make cheese and yogurt, and sometimes butter if she had an immediate use for it.

The foods she prepared were not particularly sweet. There was no cane sugar at that time. Honey was the sweetest food available. An Old Testament woman would have had to dig the honey, made by wild bees, out of the ground or from in between rocks. A New Testament woman probably had access to honey

These cooking pots from Herculaneum date from around the time of Jesus. With their "marble work surfaces," this would have been considered a high-class kitchen at the time.

that was cultivated from bees. A woman could also make her own honeylike nectar by boiling down dates or other sweet fruits.

CLOTHES

Biblical women were responsible for providing clothes for their families. This included first weaving the actual fabric from materials such as wool or flax. She could do this spinning and weaving herself, or she might get to use a large outside loom and join with the other women of her community, working as they visited together, perhaps like a quilting bee in more recent American history.

Once the fabric was made, the woman then fashioned it into simple tunics and cloaks. Making clothes was not a daily task for a woman—Samuel received one new cloak a year from his mother—but cleaning and repairing clothes may have been. Keep in mind, however, that this was not a time of daily showers and electric washing machines. Clothes needed to wear well and last as long as possible, even when worn day after day. Washing clothes involved stomping them or beating them with a stick in a tub of water, probably laboriously gathered from a well. Soap or other cleansing agents such as soda or chalk were also used.

This stained-glass window from the early twentieth century shows Egyptian women spinning and weaving as a group activity.

THE MOTHER OF INVENTION

You can be sure that a biblical woman's daily plate of chores was full and that a problem-solving woman was always looking for ways to get her tasks done more effectively. Because of this, women were at the forefront of creating new and improved tools to help with their work. They may not have always gotten credit for their inventions or been able to market them by themselves, but items like looms and spindles; needles, scrapers, and tanning tools (for use with animal skins); and dyes for coloring clothing were all a part of the woman's domain in Bible times. The advances made in these "technologies" were most likely made by women.

ANIMAL CARE

Women shared in the tending of a family's animals, such as sheep and goats that provided meat and milk as well as material for clothing. This work might have included leading the animals to pasture, feeding and watering them, and watching over them at night. We traditionally think of shepherds as men. Certainly by trade they were. But the women tended to the family's animals, which required a broad knowledge and a variety of care.

Early multitasking: In this nineteenth-century painting by Jean-Francois Millet, a shepherdess knits while keeping her flock.

Work Outside the Home: Specialized Skills

We stereotypically think of women in the ancient world as quiet, often beaten-down subjects of their husbands. But the greater reality is that these women were social creatures, part of a larger family. Some of them were married to difficult men, but others were married to honorable men who cared for their families and treated their wives with respect. The survival of these women required their having many skills.

Just as today, when a woman proved particularly efficient at a skill, she got the attention of the community. A woman who made particularly beautiful cloth might eventually be asked to sell some of her cloth. Thus, cottage industries were alive and well. Eventually a woman could barter her goods in the marketplace or among her neighbors. She could even train her children, enabling them to contribute to her efforts.

Of course, the most primary role a woman could fulfill was that of a caretaker. As is still true today, women hired themselves out to care for the children of wealthy families. They also hired themselves out to care for the homes of those who could afford household help. This was different

This third-century Greek statue shows an older woman who seems to have made a career of "wet-nursing" other people's children.

most cases a person's vocation was woven into his or her life. Children could be easily cared for by extended family so a woman could be away from home if necessary. A woman could even take her children with her, teaching them as she worked. The roles of other members of the household could ebb and flow to accommodate any activity that contributed to the wealth and well-being of the family.

GOING TO MARKET

The market was a lively, bustling place, often at the gates of a city. It was lined with open-air stalls and rich with aromas of foodstuffs, live animals, and exotic perfumes, boisterous with the sounds of conversation, haggling, and laughter. While it was filled primarily with men, women were not unseen; the degree of their presence and involvement varied significantly from culture to culture, as well as by class and over time.

from indentured servitude, though certainly there were people of all ages who sold themselves as servants in order to work off debt. But there were also women who made household income by serving as maids and nannies.

Keep in mind that this was not a culture with a corporate mindset as we have today. This was still a rather tribal, clanlike family structure. In

By the days of the New Testament, women had gained many more rights and a higher profile. As cities developed, women found they could enlarge their trade by increasing the volume of items they made at home, whether baked goods or other food, textiles, or pottery. If they were unable to sell in the market, they could do so on the ever-expanding trade routes.

One commonly sold food was bread, which was a part of virtually every meal. The baking of barley bread also was required for the brewing of beer, which was popular in many ancient cultures. Wine, also made in the home, was another beverage that could be sold at market. Women distinguished themselves as bakers, brewers, and winemakers as well.

typical household duties for wealthy women, including child care, cooking, making clothes, doing laundry, and in some cases actually managing the household. They also served as nurses, wet nurses, and midwives. Some female slaves were forced to submit to sexual relations with the master of the house.

Slavery and prostitution were often interlinked. Prostitutes were often members of the lower classes, lacking marketable skills. In some cases female slaves were forced into becoming prostitutes; other women became prostitutes to support themselves and perhaps buy their way out of slavery. Prostitution, commonly referred to as the "oldest profession," has been a part of the social fabric since the earliest civilizations. It was

The Machne Yehuda market in Jerusalem.

SLAVERY AND PROSTITUTION

At the other end of the spectrum, many women of Bible times were slaves and prostitutes. While some women hired themselves out as slaves, others had no choice. Slave women performed many

legal in cultures including the Canaan of the Old Testament, and in some cases was sanctioned and taxed by the government. It was also a part of some pagan religions. Jericho's Rahab, who helped the Israelite spies, is believed to have been a prostitute.

A young Greek slave faces her deceased mistress in a funeral image from approximately 380 BC.

Jesus watches a widow throw two small copper coins into the temple offering. Later, He'll tell His disciples that the poor woman gave more than the rich people had, because she had given "all that she had, even all her living" (Mark 12:44 KJV).

Aging and Widowhood

Two of the more poignant biblical stories involving Jesus and women center on widows. While in the town of Nain with His disciples, Jesus encountered a widow who had just lost her only son. Touched by her grief, the Lord resurrected the young man, who immediately began to talk and was returned to his mother (see Luke 7). In another story, Jesus gave His disciples an instant lesson in spiritual economics when they witnessed, among the ostentatious offerings of the rich, a poor widow's contribution of two small copper coins. Her gift was greater than all the others, Jesus said, for she gave everything she had to live on (see Mark 12; Luke 21).

The plight of a widow in ancient times could be cruel. They are often mentioned in the Bible with the orphans and fatherless. When a woman had lost her husband, who generally was the primary breadwinner in the household, she faced a life of uncertainty. With limited job prospects (at least honorable ones), no pension, no social security, and no life insurance, she was prone to poverty and, in many cases, the threat of being robbed or otherwise taken advantage of by unscrupulous characters. The prophet Jeremiah compared the once-great city of Jerusalem—which after turning from God had fallen to Babylon and seen its temple destroyed—to a widow. Jerusalem is described as a queen who has become a slave (see Lamentations 1:1).

DEFENDER OF WIDOWS

Psalm 68:5 describes God as a defender of widows.

EXPECTATIONS AND PROTECTIONS

In the ancient world, it was common for a woman to become a widow at a young age, largely because of two factors: 1) the lower life expectancy, in general, for people in early civilizations and 2) the tendency for many men to marry women ten or fifteen years younger than them. Quite often a young widow would have no trouble remarrying, and in fact levirate law provided for such situations. If she had no children, she was expected to remain with her in-laws and to marry her husband's brother or other close relative, both to ensure that she was provided for and to continue the bloodline.

Ruth is a good example of a widowed woman who chose to stay with her widowed mother-in-law. Ruth, in fact, traveled back from her native Moab to Naomi's hometown of Bethlehem. There, Ruth married one of her closest relatives by marriage. She and Naomi were both provided for then by the levirate law. In such cases, the deceased husband's property stayed in the family. If a close relative could not be found to marry the widow, the woman did have the option of marrying someone from another clan or returning to her own family.

In other cases, the widow might have a grown son who would be able to help care for her. Many ancient homes, even extending back to prehistoric times, included structures that apparently served as "widow's quarters." And many families lived in more of a compound rather than a single-family dwelling so that the extended family had a place together.

John comforts his new "mother," Mary, as Jesus dies.

Jesus gave us an example of caring for a widow. As He hung, dying, on the cross, He made provisions for the care of His own mother, by then evidently a widow. Seeing His mother, Mary, standing nearby, He committed her to the care of one of His disciples. From that point on, Mary became a part of that disciple's home (see John 19:26–27).

In some cases, a widow might have become wealthy enough that she did not need someone to provide for her and therefore could live on her own. However, in the event she was not wealthy, was unable to remarry, and had no family to care for her, she was in dire straits. Because of the hardships facing widows, there are a number of laws and exhortations in both the Old and New Testaments to care for widows, as well as for orphans. Exodus 22:22, for example, warns against taking advantage of a widow or orphan. Moses, in Deuteronomy 10:18, describes God as one who will defend the cause of widows and orphans, and later, Deuteronomy 14:28–29, gives instructions for collecting and storing tithes (10 percent) of the year's produce at the end of every three years to feed widows, orphans, and foreigners.

A WIDOW'S SOCIAL LIFE

Socially, there were certain advantages afforded a widow. For example, she was free from at least some of the strictures that applied to younger, unmarried women. She could operate more independently, was less subject to male authority, and perhaps not as bound by rules of dress and behavior as married women. On the other hand, one of the difficulties of widowhood was that, because widows significantly outnumbered widowers, they had fewer options for remarrying than did men whose wives had died.

Widows in ancient times were easy to recognize, as they wore distinctive clothing—Genesis 38 refers to Tamar taking off and putting back on her "widow's clothes." Although sackcloth and ashes may have been the customary attire during an actual mourning period, it is not clear exactly how the widow's post-mourning clothing differed from that of a married woman. Deuteronomy 24:17 mentions a widow's cloak, but not how that might differ from any other

JUSTICE FOR WIDOWS

Among the curses included in Deuteronomy 27 is a curse for anyone who withholds justice from a widow.

Different cultures have different dress codes. This Calcutta woman is indicating her widowhood by wearing a white sari.

woman's cloak. Apparently a widow's garb did not include a veil; Genesis 38 relates how Tamar, who was disguising herself, put on a veil only after shedding her widow's garments.

WIDOWS AND THE EARLY CHURCH

Evangelism and outreach/ministry have been dual goals of the Christian church since its beginning, and widows were the primary focus of these early charitable efforts. Acts 6 recounts an internal problem in the early church: complaints by some of the Greek Jews that their widows were being neglected in the daily food distribution. To address this issue, the disciples chose seven men, including Stephen, to operate a full-time food ministry serving the widows; this allowed the disciples to maintain their focus on prayer and preaching, and the church continued to grow.

Paul devoted more than half of First Timothy 5 to the subject of widows: how they should be treated and how they should act. While commanding the church to care for those widows who were truly in need, he made it clear that a widow's family should be the first source of her provisions. He also called for the creation of a list of needy widows, consisting of those who met certain require-ments: 1) She was at least sixty years old; 2) she had been faithful to her husband; and 3) she had been known for good deeds, such as raising children, exhibiting hospitality, and helping others. Further, he advised younger widows to remarry rather than counting on the church to care for them and becoming idlers, gossips, and busybodies. Those who did make the list were expected to serve the church.

As the church grew, widows played a key role in its ministries. During the second and third centuries, an order of widows was created to look after other needy women in the congregation.

A young widow makes her offering at the temple.

WIDOWS IN DISTRESS

Dorcas was a woman known for helping the poor. Acts 9 describes the women who came to grieve Dorcas when she died. When Peter arrived, (in the hopes that he could bring Dorcas back to life) widows gathered around him, showing him the clothes she had made for them.

WEEK-TO-WEEK VIEW

For women of Bible times, or at least those in the Judeo-Christian arc, the Sabbath would have defined the rest of the week. With six days devoted to household chores, child care, and perhaps even outside work, the seventh was meant for tending to more spiritual concerns. Women played a major role in preparing the family and the household for worship.

Judaism was far from the only religion in biblical times: From the early Mesopotamians on, people worshipped gods of such things as the sun, the moon, water, weather, and fertility; gods included El and Baal (Canaanites), the sun god Ra and the sky goddess Nut (Egyptians), Zeus (Greeks), and Apollo (Romans). Judaism, however, was the first to demand exclusivity, as it forbade the worship of all gods and goddesses except Yahweh. Under Mosaic Law, the Sabbath—which would have corresponded with Saturday, the seventh day of our modern calendar—was designated as a day of rest, "holy to the LORD" (Exodus 31:15 NIV). This passage goes so far as to require the death of anyone who did any work on the Sabbath. The Israelites were to observe and celebrate the Sabbath "as a lasting covenant" (Exodus 31:16 NIV) in recognition of the fact that God had created the heavens and earth in six days and rested on the seventh.

In Old Testament times, the family would visit the local shrine, make a sacrifice, and be instructed by a priest. In New Testament times, the Sabbath began at sunset on Friday and ended at sunset on Saturday. The meal served at that time would be the culinary highlight of the week, with the best bread, meat, and other items a family could afford to serve.

The copper blech is covering the lit burners of the stove to keep the precooked food warm so no cooking need be done on the Sabbath.

The complexities and rigors of Mosaic Law would no doubt have been a challenge to a woman responsible for running a household. For example, the prohibition on working on the Sabbath meant wives and mothers had to have meals prepared by sundown Friday for that evening and the next day, a day in which they were forbidden to even start a fire, all the while being mindful of Jewish dietary law. A typical meal for a family of modest means might have consisted of some sort of homemade flatbread, with olive oil for dipping, and maybe onions or leeks; a simple stew such as lentils; a salad with lettuce or spinach and other vegetables; perhaps some dates or figs; and wine. Such a meal could be prepared ahead of time, and the dishes that were cooked could be packed in straw to keep them warm.

For families who obeyed Jewish law to the fullest, the Sabbath included sacrifices brought to the local temple. The sacrifices outlined in Numbers 28:9–10 included two lambs. In Leviticus 24 guidelines are given for an offering of twelve loaves of bread, a sacrifice that would have been prepared by the women of the household.

For Jewish families who lived after the great exile in Babylon, part of the Sabbath included a trip to the synagogue or local teaching center. Once at the synagogue, many scholars now believe, women played an active role in worship, although other authorities have traditionally assumed this not to be the case. There was a fair amount of diversity within Judaism, as there later would be within Christianity, and as continues to be the case within both faiths. Biblical women are portrayed as dancing, singing, and playing musical instruments in praise to God. The Song of Moses and Miriam, relates how, after the Israelites had crossed the Red Sea and escaped the Pharaoh's army, "Miriam the prophetess, Aaron's sister, took a

DAY-TO-DAY RELIGION

Religion was not simply relegated to one day of the week, however; prayer, instruction, and remembrance were intended to be a part of day-to-day life, permeating the fabric of one's existence. Mothers and fathers were charged with the responsibility of keeping their children informed about their history, laws, traditions, and beliefs. Children memorized scriptures and heard stories of spiritual heroes that became a part of the Bible, and much of this teaching rested on the shoulders of mothers who tended to the children all day while the men were in their fields and shops. Jewish families offered benedictions to God each morning, afternoon, and evening.

OBSERVING THE SABBATH

As religious leaders became more and more specific about how a person was to honor the Sabbath, the rules and regulations about what a person could or couldn't do on that day became quite burdensome. For instance, there were guidelines for what kind of knot a person could tie on the Sabbath and what kind of knot was considered work. If a woman could tie a knot with one hand, then it was allowed. Such guidelines pertained to her clothing as well as to small household chores. They also affected the materials she could use around the house. She could draw water from a well if the well was close enough to the house, but she had to use something other than rope to lower the skin or jar.

tambourine in her hand, and all the women followed her, with tambourines and dancing" (Exodus 15:20 NIV). In the story of Lydia, women gathered for prayer in the synagogue. While it was rare for women to be synagogue leaders, it was not unheard of. Lydia, Phoebe, and Priscilla occupied positions of authority in the early Christian church, which had its roots in the Jewish synagogue. They may have been exceptions, but they weren't the only ones. And archaeological evidence points to women who held such synagogue titles as priest, leader, elder, and "mother."

YEAR-TO-YEAR VIEW

The Israelite woman's year was marked by a series of festivals. Much like the Western culture prepares for Thanksgiving and Christmas holidays, she would prepare for these holy days. They came so often that she may have felt she was always preparing for one or the other.

These celebrations, originally associated with the planting and harvest seasons, eventually became commemorations of God's mighty acts of provision throughout the history of the nation.

The terms *feast* and *festival* are often used interchangeably in most Western translations of the Bible. In technical terms, however, a feast was a specific meal, while a festival was a celebration lasting an extended period of time and could include more than one feast through the course of the celebration. Passover, which was celebrated on one night, included a feast, but it was a part of the Festival of Unleavened Bread, which lasted a week.

A feast day in a synagogue—the Feast of the Rejoicing of the Law.

These festivals and holy days in Israel were times when friends and distant family could gather, much like family reunions today. For some of the festivals, as many people as were able would travel to Jerusalem just as, according to Luke 2:41, Mary took Jesus year after year. It was on one such trip, when Jesus was twelve, that Mary and Joseph mistakenly left their Son behind talking with the teachers in the temple courts. The reason it was easy for these parents not to notice their missing child is that extended family would all caravan together on these pilgrimages. As far as His parents knew, young Jesus could have been with any one of many traveling families and probably in any one of many places in Jerusalem where friends and family were. Thus, it took them three days to find Him.

Overwhelming Details

Whether the festivals were to be celebrated in Jerusalem or at home, they required preparation. Just as a woman had to prepare ahead of time for the Sabbath, a day when minimal food preparation was allowed, the festivals required attention to many details: gathering food, transporting family, and carrying clothes. All this took place in an age before automated vehicles or refrigeration. You can imagine what a time of joy it must have been to see family you'd been separated from without the connection of e-mail, a telephone, or even a telegraph line with which to communicate.

WHICH FESTIVALS?

Below is a list of festivals that would have held a special historical and spiritual significance for the ancient Israelite woman. As you can see, except for July and August, there is some holiday every sixty days. This list doesn't include the monthly New Moon festival.

For each of these events, a woman in the Bible would need to prepare food either for travel or for guests. If traveling, she would need to pack clothes for her children and husband as well

In this nineteenth-century painting by William Holman-Hunt, a relieved Mary finds Jesus at the Temple.

as carry gifts for family she would be seeing. If staying at home, she would need to make special arrangements, prepare special clothing or food that the holiday might require, prepare grain for the offerings, or otherwise make provisions to host visiting guests.

Israelite Annual Festivals

Passover and the Days of Unleavened Bread
- 14th day of the first month, Nisan (March–April)
- Leviticus 23:4–8
- This feast commemorated the night before Israel's escape from Egypt when the blood of an innocent animal was sprinkled on the door frames of the houses so that the angel of death would "pass over" (see Exodus 12:1–14). In celebrating this festival, lambs were sacrificed and eaten with a meal that included specific foods symbolizing the quick flight of the Israelites (see Exodus 12:5–8; Deuteronomy 16:2).
- 15th–21st days of Nisan
- When the Israelites were delivered from Egypt they ate unleavened bread because they were in too much of a hurry to make bread that would require time to rise (see Exodus 12:39). During the days of this festival, the women were to serve only unleavened bread to their families to remember the journey of their ancestors (see Exodus 12:8; Deuteronomy 16:3).

Feast of Weeks (Pentecost)
- Leviticus 23:15–22
- 6th day of Sivan (May–June)
- This one-day feast celebrated the wheat and barley harvest, as well as the ripening of early figs and grapes (see Exodus 23:16; 34:22). The priests offered two loaves made of new flour and made animal sacrifices (see Leviticus 23:17–18; Numbers 28:26–31). People also brought freewill offerings to show their recognition of God's provision and their gratitude (see Deuteronomy 16:10).

Feast of Trumpets
- Leviticus 23:23–25
- 1st day of seventh month, Tishri (September–October)
- This feast marked Israel's new year, Rosh Hashanah (head of the year). The celebration included a day of rest and sacred assembly with trumpeting and special sacrifices (see Leviticus 23:24; Numbers 29:1–6). It

commemorated God's giving of the Ten Commandments on Sinai. As with other festivals, it included a grain offering for which the wife would prepare the grain.

Day of Atonement
- Leviticus 23:26–32
- 10th of Tishri (September–October)
- Known as Yom Kippur, this highest of holy days reminded the Israelites of their need for God's forgiveness (see Leviticus 16:29–34; Numbers 29:7–11).

Festival of Tabernacles and the Last Great Day
- Leviticus 23:33–43
- 15th–21st of Tishri (September–October)
- This festival recalled, if not reenacted, Israel's nomadic life in the wilderness after leaving Egypt and before entering Canaan—the people camped out in temporary shelters—as well as celebrated the gathering of the year's main harvest of fruit and olives (see Deuteronomy 16:13 -15; Leviticus 23:42; Numbers 29:12–34). While a woman's typical household duties were labor-intensive,

during this week they were even further disrupted.
- 22nd of Tishri
- This date was the final annual Sabbath of the Hebrew festival year (see Exodus 34:22; Leviticus 23:36; Numbers 29:35–39).

Dedication (Lights, Hanukkah)
- John 10:22
- 25th of Kislev (November–December)

Purim (Lots)
- Esther 9:21, 27–28
- 14th and 15th of Adar (February–March)
- This festival was inaugurated by Queen Esther. As a Jewish exile, she disguised her nationality and became queen of Persia. As queen, she had the opportunity to thwart the efforts of an enemy who would have put her people to death. In commemoration of this great rescue on her part through God's providence, this feast gave the Jewish women who lived after the exile an opportunity to celebrate a female champion of Israel.

Golda Meir (1898 1978) was the first woman to serve as prime minister of modern Israel (1969–74). Perhaps surprisingly to some, Israel had female leaders millennia earlier.

Women's Roles and Jobs

INTRODUCTION: ROLES AND JOBS OF OLD TESTAMENT WOMEN

The Old Testament reveals women who were leaders, prophets, tabernacle workers, artists, musicians, poets, and queens. Others filled roles of lesser status—as midwives, harlots, mothers, and simple wives—but were heroes, nonetheless. Then there are the women whose names are not included in the biblical text but whose stories live on to teach, guide, and instruct us in life. Scripture also reveals symbolic women, as examples of what to be or what not to be. And lastly are the goddesses—larger than life pagan idols of the people in that ancient culture.

From the myriad of women presented in the pages of the Bible, readers will find a message from days gone by that, named or unnamed, women played a vital role in the story of God and humankind, as they continue to do today.

CHURCH AND GOVERNMENT

Wise and wily, winsome, and woebegone women of the Old Testament showed quite a bit of chutzpah in days gone by. Revealed to us is the courage of Deborah, the boldness of Huldah, the effrontery of Miriam, and the intelligence of Abigail. Then there are the women who quietly went about the business of serving God with their artistry, special skills, and musical abilities. In the midst of all this are the stories of women who were false prophetesses, scheming queens, and members of royal families caught up in intrigue. No matter how big or small their roles, each of these women were an integral part of the Old Testament story.

Judge

There were very few women in this category. Actually, Deborah was in a category unto herself.

DEBORAH

Judges 4–5

Deborah was the only woman with the official title of "judge" in the Old or New Testament. For decades, she held court under a palm tree in northern Israel. Her husband, Lappidoth, permitted Deborah to fulfill her God-given role. His support was never more evident than when his wife initiated a military campaign against powerful King Jabin of Canaan. Led by his cruel general, Sisera, Jabin's army had terrorized Israel twenty years. Deborah summoned Barak and told him to recruit soldiers from the tribes of Naphtali and Zebulun to march to Mount Tabor. Although Barak's name meant "lightning," he refused unless Deborah accompanied him. She agreed, but informed him the honor of capturing Sisera would go to a woman. Together, Deborah and Barak motivated ten thousand soldiers to follow them.

Judge Deborah addressing the people.

According to Deborah's warlike victory song, one of the oldest in the Bible, Barak's gallant few fought like heroes. God intervened with a supernatural storm, and the flooded river Kishon swept away Sisera's large army with its nine hundred chariots of iron. Sisera himself was killed by Jael, who executed her sleeping guest with a hammer and tent peg. Thus, Deborah's prophecy came true.

Thanks to Deborah's faith, courage, and leadership abilities, Israel experienced a rare period of peace for forty years.

Prophetesses and Worship Leaders

Though we know a couple of these women by name, the majority are described in the Bible simply by their function. And what an important function it was, assisting in the worship of God.

MIRIAM

Exodus 15:20, 21; Numbers 12:1–15; 20:1; 26:59; Deuteronomy 24:9; 1 Chronicles 6.3, Micah 6:4

Miriam, the sister of Moses and Aaron, was the first woman in the Bible designated as a prophetess. Although Exodus 2 does not name her, Miriam is usually identified as the sister who watched over baby Moses, hidden in the reeds along the Nile River bank because Pharaoh decreed the killing of Hebrew newborn males. When Pharaoh's daughter rescued the crying infant, quick-thinking Miriam offered to bring "one of the Hebrew women" (Exodus 2:7 NIV)—their mother Jochebed—to nurse him. In rescuing Moses, Israel's future leader, Pharaoh's daughter rescued an entire nation.

Miriam leads the Hebrews in praise in this eighteenth-century painting by Paulo Malteis.

Eighty years later, after the parting of the Red Sea, Miriam led thousands of Hebrew women in singing praise to God, playing tambourines, and dancing for joy. She no doubt ministered to women during the trying years of their desert journey and, perhaps like other prophetesses later in the Bible, spoke God's messages to the general congregation.

The Bible mentions nothing of a marriage. Perhaps Miriam remained single, highly unusual during her era.

Like many leaders, Miriam struggled with envy, as did her brother Aaron, the high priest. The two scorned Moses' marriage to a Cushite woman and questioned his leadership. Miriam may not have felt close to Moses. Although she watched over him when he was a baby and knew him as a toddler, she probably did not see Moses again until both were elderly adults, when he returned to Egypt to demand Israel's freedom. Because her name is uncharacteristically listed first—before Aaron's—in the account of this family quarrel, some believe Miriam played instigator (see Numbers 12). She also may have assumed headship as the eldest. Despite both siblings' sin, Miriam appears to be the only one who suffered leprosy and a week's banishment outside the camp. Critics point to this seeming inequity of justice as sexism. But Miriam expressed no repentance, even after being struck with leprosy. Aaron, on the other hand, readily admitted their sin and begged Moses to pray for their sister.

Although wronged, Moses did, and the Lord, while temporarily isolating Miriam, responded with healing and restoration.

Centuries later, God affirmed Miriam's ministry through the prophet Micah as He reminded His people of His love for them: "For I brought thee up out of the land of Egypt, and redeemed thee out of the house of servants; and I sent before thee Moses, Aaron, and Miriam" (Micah 6:4 KJV).

ISAIAH'S WIFE
Isaiah 8:3–4

Isaiah and his prophetess wife contrast vividly with other prophets such as Jeremiah, single by God's command; Ezekiel, whose beloved wife died as a sign to His idolatrous people; and Hosea, who married Gomer, a prostitute, to illustrate God's forgiveness. On one hand, Isaiah and his wife shared God's truth and the common joys and burdens of ministry. On the other, they may have struggled, learning to accept each other's unique gifts and roles.

God used their two sons to communicate His messages. One they named Shear-Jashub, who met King Ahaz (see Isaiah 7:3). His name meant "a remnant will return," predicting Israel's journey back to God and to their land after exile.

They named their second son Maher-Shalal-Hash-Baz, meaning "haste, spoil, speed, prey," which implied Syria and Samaria would flee before Assyrian enemies. This prediction came true in 732 BC when Tiglath-pileser III conquered Damascus.

While we do not know the name of this prophetess who loved and served God, her family, and God's people, He does.

HULDAH

2 Kings 22:14–20, 23:1   25; 2 Chronicles 34:22–33

The prophetess Huldah was married to Shallum, who oversaw King Josiah's wardrobe. When priests repairing the temple found the long-neglected Mosaic Law, the young king sent a delegation to Huldah to inquire of God about its message. Interestingly, he did not ask Jeremiah or Zephaniah, who also prophesied during his reign.

Unlike messages from earlier prophets, Huldah's words related to those already in print, part of the book of Deuteronomy. She verified God's solemn message: Judah would be destroyed because of disobedience. Although politically risky, Huldah's prophecy fanned the spark of revival in Josiah's heart. He began an aggressive campaign to destroy idolatry in Israel and lead his people back to God.

TABERNACLE ARTISTS

Exodus 35:25–26

The Tabernacle, constructed after the Exodus, required enormous community effort. Although isolated in the desert with little prospect of acquiring more treasures, families willingly donated those received from the Egyptians before their flight. These included jewels, gold, silver, brass, linen,

An illustration of the Tabernacle with gifts of gold and fine, newly woven drapes and curtains.

hides, and wood for the tent and furniture God designed. Moses invited all artists to use their God-given gifts to create the beautiful place where His Presence would dwell. Spinning was women's work, so they produced all the blue, purple, scarlet, and fine linen thread needed, as well as that spun from goat hair. Others wove the thread into cloth and sewed curtains for the Tabernacle and exquisite clothing for the priests, as the Tabernacle grew from a plan in the mind of God to a reality where they could worship Him.

MUSICIANS AND POETS

1 Chronicles 25:1–8; Ezra 2:65; Nehemiah 7:67; Psalm 68:24–26

In everyday life, Old Testament women celebrated family and national events through composing and singing songs, often accompanied by instruments and dance. Miriam is the first woman in the Old Testament mentioned as praising the Lord through music, leading thousands of women in celebration of Israel's escape from Pharaoh through the Red Sea. Deborah, Hannah, and others also worshipped God through composing and/or singing.

In 1 Samuel 18:6, the women of Israel sang, danced, and played tambourines and lutes to commemorate the victories of David and Saul.

As king, David supported a music school in which composers and singers praised God and prophesied to the accompaniment of harps, lyres, cymbals, trumpets, and flutes. Most musicians listed in the Bible are men, as would be expected in a patriarchal society, but some scholars point to the inclusion of Heman's daughters as an indication women Levites also participated. They followed the tradition of earlier prophetesses, studying and serving in this capacity, as temple musicians were chosen not by age, experience, or sex, but by drawing lots. Psalm 68:24–26 describes a holy procession entering the sanctuary that specifically included maidens playing tambourines.

Centuries later, when King Josiah died in battle, women singers, as well as men, sang Jeremiah's laments in his honor (see 2 Chronicles 35:25).

Sing praise to the Lord—whether in an organized choir or by yourself—and you will share the joy felt by those earlier women.

After the Exile, Zerubbabel took two hundred men and women singers with him to Jerusalem (see Ezra 2:65). Eighty years later, Nehemiah (see Nehemiah 7:67) likewise took 245 men and women singers to lift praises up to God and encourage people trying to follow Him.

The heritage of musical praise nurtured by Old Testament women laid the foundation for the women of the first-century Church, as well as contemporary women who love to praise the Lord with musical gifts He gave them.

TABERNACLE WORKERS
Exodus 38:8; 1 Samuel 2:22–25

Although God did not divide worshippers according to gender, Solomon's temple and later temples maintained a separate court of women. In the Old Testament, however, two passages tell us women served at the entrance of the Tabernacle. (All men other than the priests remained outside the Tabernacle, as well.) Exodus 38 highlights female workers who sacrificed their treasured bronze mirrors as materials for the cleansing basin and stand. Upon the Tabernacle's completion, they gathered at its doorway and presented sacrifices,

perhaps washing feet and hands in the laver to which they had contributed, before serving God and their fellow Israelites. We do not know these women's specific functions, but they were encouraged to exercise them.

Hannah presents her son Samuel to Eli in a seventeenth-century painting by Gerbrand van den Eeckhout. Samuel would later denounce Eli's son's for abusing the temple women.

Centuries later, other Tabernacle workers violated this standard of sacrifice, purity, and worship. Hophni and Phinehas, the sons of Eli, the high priest, took sexual advantage of the women who served. God sent the child Samuel to deliver his first prophecy— one of doom for Eli's house—because Eli did not dismiss his sons from service, thus he honored them above the Lord.

FALSE PROPHETESSES IN THE OLD TESTAMENT

FALSE PROPHETESSES WHO SEWED CHARMS

Ezekiel 13:17–23

These prophetesses gave "inspired" messages from their own imaginations. As a result, evildoers often prospered while the righteous lost their lives. These con-women also made and sold charms in the form of veils and wristbands or bracelets that affirmed the lies of the wicked and disheartened those who tried to follow God. The Lord warned the false prophetesses of their destruction if they continued to deceive and exploit the Israelites.

NOADIAH

Nehemiah 6:14

In this case, Noadiah's name, which means "convened of God," proved a complete contrast to her true nature. She used her influence against Nehemiah, who was rebuilding Jerusalem's protective wall, destroyed when Nebuchadnezzar, the Babylonian king, had taken Judah captive nearly 150 years before. Noadiah joined forces with other false prophets, as well as Nehemiah's enemies Tobiah and Sanballat, in an attempt to frighten him away from his godly task. Fortunately, Nehemiah refused to listen to Noadiah or her evil compatriots.

ROYALTY AND WEALTH

Women of royalty and wealth were as varied in biblical times as they are today. Some defied their fathers. Others, although seemingly intelligent, married fools. One famous queen searched for wisdom; another went to the dogs. Some rescued princes; others put them to the sword. Regardless of their faults and fates, each of these biblical women have something to teach us—such as how power can bring one down and godliness can raise one up. Through their simple actions, power plays, political intrigues, rescue efforts, and kindness, they changed their world and continue to influence ours today.

PHARAOH'S DAUGHTER

Exodus 2:5–10; Acts 7:21–22; Hebrews 11:24

The Bible does not name this compassionate woman who dared oppose her father's edict by rescuing baby Moses from the Nile River. She gave Moses a royal education. His studies in Egyptian literature, law, and religion probably contributed to his skill in writing the first five books of the Old Testament and leading his nation. The Bible does not indicate whether Moses saw his adopted mother after his escape to Midian, or whether she saw him when he returned to

Pharaoh's daughter reaches for the baby she would call Moses. The painting is by nineteenth-century artist Konstantin Dmitriyevich Flavitsky.

demand freedom for the Hebrew slaves. We do know her influence made all the difference in Moses' life and in the history of Israel.

ABIGAIL
1 Samuel 25:2–43; 27:3; 30:5;
2 Samuel 2:1–3; 3:2–3;
1 Chronicles 3:1

Abigail was the wise, beautiful wife of a spiteful, but wealthy man named Nabal. David and his band of followers had protected Nabal's flocks and shepherds from thieves. When David's representatives requested supplies in exchange, Nabal hurled insults at them. His response, which broke every rule of ancient hospitality, brought David's wrath upon the household. He

and his four hundred men prepared for battle.

Nabal's servants warned Abigail of the impending disaster. Without consulting her husband, she ordered servants to load bread, wine, mutton, grain, and cakes of fruit onto donkeys. Abigail led the supply train to David's territory, hoping to stop inevitable war. When he and his fierce men faced them, Abigail apologized profusely for Nabal's behavior and offered her gift. She also affirmed David's anointing from God and cautioned him to avoid staining his conscience with unnecessary bloodshed. Abigail's beauty, diplomacy, and food won the day. David blessed her good advice and granted her request not to avenge himself against Nabal. Upon returning, Abigail said nothing to her husband, as he was very drunk. The next morning, she told him the truth. Nabal apparently suffered a strokelike illness and died ten days later.

David lost no time in asking Abigail to be his wife. She accepted his proposal and went on to share his dangerous life, which included King Saul's pursuit and life in hostile territories. During one enemy raid,

Amalekites captured Abigail, along with the families of David's men. Thankfully, her husband and his band rescued them.

Abigail's servants (rear) take supplies to David's men in this nineteenth-century painting by Antonio Cortina y Farinós.

Scripture says little about Abigail after this point, other than her giving birth to a son, Daniel (Kileab). Hopefully, her wisdom and winsomeness continued to help David as he began to rule Israel.

QUEEN OF SHEBA
1 Kings 10:1–13; 2 Chronicles 9:1–12; Matthew 12:42

Some consider the queen of Sheba a legendary figure, but Jesus treated her as a historical person. A descendant of Sheba, the grandson of Abraham and Keturah, she ruled a portion of Arabia or northern Africa.

The queen, having heard rumors of King Solomon's exceptional wisdom and wealth, traveled to Jerusalem to see if they were true. She wanted to ask Solomon the difficult questions she had stored up in her heart. His intellectual and spiritual prowess, as well as his kingdom's magnificence, elicited high praise from the queen. She not only affirmed Solomon's superior wisdom, she reverenced God's greatness and praised Him for giving Israel such an able leader.

Before the queen of Sheba returned to her own country, she gave Solomon extravagant gifts of jewels, spices, and 120 talents of gold. He gave even more gifts to her.

The queen of Sheba and her entourage arrive at Solomon's court. The nineteenth-century painting is by Giovanni Demin.

The fact Jesus held the queen of Sheba up as a positive example confirms her value in His eyes—and the value of all women who seek His wisdom.

WEALTHY WOMAN OF SHUNEM
2 Kings 4:8–37; 8:1–6

Elisha the prophet met this unnamed wealthy woman in the town of Shunem in northern Israel. Although married, she owned land rights, unusual during this era. She invited him for a meal several times, then urged her husband to extend their hospitality to this man of God. They built and furnished an addition where the tired prophet could rest and pray.

Grateful for their kindness, Elisha asked if he could use his influence in the king's court or with military authorities to help them. Despite the unstable times, she declined. Elisha asked Gehazi, his servant, for suggestions. Although wise in the things of the Lord, Elisha did not notice the obvious: his benefactor had no child! When he bestowed this blessing upon the Shunammite, she begged him not to get her hopes up. But a son arrived, just as Elisha predicted.

Later the boy suffered a sudden illness and died. Her husband, seemingly unaware of the child's death, objected to her seeking help from Elisha. Nevertheless, the Shunammite left for Carmel. When Elisha's staff, laid upon her son's face by Gehazi, did not bring him back to life, Elisha himself traveled to her home. He prayed, then twice stretched himself over her child. The boy sneezed seven times, opening his eyes, and Elisha presented him alive to his grateful mother.

Later, when Elisha foresaw a seven-year famine and advised her to take her family to another country, the woman obeyed, putting her land and possessions in jeopardy. Just as she returned to petition the king for her rights, Gehazi was telling the king how Elisha had resurrected her son. Impressed, the king helped her recover all.

Although unnamed, the Shunammite woman's faith and kindness surpassed that of many better-known characters in the Bible.

JEHOSHABEATH OR JEHOSHEBA

2 Kings 11:2; 2 Chronicles 22:11

Jehoshabeath's story reflects the intrigues often resulting from polygamy and intermarriage of royal families during Bible times. The daughter of deceased King Jehoram of Judah, she was the only princess the Bible mentions who married a high priest. Jehoshabeath's marriage to godly Jehoiada seems especially unusual because her father "did evil in the sight of the LORD" (2 Kings 8:18 KJV). As the child of one of Jehoram's lesser wives, Jehoshabeath may

RICH, BUT POOR: POTIPHAR'S WIFE

Genesis 39:1–20

This unnamed woman possessed many advantages of her time, as she was married to a royal official, the captain of the Egyptian guard. However, she used her position to harass Joseph, her husband's slave and household manager. Young, well-built, and handsome, he became the target of her unwanted attentions, despite his continual resistance. Finally, she cornered him. Joseph escaped, leaving his cloak behind. She used it as evidence of his supposed attempt to rape her, and Joseph's master put him in prison. Potiphar's wife gained nothing, except perhaps her husband's suspicion. (It is noteworthy he imprisoned Joseph, rather than execute him for his alleged crime.)

Potiphar's wife won't take Joseph's "No" for an answer.
Giovanni Francesco Barbieri painted the picture in 1649.

In Antoine Coypel's seventeenth-century painting, Jehoida drives Athaliah from the throne while Jehoshabeath protects her son.

not have been close to her half brother, Ahaziah, the new king. She certainly was not close to his mother, Athaliah, who after Ahaziah's early death, murdered all but one of her grandsons and seized the throne. Jehoshabeath rescued her year-old nephew Joash from among the doomed princes and, along with Jehoiada, concealed the baby in the temple. For six years, they hid him from his evil grandmother until Jehoiada staged a rebellion, and seven-year-old Joash was crowned king.

If Jehoshabeath had not risked her life to save baby Joash, David's—and Jesus'—royal line would have disappeared forever.

ESTHER (HADASSAH)

Book of Esther

Esther was a Jewish orphan who married Xerxes, king of Persia. (See Section 4—Bible Women and Their Interactions with Men.)

EVIL OLD TESTAMENT QUEENS

JEZEBEL

1 Kings 16:31; 18:4, 13, 19; 19:1–3; 21; 2 Kings
3:1–2, 13; 9:7, 10, 22, 30–37

The Bible states King Ahab of Israel did more to anger God than any king before him then introduces Jezebel, his queen, as evidence of his evil choices (see 1 Kings 16:30–31). The daughter of Ethbaal, king of Sidon, she brought idolatry to Israel and influenced her weak husband to build a temple to Baal Melqart. She supported 850 prophets who worshipped Baal and Asherah, the pagan god and goddess. Together they led Israel astray. Jezebel hunted down God's prophets, including Elijah, who, after defeating Baal's prophets, fled from her. She masterminded the death of Naboth, when he refused to sell his inheritance to Ahab. As a result, Elijah prophesied dogs would eat Jezebel's corpse. Later, Jehu commanded she be thrown from a window. Afterward she was trampled by horses and most of her remains eaten by dogs; thus the prophecy came true. Jezebel's legacy of heresy and spiritual prostitution lives again in Babylon, the queen described in the New Testament's Revelation 2:20.

A dog sniffs the remains of Jezebel, in this nineteenth-century engraving by Gustave Doré.

ATHALIAH

2 Kings 8:16–18, 26; 11; 2 Chronicles
21:4–6; 22:2–3, 10–12; 23:12–21

Athaliah, the daughter or granddaughter of evil King Ahab of Israel. Some suggest she was the daughter of Jezebel, whose character she reflected. She wed Jehoram, Judah's king, who, upon gaining the throne, killed all his brothers, after which Elijah predicted Jehoram would contract an intestinal disease. Jehoram was indeed struck with disease; two years later his intestines fell out and he died in great pain, "to no one's sorrow" (2 Chronicles 21:20

The profile of Athaliah, queen of Judah, is drawn here as if on a coin by Guillaume Rouille for a book published in the sixteenth century.

NKJV), leaving Athaliah a widow. Ahaziah, their son, ruled only one year, following the ways of Ahab's family because his mother actively encouraged him. After Ahaziah's early death, Athaliah, following in the ways of her dead husband, grabbed power after executing all her relatives, including all but one of her grandsons. Jehosheba, Ahaziah's half sister, rescued prince Joash and his nurse. Six years later, Jehosheba's husband Jehoiada, a priest, led a rebellion that included the priesthood, as well as military leaders. Jehoiada commanded Athaliah be executed. She was killed at the Horse Gate, and seven-year-old Joash, guided and protected by the priest, ruled instead. The Bible says the people of Judah rejoiced at the end of Athaliah's evil reign.

EVERYDAY HEROINES

The word *heroine* implies one who has acted with courage, done some daring deed, or accomplished an amazing feat. Some of these biblical women became heroines by simply acting with compassion, standing up for what was right, sticking close to family, hammering a tent peg, or dropping a millstone. They were nurses, midwives, daughters, housewives, harlots, villagers, daughters-in-law, and servant girls, revealing that God can use anyone to accomplish His purposes, if she is only brave enough to trust and obey. These courageous women were obviously up for the challenge, and so became heroines of yesterday that live on today.

DEBORAH (REBEKAH'S NURSE)
Genesis 24:59; 35:8

Probably born into Laban's household as a slave or servant, Deborah cared for Rebekah as a child. She accompanied her to Canaan when Rebekah married Isaac and remained with the family all her life. When the children of Rebekah's son Jacob were born, Deborah probably cared for them as well, stabilizing the often stormy family with her love and service. When the elderly Deborah died, the family buried her under an oak tree. Jacob referred to this place as Allon Bacuth, "Oak of Weeping"—a tribute to the tenderness Rebekah's descendants felt for Deborah.

PUAH AND SHIPHRAH, MIDWIVES
Exodus 1:15–20

Puah and Shiphrah were two midwives who, because they feared God, saved male Hebrew newborns alive, in direct violation of an Egyptian ruler's edict to kill the baby boys at birth. Some confusion exists as to whether these brave women were Egyptians who served Hebrew women or Hebrews themselves. It appears unlikely Pharaoh would assign Hebrew women to kill Hebrew children, or that he would communicate with slave midwives about their disobedience to his law. Such defiance usually brought immediate execution.

A modern-day Shiphrah or Puah.

According to Aben Ezra, a Jewish scholar, Puah and Shiphrah were likely midwife instructors, with perhaps five hundred others following their lead. When Pharaoh questioned their refusal to kill Hebrew male babies, the midwives replied that they rarely attended Hebrew mothers because they gave birth quickly.

Shiphrah and Puah accepted at least some aspects of Judaism, because they "feared God" (Exodus 1:21). Despite the half-truths they told Pharaoh, God honored their refusal to kill His people and gave them families of their own.

Lord readily granted them their inheritance, protecting these young women and future female heirs from poverty. The only stipulation: They were to marry within their tribe, and thus keep the land and possessions in the family.

The daughters of Zelophehad fight for their rights in a male-dominated system.

DAUGHTERS OF ZELOPHEHAD: MAHLAH, NOAH, HOGLAH, MILCAH, AND TIRZAH

Numbers 26:33; 27:1–11; 36:1–12; Joshua 17:3

When Zelophehad died in the desert on his way to the Promised Land, he had no sons. By established tradition, his daughters were not allowed to inherit his property. But the five girls refused to accept this edict. Together they petitioned Moses and the elders, standing before God at the entrance of the Tabernacle. The

RAHAB

Joshua 2; 6:17–25; Matthew 1:5; Hebrews 11:31; James 2:25

Rahab lived in the city of Jericho at the time God told Israel to enter the Promised Land. Some have translated the word that describes her occupation as "innkeeper," but in the New Testament, Paul and James both refer to her as a harlot. Despite her life of sin, she hid Hebrew spies from her king's soldiers because she believed in Israel's God of miracles. Through travelers, Rahab had heard how Yahweh dried up the Red Sea and gave His people victories over

Sihon and Og, kings who had ruled east of the Jordan River. So when the spies asked for sanctuary, Rahab hid them on her roof, covering them with stalks of flax.

When soldiers arrived and demanded their whereabouts, Rahab urged their pursuers to hunt elsewhere. Afterward, she expressed more faith in God than many of His own people, predicting their triumph over Jericho, a fortified city many regarded as impregnable. Rahab begged not only for her own life, but for those of her family. In exchange for her silence regarding the Israelites plans to conquer Jericho, the spies swore they would spare her family. Rahab was to hang a scarlet cord in her window, and if her relatives gathered in her house during the battle, they would survive. After urging the spies to hide in hills outside the city, Rahab helped them escape down the scarlet cord tied in her window (her house comprised part of the city's wall). Later, Joshua honored their oath. Rahab and her household survived Israel's destruction of Jericho.

In the New Testament, Matthew states Rahab married Salmon, a chief of the tribe of Judah. God raised her from pagan degradation to life in a leading Hebrew family who worshipped Him. Rahab gave birth to Boaz, and King David and Jesus Himself were her descendants.

Paul includes Rahab as one of only two women in his "roll call of faith." James points to her courageous action that demonstrated her faith and willingness to abandon her immoral past. Many view Rahab's scarlet cord as a symbol of Christ's future atonement for sin and her life as true evidence of God's infinite grace.

Rahab helps Joshua's spies to escape from Jericho. This 1860 woodcut is by Julius Schnorr von Carolsfeld.

JAEL

Judges 4:17–24; 5:24–27

Jael was the wife of Heber the Kenite. Although both she and her husband were Hebrews, Heber maintained friendly relations with King Jabin of Canaan, Israel's

Jael claims Barak's victory in an eighteenth-century painting by Jacopo Amigoni.

enemy. When Sisera, the defeated general of Jabin's army, abandoned his chariot and fled on foot, he assumed he would find sanctuary in Jael's tent. She brought him refreshments and hid him under a blanket. Exhausted from battle and Israel's pursuit, he fell asleep. Jael hammered a tent peg through his temple—a doubly daring act because Israel had not completely subdued King Jabin. Jael fulfilled the judge Deborah's prediction Sisera would fall at the hands of a woman, and she commemorated Jael in her song of victory.

RUTH

Book of Ruth, Matthew 1:5

Naomi's son Mahlon married Ruth, although she was a Moabite and prohibited from the congregation of Israel for ten generations (see Deuteronomy 23:3). But Mahlon, along with his family, probably shared his Jewish faith with Ruth. Mahlon means "sickly one." Apparently the name fit him, for he died, leaving her a young widow without resources.

Ruth, however, did not drown in self-pity. Instead, her pledge to accompany Naomi from Moab to Israel echoed her new faith in God. Ruth did not resent caring for her mother-in-law, nor working hard in the fields, gathering food for them. God honored her love and faithfulness by providing a kinsman-redeemer, Boaz. The son of Rahab, the prostitute from Jericho who rescued Hebrew spies, Boaz could appreciate Ruth's faith, despite her foreign heritage. They married and had a son, Obed. Naomi, who gained a home as well, joyfully cared for the baby, whose name means "a servant who worships," a reflection of Ruth's decision to worship the true God.

Ruth was not a native Israelite, but she was God's child in faith and righteousness. Not only did God bless her with a caring husband and a son, but her name is listed in Jesus' genealogy in the New Testament. God's sovereign grace embraced her with a love that surpassed all racial prejudice.

Jews often read the book of Ruth at the Feast of Pentecost (harvest).

Another image of Ruth, gathering up the remains of the harvest. The nineteenth-century painting is by Antonio Cortina y Farinós.

NOBODIES: UNNAMED WOMEN OF FAITH AND ACTION

WOMAN OF THEBEZ
Judges 9:50–57; 2 Samuel 11:21

In defeating Abimelech, the murderous son of Gideon, this unnamed woman helped preserve Israel. Gideon—also known as Jerub-Baal, the hero who routed Midian with only three hundred men—had seventy sons by many wives, plus one named Ahimelech by his concubine. With the help of men from Shechem, his hometown, Abimelech executed sixty-nine of his brothers in an effort to seize power. Only Jotham, the youngest, escaped his clutches. Abimelech raided cities and even destroyed Shechem. He then marched on Thebez, where the inhabitants ran to a tower for refuge. Abimelech intended to burn the people to death. However, an unnamed woman threw down a millstone and cracked his skull. Abimelech ordered his armor bearer to kill him so he would not suffer the humiliation of dying at the hands of a woman.

WOMAN OF BAHURIM
2 Samuel 17:17–21

Jonathan and Ahimaaz, King David's spies, had discovered important information about his rebel son Absalom's plans. They then had to run for their lives because a boy spotted and betrayed them to Absalom. Jonathan and Ahimaaz hid from Absalom in the courtyard of a Bahurim man. This man's wife secured their safety by covering their hiding place (a well) with a cloth as if she'd been drying grain there. She also misdirected the soldiers when they arrived, so the spies survived to share their information with King David and ultimately defeat Absalom's army.

continued on next page

continued from previous page

In this thirteenth-century depiction from the Morgan Bible Joab chases Sheba to Abel. The wise woman of Abel can be seen dropping Sheba's head from the tower.

WISE WOMAN OF ABEL
2 Samuel 20:14–22

After Absalom's rebellion, King David's general Joab and his army surrounded the town of Abel, searching for a rebel named Sheba. A woman who described herself as a "mother in Israel" (2 Samuel 20:19 KJV) challenged Joab, asking why he sought to destroy her city. When no one else stepped forward, this wise woman told Joab he was attacking the "peaceable and faithful in Israel" (2 Samuel 20:19 KJV). Joab described his mission: to hunt down the rebel Sheba. If the city would turn the criminal over to him, the army would attack no one. She promised Sheba's head would be thrown over the wall—and it was. With her forthright gifts of communication and diplomacy, the wise woman saved her entire city. Her action also helped support David's shaky kingdom and established peace.

MAID OF NAAMAN'S WIFE
2 Kings 5:1–23

Her name is not known. Raised in a godly Hebrew home, this young girl had been kidnapped in an Aramean raid and no doubt witnessed brutal attacks on her family and the terrors of the Damascus slave market. Yet she did not hesitate to express her concern for her captors' welfare or direct them to God's prophet. When her master, Naaman, an army commander, suffered from leprosy, she told his wife Elisha the prophet could cure him. Despite Naaman's initial stubborn refusal to wash in the Jordan River, as Elisha instructed him, his servants persuaded him to cooperate, and he was cured of his disease. Naaman wanted to reward Elisha after his healing. Hopefully, he also rewarded the little maid whose compassion changed his life.

SHALLUM'S DAUGHTERS
Nehemiah 3:12

After Israel's exile, Nehemiah led a large group of Jews back to Jerusalem, calling on families to repair sections of Jerusalem's protective walls. Shallum, who governed a half-district of the city, had no sons to help him refurbish his assigned segment. So, it was his daughters, disregarding their high status and women's traditional roles, who provided the much-needed *man*power.

Men are to the fore in this picture of the re-building of Jerusalem's walls, but at least one woman is there to the right-hand side. She appears to be drawing a sword to help repel their enemies.

MOTHERS WHO MADE A DIFFERENCE

Mothers are a unique breed. Although considered a part of the "weaker sex," they are also compared to lionesses. For they will do anything to produce, protect, promote, and provide for their young. Here are some biblical women who persevered in the midst of adversity and, for their efforts, made a difference in the lives of their children, their families, their communities. Some hid from God, laughed at His promise, and cried out to Him in frustration. To each one God listened, then answered—something He is still doing for women today, who, in raising up heroes, become heroes themselves.

EVE
Genesis 1:26–31; 2:18–25; 3; 4:1–2, 25–26; 1 Timothy 2:13

In the beginning, the Lord declared it was not good for Adam to be alone, so He created a helpmate that fit him—the woman. The word for "help" in Genesis 2:20, *ezer*, is also used in passages such as Psalm 70:5 to describe God as our Help or Deliverer, so no inferiority is implied. God created Eve in His image and commanded her to have dominion over the earth and to be fruitful and multiply, just as He did her husband Adam.

The first couple enjoyed their work in the Garden of Eden together with only one stipulation from God: They were not to eat fruit from the Tree of the Knowledge of Good and Evil. Unfortunately, they listened to Satan, in the form of the serpent. He represented God as a devious, selfish deity who feared they would steal His exclusive wisdom. Satan scoffed at God's warning they would die if they disobeyed. Despite God's kindness to them, Adam and Eve believed Satan. They ate the fruit and suffered the consequences.

Cain offers a gift but Abel gets all the attention—a prelude to the very first instance of sibling rivalry.

Eve is remembered as the first human being to sin. But she also was the first mother. In the birth of Cain, Eve experienced the pain her Maker had wanted to spare her. But she also experienced the joy of participation with the Creator in producing new life. No mother or other woman assisted her in pregnancy, childbirth, or in raising her first children. Perhaps she had no daughter or woman friend to comfort her when her elder son murdered the younger. Still, when Eve gave birth to Seth, she praised God. She and Adam must have passed down their imperfect but genuine faith to their descendants, because after the birth of Seth's son Enosh, "men began to call on the name of the LORD" (Genesis 4:26 NIV). In the suffering and uncertainty of a newly fallen world, Eve persevered, and the human race survived.

SARAH (SARAI)

Genesis 11:29–31; 12:5–20; 16:1–9; 17:15–21; 18:1–15; 20:2–18; 21:1–12; 23:1–19; 24:36, 67; 25:10, 12; 49:31; Isaiah 51:2; Romans 4:19; 9:9; Galatians 4:21–31; Hebrews 11:11; 1 Peter 3:6

Sarah was, without doubt, a historical figure. Her birth name, Sarai, indicates a distinguished Babylonian family background. She lived in Ur of the Chaldeans in Mesopotamia. The daughter of Terah, Sarah was Abraham's half sister (see Genesis 20:12) and also his wife—not unusual in ancient societies, in which intermarriage was common. When Terah and his family migrated hundreds of miles north to Haran, Sarah already had passed middle age without having children. When God told Abraham to go to Canaan, she was in her sixties.

Despite age and exposure to the desert, Sarah retained her spectacular beauty, which captivated kings and complicated their journeys. Abraham concocted a plan to ensure his own safety and insisted Sarah pose as his sister, even before Pharaoh of Egypt expressed interest in her. She cooperated with her husband's scheme. Some scholars point to her powerlessness in that society and assert she had no choice. Others say Sarah should have resisted his deception. God Himself intervened on her behalf, however, warning Pharaoh through a plague that Sarah was Abraham's wife. Years later, the Lord would have to mediate a similar scenario, when Abraham allowed Abimelech, King of Gerar, to claim Sarah—despite the fact Abraham knew she would give birth to the son of promise within the next year! The Bible does not record Sarah's reaction to these charades. She appeared far more upset about her lack of children, a terrible misfortune during that era. Ancient Mesopotamian records confirm that if a wife proved infertile, she was expected to give her husband a substitute to bear children for her. Thus, in proposing her slave Hagar as a surrogate mother (see Genesis, Sarah simply followed accepted social mores. Neither she nor Abraham knew at that time God's son of promise was to be Abraham's *and* Sarah's biological child, which was later made very clear in Genesis 17:15–19. Still, neither spouse appeared to pray about using Hagar as a surrogate or consider the ramifications in view of what God already had revealed to Abraham. He impregnated Hagar, resulting in rising tension between the women and Sarah's abuse of her slave. Abraham, also following societal dictates, abdicated responsibility for the pregnant Hagar, leaving her in Sarah's hands. Wronged by a culture that demanded sons, Sarah, in turn, victimized Hagar, who ran away. Only God's direct intervention brought her back. Hagar gave birth to a son, whom eighty-six-year-old Abraham named Ishmael.

Thirteen years later, God appeared to Abraham again and told him Sarah would be the

Sarah laughs at the idea of her impending pregnancy, in a children's Bible illustration from the early twentieth century.

mother of the child of promise. He not only required Abraham's genetic contribution to this special baby, but Sarah's as well. Abraham, age ninety-nine, and Sarah, eighty-nine, both found the news hard to believe. God first appeared to Abraham, who laughed. Shortly afterward, the Lord appeared again with two men and promised Sarah would have the son of promise the following year. Listening at the entrance of the tent, she laughed, too. Some wonder why God did not fault Abraham's amusement but seemed to reprimand her. Perhaps God especially wanted Sarah, whose schemes complicated everything, to pause and think about her attitudes and actions. When the son of promise was born, exactly when God predicted, Sarah realized she had laughed at Him in unbelief, but God literally had brought her laughter (the name *Isaac* means "laughter") and more joy than she ever imagined.

Unfortunately, the mirth did not last. Sarah no longer favored Ishmael as her adopted son. She now saw him as a threat to Isaac and the immense wealth Abraham would pass down. Sarah demanded her husband expel Hagar and her son, now a teenager. Abraham reluctantly did so—and God Himself again cared for the slave woman who had no true husband and the boy who had no true father.

Sarah may have faced an equally agonizing situation when Abraham took their only son to Mount Moriah to offer him as a sacrifice, as God required. She may not have known of Abraham's intentions until after they returned. Or perhaps she, fully aware of the wrenching prospect of losing Isaac, now possessed faith equal to Abraham's and supported his action. The Bible does not record her reaction, and only God knew her heart.

Sarah lived a 127 years and saw Isaac grow up. Her burial in a cave at Machpelah is the first mentioned in Genesis. Later Abraham, Isaac, Rebekah, Jacob, Leah, and others in their family would be buried there.

Paul extols Sarah as an example of faith in Hebrews 11. In Galatians, she represents God's grace, as opposed to the slavery of legalism. Peter praises her as a model of obedience to her husband.

At times, her submission to Abraham appeared more blind compliance than faith. Sarah's obsessive desire for a child and love for Isaac also wreaked havoc in her marriage. But the pattern of her long life consisted of true faith and obedience. Centuries later, the Lord, through Isaiah, urged His sinful people to remember not only Abraham, but Sarah, who miraculously gave birth to their nation.

HAGAR
Genesis 16; 21:8–20; Galatians 4:21–31

Single mothers today often feel helpless as they face the challenges of raising children alone. Hagar, a slave to Sarah, Abraham's wife, experienced powerlessness few in modern culture can imagine. First, she was forced to sleep with her master. The child Hagar carried as a result did not belong to her. When she unwisely gloated over her mistress, Sarah abused Hagar to the point the pregnant woman preferred the perils of the desert to life with her angry owner.

When Hagar ran away, God intervened. He spoke directly to her, assuring Hagar she and her unborn baby mattered to Him. The Lord gave him the name Ishmael, which means "God hears." He also gave

Hagar a promise similar to the one He gave Abraham: Her descendants would be too numerous to count.

Awed by this encounter with God, Hagar named Him—the only woman in the Bible to do so—"Thou God seest me" (Genesis 16:13 KJV). As the Lord commanded, she returned to Abraham's camp—even though runaway slaves usually were executed. Apparently Abraham believed the story of her God-encounter, for when Hagar gave birth, he named the baby Ishmael.

The boy grew up as Abraham's sole heir until Isaac was born

Hagar's son Ishmael is spared by divine intervention, shown here as an angelic visitation. Karel Dujardin painted the picture around 1662.

fourteen years later. Hagar, who had assumed her son would inherit wealth, suddenly faced his radical demotion. Teenaged Ishmael taunted his half brother, bringing Sarah's wrath upon him. Reluctantly acquiescing to Sarah's demand to oust the slave woman and her child, Abraham sent Hagar and Ishmael away. As a result of wandering in the desert, their water was soon gone. A tearful Hagar withdrew a few yards from Ishmael because she could not bear to watch her child die.

Again, God intervened, assuring Hagar he had heard her son's cries. He opened her eyes to a well, and she was able to revive Ishmael. The Bible states God was with the boy as he grew up. The Lord did not ignore Ishmael, who had no control over his origins.

We do not know about Hagar's lifelong spiritual condition, but the Bible makes it clear God cared for her and Ishmael. When she was wronged, He did not change her cir-cumstances. Instead, God spoke personally to her, a privilege few prophets in the Old Testament experienced. And when the only person in the world Hagar loved was threatened, God rescued and validated him. Hagar stands as an encouragement to disadvantaged and oppressed mothers in every culture.

LEAH

Genesis 29:15–35; 30:1–24; 31:1–18; 33:1–7; 35:23; 46:8–15; 49:31; Ruth 4:11

Leah was the daughter of Laban, Rebekah's brother. These family connections brought Jacob, Leah's cousin and future husband, from Canaan to Haran. Jacob had tricked his vengeful brother Esau. Their mother Rebekah suggested Jacob visit her relatives far away and find a wife.

Jacob loved Leah's beautiful younger sister, Rachel, and worked seven years for his future father-in-law in order to marry her. But on the wedding night, Laban substituted the less attractive Leah for Rachel. We do not know whether Leah willingly participated in this deception—successful because the bridegroom probably celebrated with too much wine and because wedding tradition dictated the bride be brought to her new husband's room in darkness and silence. Jacob, not surprisingly, resented the arrangement, but worked seven more years for Rachel, whom he married the week after his and Leah's wedding.

All her days, Leah struggled with Jacob's preference for her sister. The Bible states God saw Leah was not loved and gave her children to delight her and raise her status.

Leah named them, unusual in that patriarchal society. Despite her pain, she gave her offspring positive names that denoted her faith in God:

Reuben: "Behold, a son!" She praised the Lord because He had blessed her.

Simeon: "Hearing." Despite her sister's attacks, God had listened to her hurt.

Levi: "Joined." She believed she and Jacob would grow closer because, counting Levi, she had born him three sons.

Judah: "Praise." Leah declared, "I will praise the Lord."

Issachar: "Reward." Modern women might not understand the value ancient societies placed on

A statue of Leah carved by Michelangelo.

many sons, but Leah felt God had granted her this child because she had given her maid to Jacob to wife.

Zebulun: "Honor." Leah hoped her husband would honor her, having produced six sons.

Dinah: "Acquitted." Perhaps Leah, who keenly felt her lack of beauty, felt vindicated by her lovely daughter's birth.

Her barren sister Rachel named her maid Bilhah's son Naphtali ("my struggle"), with a less-than-subtle hint of the discord in the polygamous household: "With great wrestlings have I wrestled with my sister, and I have prevailed" (Genesis 30:8 KJV). While Leah continually sparred with Rachel's hostility and Jacob's indifference, she loved him and remained a faithful wife and mother. Interestingly, Jacob buried Leah, not Rachel, in the family burial cave at Machpelah, along with Abraham, Sarah, Rebekah, and Isaac, bestowing the honor in death he denied her in life. And it was Jacob and Leah's son Judah that would be named in the genealogy of Jesus (see Matthew 1:2; Luke 3:33–34).

Jochebed braces herself before committing her son to the river. The 1884 painting is by Pedro Américo.

JOCHEBED

Exodus 2:1–11; 6:20; Numbers 26:59; Hebrews 11:23

Jochebed, a Levite, was the mother of Miriam, Aaron, and Moses. She married her nephew Amram, also a Levite, which was not unusual at the time. Jochebed gave birth to her children during the era when Israelites toiled as slaves for Pharaoh of Egypt. Despite impossible circumstances, the family followed Yahweh. When

Pharaoh decreed all Hebrew male newborns must die, they refused to obey and hid baby Moses three months. Hebrews 11:23 even declares "they were not afraid of the king's commandment" (KJV). When they could no longer conceal Moses, Jochebed coated a basket with tar and pitch and hid her baby along the banks of the Nile River. Her daughter Miriam stood guard because she could not. Only a mother can understand the joy and relief Jochebed felt when Pharaoh's daughter discovered her baby and actually paid her to nurse him. Only a mother can comprehend the pain she felt in giving him up when Pharaoh's daughter claimed him as her son.

The Bible does not state whether she ever saw Moses again. But Jochebed's daring and faithfulness to God and her child preserved Israel's great leader who later wrote the Pentateuch, the first five books of the Bible.

HANNAH

1 Samuel 1; 2:1–11, 18–21

Hannah was married to Elkanah, a Levite (see 1 Chronicles 6:27) from the hill country of Ephraim. When Hannah remained childless, Elkanah married Peninnah, who gave birth to many sons and daughters. While polygamy carried on Elkanah's family line, it did not ensure a peaceful home. Peninnah mocked Hannah's barrenness, intensifying the latter's grief. Elkanah only aggravated the situation when he expressed his special love for Hannah by giving her a double portion of his yearly sacrifice. Perhaps he did not understand her vulnerability, for if he died, Hannah would retain no financial support because she had no son. Powerless, she enlisted God's power to help her.

Hannah took bold initiative with her prayer at the tabernacle in Shiloh. She requested God take action in her situation. She even offered God what she did not possess: a son.

Her intense emotion brought censure from Eli, the high priest. He thought she was drunk. But she pleaded her case so convincingly, he blessed her, praying God would grant her request.

No longer depressed, Hannah went home and soon became pregnant. She named her baby Samuel, which means "heard by God," a fit name for the little boy— the answer to Hannah's prayer. Hannah nursed Samuel until approximately age three. How difficult it must have been for her to give up her only son! Hannah's sacrifice mirrors God's surrender of His only Son centuries later. She freely brought Samuel to the tabernacle and reaffirmed her vow with a poetic, prophetic prayer that resembles the Magnificat, the song of praise sung by Mary in Luke 1. Cosmic in scope, Hannah's song of thanksgiving goes beyond her small world and speaks of God's power, sovereignty, and compassion for the oppressed. Some doubt an uneducated woman could have composed this poem, but Hannah's heritage was rooted in oral tradition, which included many such songs. Perhaps she borrowed from Miriam's and Moses' triumphant lines after the Israelites crossed the Red Sea.

God not only gave Hannah a son and a song of praise, but also three additional sons and two daughters.

RIZPAH
2 Samuel 3:7; 21:1–14

As King Saul's concubine, Rizpah gave birth to her sons Armoni and Mephibosheth (the latter not to be confused with Jonathan's son with the same name). After Saul's death, Rizpah, like many other widows of her era, found herself vulnerable. Ishbosheth, Saul's heir, accused Abner, his general, of sleeping with Rizpah. She somehow survived his claim.

Still, she and her family suffered because of Saul's sin. Saul had broken an ancient treaty Israel had made with the Gibeonites in the Lord's name and nearly destroyed this ethnic group. God told King David Israel was suffering a famine because of this treachery. After

The Dutch painter Rembrandt van Rijn asked his own mother to model for his portrait of Hannah, mother of Samuel.

Saul's death, the Gibeonites called for vengeance, requiring David to turn seven of Saul's descendants over to them. He protected Mephibosheth, Jonathan's son, because of their deep friendship, but gave the Gibeonites the five sons of Merab, Saul's daughter, and Rizpah's two sons. The Gibeonites hung them high on a hill, exposed for days, contrary to the Law, which dictated they should be buried by sunset the day of execution.

A grieving Rizpah protecting her son's bodies.

Rizpah, heartbroken, refused to allow further abuse of her children and relatives. She remained on guard night and day for several months, permitting no bird or beast to touch the bodies. David heard of her loyalty. He obtained the bones of Saul and Jonathan, exposed in a Philistine town after Israel's defeat, and gathered those of Rizpah's sons and nephews, burying them all with proper respect.

Rizpah, a victim of her violent, barbaric era, remained faithful to those she loved.

NAMELESS NURTURERS

NOAH'S WIFE, SONS' WIVES

Genesis 6:18; 7:1, 7, 13; 8:16, 18; 9:19;
1 Peter 3:20; 2 Peter 2:5

Noah's wife and his sons' wives must have loved and followed God; otherwise, He would not have saved them from the Flood. During the years Noah built the ark, his wife supported him when others ridiculed him. Noah's daughters-in-law also forsook their families and friends while helping their husbands—Shem, Ham, and Japheth. All the women no doubt contributed to preparations for their voyage and care of the animals aboard. After the Flood, the young women raised a brand-new generation in brand-new surroundings. Unlike earlier Genesis accounts, we find no mention of Noah's having more sons and daughters. So the fate of humankind—including Jesus' birth, as He descended from Noah's son Shem—rested upon the mothering skills of these brave young women, the support they received from their mother-in-law, and the grace and strength God gave them.

Noah makes a sacrifice to God with his wife and daughters-in-law beside him. One young woman appears to be pregnant and the first child of the new generation has already been born, in this seventeenth-century painting by Giovanni Martinelli.

MANOAH'S WIFE/ SAMSON'S MOTHER

Judges 13; 14:1–9

Although the Talmud states she was Hazzelelponi or Zelelponi (see 1 Chronicles 4:3), of the tribe of Judah, we are not certain either is her name. But God certainly knew her. Manoah's barren wife was visited by the "angel of the LORD" (Judges 13:3 NIV), usually assumed to be Jesus, who told Manoah's wife that she would have a son and that "No razor may be used on his head, because the boy is to be a Nazirite" (Judges 13:5 NIV). The angel of the Lord spoke with her alone twice before Manoah saw him, predicting the birth of their son. The angel affirmed his earlier command that Manoah's wife avoid alcohol and unclean foods, as the boy would be a Nazirite, set apart as holy to the Lord.

Manoah still did not realize he was speaking to the angel of the Lord. But when

Manoah and his wife are visited by an angel in this painting by the classic Dutch artist Rembrandt.

He ascended to heaven in the flame of their sacrifice, both fell down in worship. Manoah feared they would die. His sensible wife, however, said God had told them great things and accepted their sacrifice. Why would He judge them so harshly?

She followed the angel's instructions and gave birth to a son. Manoah's wife called him Samson, which means "strength of the

continued on next page

continued from previous page

sun," a fitting name for a judge whom God endowed with supernatural physical power.

She and Manoah must have suffered untold grief when Samson wanted Philistine women as wives. The Bible does not mention Samson's parents again after his first disastrous marriage. Perhaps they died before Delilah tricked Samson into revealing the secret of his strength, his long hair, and did not have to witness his subsequent enslavement and death.

LEMUEL'S MOTHER
Proverbs 31:1–9

Queen mothers were widely respected in the Middle East, and Lemuel's mother demonstrated why. Some scholars have tried to link Lemuel with King Solomon, but no evidence supports this claim.

His wise mother gave her royal son frank advice about destructive relationships with women and alcohol abuse. She also reminded King Lemuel of his responsibility to exercise justice, defending the poor and helpless. Some attribute the picture of the Ideal Woman in Proverbs 31:9–31 to Lemuel's mother.

TWO PROSTITUTE MOTHERS WHO VISITED KING SOLOMON
1 Kings 3:16–28

The Old Testament describes a strange scenario in which a prostitute, who accidentally smothered her newborn son, tried to steal that of her roommate, also a prostitute. That immoral women would dare approach King Solomon with their quarrel is amazing, as the Law punished fornicators with death by stoning. The fact their argument involved children that resulted from their sinful lifestyles—including the death of a baby, with a possible accusation of murder—gives pause. Perhaps, arrested and facing execution, the women, pleading for mercy, somehow obtained an audience before their wise king.

Solomon instructs his guard to cut the living baby in half. One woman stands by. The other intervenes so that the baby might be spared. The painting is by nineteenth-century Russian artist Nikolaj Ge.

Postpartum emotions ran high as each claimed the living child. When Solomon threatened to divide the baby in half, the false mother suddenly reversed her demands and heartlessly agreed. Thus, Solomon detected the identity of the true mother, who begged him to give the baby to the other.

While the vindicated mother lived an immoral lifestyle, she thought first of her child's welfare, even if it meant she might never see him again. God gave her mercy through the just ruling of Solomon, His servant-king.

SYMBOLIC WOMEN

Moral or immoral, wise or foolish, idyllic or idolatrous, the following biblical "women" are symbols of what God wants—and what He does *not* want—His daughters to be or do. Be they of proverbs, prophets, or pagan priests, they are presented to teach us what God believes to be ideal and what just might break the deal. Here they are . . .for your consideration.

LADY WISDOM

Proverbs 1–4; 8; 9:1–12

The instruction of Lady Wisdom dominates the first chapters of Proverbs. The fact she commands male attention makes her pleas all the more significant. Lady Wisdom declares a clear goal: to instruct a young man. Will he listen and obey?

Proverbs 8 paints a vivid poetic portrait of Lady Wisdom, whom God brought forth before creation. Many link her and scriptures in the New Testament that speak of Jesus before His earthly birth (see John 1:1–4; 1 Corinthians 1:24; Colossians 1:15–20). Some, reading these passages, conclude Jesus, too, was a created being. Others have compared Lady Wisdom to the Egyptian goddesses Isis and Ma'at. But she was not a historical person, nor a deity. Lady Wisdom was a larger-than-life allegorical figure who represented this attribute of God as He spoke the universe into existence. In Proverbs 8:22–31, she gives her pre-creation account of close communion with God, a relationship that validates her advice.

The Egyptian goddess Isis was one culture's personification of Lady Wisdom.

Lady Wisdom is connected to the portrayal of a loving wife in Proverbs 5:15–19 and the Virtuous Woman of Proverbs 31. Proverbs 7 and 8 also place the Immoral Woman and Lady Wisdom in side-by-side contrast. Wisdom states her case and makes it clear the young man must make his choice. But she also urges him to seek her help, as well as her information.

THE IMMORAL WOMAN

Proverbs 2:16–19; 5:1–14, 20–23; 6:20–35; 7; 9:13–18; 22:14; 30:20; Ecclesiastes 7:26

Solomon, who broke God's law by marrying hundreds of pagan women, still had much to say about the trap they presented. In these passages, a father warns his son of the Immoral Woman, whose wiles led another young man down a gradual path of death and destruction. She is identified more as an adulteress than a prostitute, the personification of seductive evil, related to the serpent in the Garden of Eden and the predatory lion described in 1 Peter 5:8.

THE VIRTUOUS WOMAN

Proverbs 31:10–31

While Proverbs discusses the negative side of womanhood, it ends with the celebration of the Virtuous Woman. Like other representative figures in the book, this wise, industrious wife and mother appears a larger-than-life ideal rather than a real person. Nothing is said about her appearance. Dedicated to her family, she runs her household, buys real estate and other commodities, manages a farm, uses her "craftiness" to clothe her family and beautify her home, and still takes time to educate those around her

In this painting by Dante Gabriel Rossetti, a farmer visting the city finds a childhood friend who has resorted to selling herself on the street. He tries to take her back to virtue (as represented by the lamb), but she is too ashamed to go.

and show kindness to the poor. Her husband and family celebrate her accomplishments.

ISRAEL, THE WIFE OF YAHWEH

Isaiah 50:1–2; 54; 62:1–5, 12; Jeremiah 2; 3:1–5, 14; 31:32; Hosea 1–4; Ezekiel 16; Revelation 12

In Exodus 6.7, God told Moses, "I will take you [the Israelites] to me for a people, and I will be to you a God" (KJV). He likened the intimate covenant between them to marriage.

Unfortunately, His prophets often painted sad pictures of Israel's and Judah's spiritual adultery. The people worshipped the gods of the nations around them, forsaking the vows they had made to Yahweh. God even commanded His prophet Hosea to marry a prostitute, Gomer, in an effort to help His people understand their sin. But God also offered grace and restoration in the "rest of the story," when, despite her unfaithfulness, Hosea rescued Gomer from miserable destitution and reaffirmed their marriage. God celebrated Jerusalem's restoration

The pregnant woman under attack in this nineteenth-century painting by William Blake is the personification of Israel from the book of Revelation.

in Isaiah 54:7, saying, "For a small moment have I forsaken thee; but with great mercies will I gather thee" (KJV).

This vivid, tender portrayal of God's love for His people continues in the New Testament when He defends Israel, represented by a queenly pregnant woman who gives birth to the Messiah, from Satan, the dragon (see Revelation 12).

FEMALE DEITIES IN OLD TESTAMENT TIMES

ASHERAH

Exodus 34:13; Deuteronomy 7:5; 12:3; 16:21; Judges 3:7; 6:25–30; 1 Kings 14:15, 23; 15:13; 16:33; 18:19; 2 Kings 13:6; 17:10–16; 18:4; 21:1–15; 23:1–15; 2 Chronicles 14:2–3; 15:16; 17:6; 19:3; 24:18; 31:1; 33:3, 19; 34:3–4, 7; Isaiah 17:8; 27:9; Jeremiah 17:2; Micah 5:14

Asherah (meaning "to stride" or possibly "shrine"), the wife of El, the chief god, was considered a mother goddess by the Canaanites for hundreds of years. Some Israelites, like the surrounding idolatrous peoples, considered Asherah a consort of Yahweh. Others linked her with Baal, as Jezebel did when she supported numerous prophets of both Baal and Asherah.

Asherah was identified closely with carved, stylized trees or poles the Israelites erected near Yahweh's altars in defiance of God's messages through His prophets. King Manasseh of Judah erected an Asherah pole in the temple itself, bringing God's judgment on him and his people in the subsequent destruction of Jerusalem and the exile of Judah.

ASHTORETH (ASTARTE)

Judges 2:12–13; 10:6–7; 1 Samuel 7:3–4; 12:10; 31:10; 1 Kings 11:1–6, 33; 2 Kings 23:13

Ancient Canaanites considered Ashtoreth (meaning "increase, progeny"), the wife of Baal, the goddess of sexual love and fertility. While she also was linked with war, Ashtoreth was better known as the "queen of heaven" and represented by Venus, the morning and evening star. God rebuked King Solomon because he and his pagan wives introduced worship of Ashtoreth to Judah.

Astarte Syriaca by Dante Gabriel Rossetti (1877).

INTRODUCTION: ROLES AND JOBS OF NEW TESTAMENT WOMEN

The New Testament introduces women with a bit more freedom than their ancestresses, yet still living under some yokes of oppression. Like the heroines of old, some were peasant girls, ministers' wives, businesswomen, crafters, leaders of their faith, and housewives. Chaste or sinful, some rose to become mothers of prophets, priests, and kings. Some who followed Jesus provided for Him materially, witnessed His miracles, cried as He hung on the cross, mourned at His tomb, began churches in their homes, and suffered imprisonment or worse. But all of them were women brave enough to follow their Master—a Man who cared for them, listened to them, healed them, and treated them as friends. From each of these brave and admirable women, we glean insight as to what it means to be committed to God—heart and soul.

WOMEN SURROUNDING JESUS' BIRTH

Before Jesus was yet formed in Mary's womb, the birth announcements were out, delivered via the angel Gabriel. And from the beginning pages of the New Testament Gospels, we witness God doing the impossible through humble women eager for the opportunity to give Him full rein in their lives—from the joyous beginning to the heartbreaking end to the hope of things to come. Here are the foremothers of faithful Christian women all over the world, examples to follow as we marvel at their courage and commitment to God.

MARY

Matthew 1; 2; 12:46–50; 13:54–56; Mark 6:2–4; Luke 1; 2; John 2:1–12; 19:25–27; Acts 1:14

Many are familiar with Gospel accounts that relate how an angel told this teenaged peasant girl she would give birth to the Jewish Messiah. An angel also visited her fiancé, Joseph, who chose to believe her claim that the child was conceived by the Holy Spirit. Near the end of her pregnancy, Mary made an exhausting trip to Bethlehem, her husband's hometown, because of Roman tax law. There, her Son Jesus was born in a stable, worshipped by angels and awestruck shepherds as He lay in an animal feeding trough.

Simeon and Anna, elderly worshippers at the temple in Jerusalem, praised God for Jesus' birth and prophesied of His future. Wise men from the East brought gold, frankincense, and myrrh as gifts to honor Him. Soon, however, Mary and Joseph fled to Egypt with their baby, as Herod the Great sought to destroy Him. They remained there until Herod died around 4 BC, then returned to Nazareth, where they went about the wonderful, puzzling business of raising God.

Because of her poverty, Mary could not give Jesus great educational or cultural advantages. But she nurtured Him, modeled true holiness, and reinforced the scriptures Jesus learned in the village school. The Bible gives no indication of supernatural activity during His childhood.

Jesus was called Mary's firstborn (see Luke 2:7), implying she gave birth to other children. Matthew 13:55–56 and Mark 6:3 list them: James, Joseph, Judas, and Simon, as well as unnamed daughters. Perhaps as Mary cared for children,

Mary, as a young girl, is visited by an angel. Understandably, she is a bit nervous. Dante Gabriel Rossetti painted the picture in 1850.

cleaned house, and scrubbed laundry, she almost forgot the amazing events surrounding Jesus' birth. When her twelve-year-old Son did not accompany the family home after Passover, but remained in the temple, Mary reacted as any mother would—sheer panic, then "How could you do this to us!"

When Jesus gave an answer that resonated with both Son-of-God perspective and junior high angst ("Didn't you know I had to be in my Father's house?"[Luke 2:49 NIV]), Mary did not understand. Still, the Bible says she treasured these things as she watched Jesus grow from a Child to a Man.

In Mary's culture, most people married and settled in their parents' town. But her eldest left home at age thirty to minister. Mary must have struggled, especially if Joseph had died. At the wedding at Cana, Jesus made it clear He was beyond her control. Despite her faith, Mary probably worried about her Son, especially when she heard of controversies He stirred up. When Jesus briefly returned to Nazareth, only to face a hometown crowd who tried to push Him off a cliff (see Luke 4:29), how Mary must have suffered! Jesus' brothers feared for His sanity and tried to take charge of Him, so Jesus distanced Himself from His family. Mary,

Mary, serene amid the confused disciples in Jean II Restout's classic depiction of Pentecost (1732).

remembering the angels, wise men, and prophecies at His birth, felt torn between His brothers' concern and what she knew in her heart. Hearing of death threats against Jesus, Mary must have feared for His life many times before Passion Week. As she wept near His cross, part of her died with Him. Even as Jesus gave her into the care of His closest friend, He did not address Mary as "Mother," but "dear woman" (John 19:26 NIV). Perhaps she realized again He was much more than her Son.

Mary was not the first who saw Him resurrected. She is mentioned only once more in the New Testament. Mary prayed in the Upper Room for the Holy Spirit's arrival, as Jesus commanded His followers to do.

Her other sons, finally recognizing Jesus' true identity, joined her in worship. Mary's long years of uncertainty and mourning were past. She now welcomed the risen Jesus as her Lord.

ELISABETH

Luke 1:5–80

Elisabeth, a Levite, was a priest's wife who lived in Judea. Although some probably blamed her infertility on sin, the Bible says she and her husband Zacharias pleased God. They followed the Old Testament Law without fail. But years passed, and the elderly couple gave up on the possibility of parenting.

One day as Zacharias ministered in the temple, the angel Gabriel appeared beside the altar of

Mary and Elisabeth with their gifts from God—Jesus and John. A little cross already lays at the children's feet in this sixteenth-century painting by Andrea del Sarto.

incense. He told Zacharias he would have a son named John, who, like the prophet Elijah, would prepare the way for the Messiah. When a bewildered Zacharias questioned the possibility, the angel told him he would not be able to speak until the baby was born.

We do not know how Elisabeth initially reacted to her husband's story. But she welcomed her geriatric pregnancy with great joy, spending five months in seclusion. During Elisabeth's sixth month of pregnancy, her relative Mary surprised her with a visit. At her greeting, baby John leaped inside Elisabeth. She was the first to welcome the Messiah and bless His mother for her faith. Uneducated Mary responded with a spontaneous poem of praise to God called the Magnificat that shares the reverent joy expressed by Hannah in the Old Testament. During the three months Mary remained with Elisabeth, the two pregnant women supported each other. Elisabeth mentored Mary with godly, mature advice, and young Mary helped her elderly relative with challenging household tasks.

When Elisabeth delivered her son, she insisted his name was John. Friends argued no one in her family bore that name. But

Zacharias requested a writing tablet and confirmed the babe's name was John. Immediately, the priest began to praise God and prophesy regarding John's mission: preparing the way for the Messiah.

Both Elisabeth and her husband probably died before Herod executed their son. But during John's formative years, Elisabeth's character and deep faith laid a foundation for his powerful ministry that began the New Testament era.

Simeon holds the baby Jesus while Anna prays over Him. Dutch artist Aert de Gelder painted the scene in the early eighteenth century.

ANNA
Luke 2:36–38

Anna was the daughter of Phanuel (Penuel), the only individual from the tribe of Asher noted in the Bible. We do not learn her husband's name, perhaps because she was married only seven years before he died. It is unclear whether Anna was widowed for eighty-four years or an eighty-four-year-old widow; regardless, Anna spent decades in the temple, worshipping, fasting, and praying while she awaited God's Chosen One. After one look at baby Jesus, Anna gave thanks that she had seen the Messiah and began to tell everyone in the temple about Him—the first woman missionary and herald of Christ's advent.

JESUS' WOMEN DISCIPLES

Overachievers, ne'er-do-wells, demonized, and pushy mothers— all are represented here among the cast of Jesus' followers. Women who were lost found new lives in Christ. From the sinful woman to sparring siblings to housewives who followed Him on foot, their stories have come down to us through the ages. Some are named. Some are not. But it does not matter, for it is in their interactions with Jesus that today's women are shown how to be disciples.

SINFUL WOMAN WHO ANOINTED JESUS' FEET
Luke 7:36–50

Luke, the only Gospel writer who mentions this woman from the city of Nain, does not humiliate her by giving her name. This sinful woman dared to enter the house of Simon the Pharisee with her alabaster jar of expensive ointment, perfume she probably used as a prostitute. To the shock of everyone, she washed Jesus' feet with her tears then dried His feet with her hair, kissed them, and rubbed them with ointment. Her actions inspired the parable of two debtors Jesus told His critical host, as well as a controversial announcement her sins had been

Jesus addresses His audience, but the unnamed woman simply wants to worship the Lord. The painting was made around 1618 by the Flemish master Peter Paul Rubens.

forgiven because she loved much. Despite the debate, Jesus assured the woman her faith had saved her. He sent her on her way in peace.

MARTHA OF BETHANY
Luke 10:38–42; John 11:1–45; 12:1–8

Martha opened her home to Jesus and His disciples. The Bible treats her as the owner, despite the presence of Lazarus, her brother (males claimed family property rights). At the least, Martha, whom some assume to be the older sibling, ruled the household. The feasts she supervised and the number of influential Jews who later mourned Lazarus also implied the family held a prominent place in the community. It is interesting to note the Bible never records words from Lazarus, though Jesus loved him. All the Lord's dialogue with the family involves Martha and/or Mary. Some scholars believe Martha of Bethany was the "chosen lady" addressed in 2 John.

Martha, a generous, hardworking woman, faced a formidable task: extending hospitality to Jesus, His twelve disciples, and others traveling with Him. She had little advance notice, so food preparation consumed her— especially since she wanted to provide the best. Her sister

Mary, on the other hand, seemed unconcerned, which infuriated Martha so much she appealed to Jesus to solicit Mary's help.

Martha seems to be asking Jesus if Mary can come and do some work. Mary thinks the Lord more important. Joseph Stark painted the picture in 1826.

Jesus, while grateful for Martha's hospitality, did not want her to worry herself about details. He said Mary, despite her seeming inactivity, was accomplishing the most important thing: listening to Him. Jesus, blasting the societal expectations of His time, made it plain that women, as well as men, should make learning about God a top priority.

Martha obviously took His words to heart. Jesus did not come immediately to heal her brother Lazarus when he became ill, yet in the midst of hurt and anger, Martha went out to meet him, then affirmed Jesus was God's Son and would raise Lazarus from the dead in the last day. Afterward, she called her sister Mary aside, telling her "The Teacher is here" (John 11:28 NIV).

Practical as always, Martha objected when Jesus told them to roll away the stone from Lazarus' grave: "He'll stink!" Martha never minced words. But when Jesus insisted, she agreed.

Jesus then resurrected Lazarus, making believers of Jews who witnessed this miraculous feat!

Six days before Passover, Martha makes her next appearance. As the resurrected Lazarus reclines at the table, Martha served, as usual, but made no snide remarks about her sister's impractical gift to Jesus—expensive perfume poured on His feet—and the embarrassing scene she provoked. Martha probably scheduled plenty of time to listen to the Teacher. Her love, loyalty, and hospitality during Passion Week must have blessed the Savior before His horrible ordeal on the cross.

In this idyllic picture by Henryk Siemiradzki, Martha is bringing wine and focusing on hospitality while Mary is focusing on Jesus. In a society where one of a woman's primary duties was to be hospitable, this must have been a difficult choice.

MARY OF BETHANY
Mark 14:3–9; Luke 10:38–42; John 11:1–45; 12:1–8

Mary stands in direct contrast to her outgoing sister Martha. Yet Mary was a woman of courage. She refused to let others' expectations distract her from what was important. She focused all her attention on the King of kings sitting in her living room, rather than fussing over household details.

Yet Jesus' delay in coming to heal her brother Lazarus, resulting in his death, shook her. When Mary heard of Jesus' arrival, she initially did not go out to meet Him, as Martha did. Yet when she heard Jesus was asking for her, she went to talk to Him. Like Martha, she reproached Jesus for His inaction. We hear no affirmation of faith from Mary, though it was the tears of Mary and other Jews that caused Jesus Himself to weep.

Her later actions spoke louder than words. At a dinner honoring Jesus, Mary perfumed His feet with pure nard that cost a year's income. Despite her prosperous family, Mary's gift represented a substantial sacrifice. In a culture in which men and women rarely spoke together in public, Mary did not hesitate to shock dinner guests by wiping Jesus' feet with her hair to express her deep love for Him.

She made no apologies when her actions were criticized by Judas Iscariot and no comment when Jesus defended and memorialized her by saying, "She did what she could. She poured perfume on my body beforehand to prepare for my burial. . .what she has done will also be told, in memory of her" (Mark 14:8–9 NIV).

Although some details in the two stories are similar, Mary of Bethany is not to be confused with the sinful woman of Nain, who also anointed Jesus' feet with precious ointment.

MARY MAGDALENE
Matthew 27:56, 61; 28:1; Mark 15:40, 47; 16:1–19; Luke 8:2; 24:10; John 19:25; 20:1–18

Some believe the name Magdalene comes from the word *Magdala,* a town known for its fish salting and dyeing industries, three miles from Tiberias on the Sea of Galilee, where Mary may have been born. Others believe her name comes from an expression found in the Talmud, which means "curling women's hair," designating an adulteress, although there is no solid evidence to indicate Mary was an adulteress or a prostitute. Little else is known about Mary Magdalene, other than that Jesus drove seven demons from her and that she possessed sufficient resources to help

Jesus warns Mary Magdalene not to touch Him as He has not ascended yet. The sixteenth-century painting is by Correggio.

Him financially. Probably single or childless, she also wandered with Him as He traveled. The Bible mentions Mary Magdalene just over a dozen times, all linked with Jesus' crucifixion and resurrection. When Jesus' women disciples are listed, Mary Magdalene's name usually heads the group, except at the foot of the cross, where, as relatives, Jesus' mother and aunt take precedence (see John 19:25).

Mary suffered intense mental/spiritual battles, but this did not indicate an evil nature or disobedience. Jesus freed her completely from demonic oppression, and Mary, in turn, never left her Lord. She was present at His trial and His crucifixion. She even asked the "gardener" where His body was, so she could take it away (although she obviously did not have the strength to do so). Of all Jesus' followers, He honored Mary as the first to talk with Him after He arose. Not surprisingly, she was the first to share with others about His resurrection.

JOANNA
Luke 8:1–3; 24:1–10

Joanna was the wife of Chuza, the household steward of Herod Antipas, the tetrarch of Galilee. Some identify her husband as the royal official of John 4:46–54,

whose son Jesus healed.

Jesus won Joanna's trust by healing her illness and/or demonic possession. She followed Him and supported Him financially. She and her husband no doubt walked a dangerous path, as Herod Antipas, having murdered John the Baptist, exhibited growing paranoia toward Jesus. Tradition says Herod dismissed Chuza because of his wife's witness in the palace.

Faithful Joanna probably stood by the cross and prepared burial spices for Jesus with the other women. Later she was among the first to discover His resurrection.

MARY, THE MOTHER OF JAMES AND JOSES
Matthew 27:55–56; Mark 15:40–41, 47; 16:1–8; Luke 24:1–11

This Mary was the mother of "James the Less" or "James the Little," who was one of the Twelve, but not the "Son of Thunder." Her son Joses apparently belonged to the larger group of Jesus' followers. Some believe Mary was the wife of Cleophas (John 19:25).

Like many other women, she had followed Jesus and helped supply His needs. She mourned for Him at the cross, brought spices to the tomb for His burial, and witnessed an angel's declaration that Jesus no longer was there.

SUSANNA

Luke 8:2–3

Susanna received healing from Jesus, gave of her financial resources to support Him, and followed Him throughout His ministry.

SALOME, MOTHER OF JAMES AND JOHN

Matthew 20:20–28; 27:55–56; Mark 15:40–41; 16:1–8

Mark is the only Gospel that records her name. Matthew identifies her as "the mother of Zebedee's children" (Matthew 20:20 KJV), the disciples Jesus called the "sons of thunder" (Mark 3:17), James and John. Some believe Salome was the sister of Mary, the mother of Jesus (John 19:25). Salome was among the Galilean women who followed Jesus, not only paying her own expenses, but helping Him and His disciples in their ministry.

She represents all doting mothers determined to obtain the very best for their children, both on earth and in heaven. Salome asked Jesus to reserve the ultimate places of honor for James and John, one on His right in His kingdom, the other on His left.

Jesus understood that Salome, despite her presumptuous request, truly believed He was God's Son. He asked the brothers, "Can you drink the cup I am going to drink?" (Matthew 20:22 NIV).

When James and John eagerly assured Him they could, Jesus reminded them the Father alone would determine such judgments.

Upon learning about this discussion, the other disciples quarreled with the Sons of Thunder. Salome's question gave Jesus an opportunity to deal with their universal craving to be the greatest.

Salome (the woman with the spice jar) and other female followers of Jesus meet an angel at the tomb. The seventeenth-century image is by Bartolomeo Schedoni.

Despite her flaws, Salome dedicated time, energy, and resources to Jesus. She was among the women who refused to leave Him during the crucifixion, and she was among those who, bringing spices for His burial, encountered an angel announcing His resurrection.

WOMEN IN JESUS' PARABLES

Jesus was a wonderful storyteller, yet each story revealed a valuable lesson that women can apply to their lives today. The characters peopling these parables are grain grinders, bread bakers, a housewife, a widow, and several virgins. Although each scenario may have been somewhat different —we no longer grind our grain, rarely knead bread, nor use oil lamps—the kernel of truth each story reveals and the lesson to be learned remain the same.

Palestinian girls grinding corn in a quern in 1912. The woman Jesus spoke to may have done much the same.

WOMEN MAKING BREAD
Grinding Meal

Matthew 24:40–41; Luke 17:35–36

Jesus told a parable about His second coming that reflected the difference between male and female tasks in His culture. On Judgment Day, people continued morning activities as they had for centuries. Two men would be in the field, while two women would be grinding grain for the day's bread, pushing heavy millstones back and forth—one of their most menial jobs. Although the women's circumstances did not differ, their faith separated them on Judgment Day. One woman lifted her vision above the drudgery and put her faith in Jesus. The other's spirit was ultimately separated from God forever.

Mixing Leaven

Matthew 13:33; Luke 13:21

Jesus told a parable about bread baking that must have puzzled His Jewish hearers. He likened the kingdom of God to the yeast a woman mixed into a large amount of flour. Yeast in the Old Testament always represented sin or evil. During the Passover, for example, all yeast was to be destroyed. Jesus Himself told His disciples to beware of the yeast of the Pharisees and Sadducees (see Matthew 16:6), and Paul later used this imagery in his epistles.

But in this uniquely positive parable, Jesus tells how a woman, using skill and experience, worked a little leaven into flour, until it permeated every bit of the dough. Jesus implied if she worked even a small amount of the kingdom of God's essence into her world, it would influence people beyond anything she could imagine.

WOMAN WHO FOUND LOST COIN

Luke 15:8–10

Jesus told this story so vividly, one wonders if Jesus' mother or one of His sisters lost a silver coin. In that era, women's dowries decorated their headdresses, the only financial resources they possessed against possible widowhood or divorce. The coin that came loose equaled approximately one tenth of the woman's life savings. Homes at the time were extremely dark, so the woman in the parable lit a lamp and swept frantically. When she finds her coin, she asks her friends and neighbors to rejoice with her. Jesus says that same joy is felt among the angels when one sinner repents.

Livia Drusilla was the wife of the Roman emperor during Jesus' lifetime. Her likeness was the first female image to appear on a Jewish coin. One like this may well have been the lost coin Jesus referred to.

PERSISTENT WIDOW

Luke 18:1–8

In this parable, a widow faced a financial crisis, perhaps the danger of losing her home, her freedom, and/or that of her children. She refused to remain passive but continued to annoy a judge with pleas for help against her adversary until the judge, weary of her endless nagging, gave her justice.

Jesus declared God is not like the callous judge. He will answer His people quickly when they persevere in prayer.

TEN VIRGINS

Matthew 25:1–13

In Jesus' era, weddings were joyous occasions with feasting, dancing, and fun. Jesus used this popular event to illustrate the importance of spiritual preparation for His second coming. In an ancient Jewish wedding, the bridegroom and his friends, accompanied by musicians, went to the bride's house, bringing her to his own home or that of his father, usually late in the evening. Relatives and neighbors joined the feast, which often lasted a full week.

The ten virgins of Jesus' parable may have been bridesmaids or guests, but probably were servants instructed to light the way for the bride and groom. All the girls fell asleep but awakened at midnight when they heard the procession approaching. The wise virgins

A young woman carefully tends her lamp. From The Parable of the Wise and Foolish Virgins *by Friedrich Schadow (1838–1842).*

had brought extra oil, but the five foolish maidens had neglected to prepare for a late arrival. They tried to borrow oil from the other five, but those with extra refused them, knowing none could greet the bridegroom if they shared. While the five foolish girls rushed off to buy oil at midnight, the wedding party arrived. The five wise girls lit the way for them and shared in the wedding banquet inside. When the others returned, they found themselves locked out. Although invited to participate in the feast, these young women missed it because they did not plan ahead.

No one in Jesus' day wanted to miss a wedding, especially women,

who enjoyed little entertainment or recreation. In the preceding parable (Matthew 24), Jesus connected with men through a story about an irresponsible servant who mistreated his fellow servants and mismanaged a household, bringing his master's wrath upon him. In the parable of the ten virgins, Jesus used a wedding story to attract the attention of women also in need of salvation. Together, these parables demonstrate His love and concern for all people, regardless of gender.

WOMEN IN THE EARLY CHURCH

Tent makers, teachers, mothers, sewers, businesswomen, and prophetesses… Although the biblical accounts of their lives may be brief and their actual positions in the church somewhat vague, all these women played a significant role in forming the first-century church. They were witnesses to the disciples' miracles and persecution. Yet they were not deterred from testifying of their faith nor from opening their homes to fellow Christians. Amid fear of reprisal, these women were truly committed to the Truth—for they stood up for their faith, risking ridicule and, in some instances, their very lives.

house—so called because she probably was a widow. The fact she welcomed groups to worship and pray there and had a maid, Rhoda, indicates it was a large upper-class abode. The fact that Jesus' followers gathered there indicates they trusted her during perilous times, including after James's execution and Peter's imprisonment. Mary, like other courageous women of the first-century churches, offered her home as a refuge where God's people could encourage each other.

MARY, JOHN MARK'S MOTHER
Acts 12:11–12

This godly woman is mentioned only once in the Bible, but she is significant in that she hosted a church in her home. Mary was the mother of the writer of the second Gospel and probably the aunt of Barnabas (see Colossians 4:10), Paul's first missionary partner. Some scholars suggest what Paul regarded as John Mark's desertion (see Acts 15:38) took place because he missed his mother.

Legend holds the Upper Room where Jesus and His disciples ate the Passover was located in Mary's

Mary's upper room must have been very busy when Jesus and The Twelve came to town. The girl bringing fresh supplies from the right-hand side of the picture might be Mary's servant Rhoda. This painting, from the sixteenth century, is by Bernardino Lanino.

TABITHA OR DORCAS
Acts 9:36–43

Tabitha lived in the coastal city of Joppa (now called Jaffa). She

Peter restores Tabitha after she has died, in a seventeenth-century painting by Giovanni Francesco Guercino.

was the only woman in the Bible referred to as *math–tria*, "disciple." Tabitha, probably a woman of means, gave generously to the less fortunate and made clothing for widows and their families. When she died of an illness, two men summoned Peter from nearby Lydda. When he arrived, weeping widows told him stories of Tabitha's kindness and showed him beautiful clothing she had made for them. Peter prayed then raised Tabitha from the dead. The Bible says Peter remained in Joppa for a time—

probably to aid a church whose growth exploded after the beloved Tabitha's resurrection.

LYDIA
Acts 16:12–15, 40

Although Paul met Lydia in a prayer group outside the city of Philippi in Macedonia, she was from Thyatira in what is modern-day Turkey. In Thyatira, a region of many ethnic backgrounds, Apollo the sun god, called Tyrinnus, was predominant. The presence of many groups of once-exiled Jews,

The site at Philippi where Paul is said to have baptized Lydia.

attracted by the city's commercial prosperity, also influenced this city where trade guilds flourished. Lydia marketed purple cloth to the wealthy, probably ran a prosperous business in Philippi, and owned a large, luxurious house with servants. Possibly a Jewess or proselyte, she heard Paul's message and became his first European convert. Lydia and her entire household were publicly baptized, after which she almost compelled Paul and Silas to stay with her.

Later, when local authorities unjustly beat Paul and Silas, imprisoned them, then relented and released them, they returned to Lydia's house to meet with Philippian Christians before they left the city.

PRISCILLA

Acts 18:1–3, 18–19, 24–28; Romans 16:3–5; 1 Corinthians 16:19; 2 Timothy 4:19

Priscilla and her husband Aquila lived in Rome until Emperor Claudius expelled all Jews from the city. They moved to Corinth in Greece, where they met Paul the apostle and invited him to stay with them. The fact that in the Bible Priscilla's name most often appears before Aquila's gives rise to the belief that she was either of an aristocratic background or that she was a more prominent leader in the church.

Priscilla, Aquila, and Paul all were tent makers. While they wove, cut, and stitched, Prisca and her husband absorbed Paul's tremendous store of spiritual wisdom. A year and a half later, when Paul left Corinth, intending to return to Syria, Priscilla and Aquila accompanied him. They helped plant a church in Ephesus, where the couple remained while Paul continued to Antioch.

While in Ephesus, a Jew named Apollos spoke in their synagogue. He possessed a thorough knowledge of the scriptures but knew only about John the Baptist's gospel. Priscilla and Aquila invited Apollos home and taught him a more complete picture of

It's possible that Priscilla, accompanied by her husband, Aquila, and the apostle Paul, walked through these city streets of ancient Corinth.

OTHER WOMEN WHO HOSTED CHURCHES

Many women shared the joys and responsibilities of hosting churches in their homes, often risking persecution by local authorities:

- **Apphia** (see Philemon 1:2) possibly the wife of Philemon, helped host her church in Colosse.
- **Chloe** (1 Corinthians 1:11) hosted her church in Corinth.
- **Nympha** (Colossians 4:15) hosted her church in Laodicea.

Nymphas, meaning "nymph given," was apparently named for the female spirits of Greek mythology. This vase, from the third century before Christ, depicts several sea nymphs.

Jesus. Apollos became an effective speaker for Christ as a result of their influence.

Later, Priscilla and Aquila returned to Rome where they led a house church (see Romans 1:3–5) then sometime later appear back in Ephesus (see 2 Timothy 4:19).

Some scholars believe Priscilla wrote the book of Hebrews; others suggest Priscilla and Aquila wrote the book together. Whether or not Priscilla wrote any portion of Hebrews, she evidenced strong, consistent faith in Jesus and a close relationship with her husband. The two acted as one, traveling, evangelizing, teaching, and encouraging young believers, as well as Paul, their dear friend.

PHOEBE
Romans 16:1–2

Phoebe, who hosted a church in Cenchrea near Corinth, was the first of Paul's friends he greeted at the end of his letter to the Romans, indicating he held her in high esteem. The word Paul uses to describe Phoebe is *diakonon*, the same word rendered "deacon" when referring to male leaders.

SISTER PROPHETESSES (FOUR DAUGHTERS OF PHILIP)
Acts 21:8–9

Little is known about these four unmarried, unnamed daughters of Philip the Evangelist, other than the apostle Paul stayed with their family on his way back to Jerusalem near the end of his third missionary journey. But their presence in scripture is significant, emphasizing truth recorded by the

Old Testament prophet Joel and preached by the apostle Peter at Pentecost: "And it shall come to pass in the last days, saith God, I will pour out of my Spirit upon all flesh: and your sons and your daughters shall prophesy, and your young men shall see visions, and your old men shall dream dreams: And on my servants and on my handmaidens I will pour out in those days of my Spirit; and they shall prophesy" (Acts 2:17–18 KJV).

JUNIA
Romans 16:7

While some Bible translations render this name "Junias," which is male, other evidence indicates Paul's relative was female. Junia became a Christian before Paul did and suffered imprisonment for the faith. He indicated she was "of note among the apostles" (Romans 16:7 KJV), an equal to himself. Some scholars suggest Junia may have been the wife of Andronicus.

Junia with Andronicus (both mentioned in Romans 16:7) flank Athanasius of Christianopolous in this Eastern Orthodox painting.

PAUL'S OTHER SISTERS IN CHRIST

Tryphena, Tryphosa, Euodias, and Syntyche probably were deaconesses in their congregations.
- **Tryphena** and **Tryphosa** (see Romans 16:12) in Rome. Tryphosa may have been her sister. According to Paul, they "work[ed] hard in the Lord" (NIV).
- **Euodias** and **Syntyche** (see Philippians 4:2–3). Both probably were prominent women who served side by side with Paul in Philippi, yet struggled in a major disagreement, which he begged them to resolve.
- **Persis** of Rome, whom Paul referred to as his "dear friend" (Romans 16:12 NIV). The Greek implies she earned the respect and love of the Roman Christians as well.
- **Eunice** and **Lois** of Lystra (see 2 Timothy 1:5). Eunice, who was married to a Greek man (see Acts 16:1) was the godly mother and Lois the godly grandmother of Timothy, Paul's protégé.
- **Julia** (see Romans 16:15) of Rome, possibly of a noble family, who may have been the wife of Philologus.
- **Mary** of Rome who, Paul said, "worked very hard for you" (Romans 16:6 NIV).

Babylon as described in the book of Revelation, with St. John and an angel looking down from above. This image of a sixteenth-century woodcut was colored by a modern artist.

SYMBOLIC WOMEN IN THE NEW TESTAMENT

BABYLON, THE PROSTITUTE QUEEN

Revelation 17; 18; 19:1–5

This vivid account of Babylon, a drunken queen astride a terrifying beast with seven horns that is covered with blasphemy, has intrigued readers for centuries. The early Christians no doubt identified her as Rome, intoxicated with power, materialism, and the blood of Christian martyrs. Indeed, the disciple John points out the beast's seven heads are the seven hills—a direct reference to Rome, famous for its seven hills. But most scholars agree the prostitute also represents evil social and political systems down through the ages— any government or force that defies God, who pleads for His people to leave her. The very kings with whom Babylon consorted destroy her out of hatred and greed. Kings who shared her wickedness and wealth mourn her, along with merchants, sea captains, and sailors who grew rich supplying her with the gold, jewels, fine clothing, spices, and the "bodies and souls of men" (Revelation 18:13 NIV) she craved.

This queen is in direct contrast to the bride of Christ, described in the final chapters of Revelation.

THE CHURCH AS THE BRIDE OF CHRIST

John 3:29–30; Ephesians 5:21–33; Revelation 19:6–9; 21; 22:1–17

When the disciples of John the Baptist warned him his followers were flocking to Jesus, he reminded them he was not the Messiah, the Bridegroom, but his friend and attendant. The bride—representing lovers of God—belonged to the Bridegroom, not him. In saying this, John perpetuated the wedding-marriage imagery of the Old Testament in which a bride or wife represented God's people, and the bridegroom/husband represented God. The portrait continues in Ephesians, with Paul's commands to husbands and wives, as their relationship represents that of Christ and His church. It culminates in the final chapters of the book of Revelation, when believers clad in fine linen and the magnificent heavenly city of Jerusalem both represent the perfected church, a bride no longer struggling with internal or external sin, but living forever in perfect harmony with God, her Husband.

ARTEMIS (DIANA) OF THE EPHESIANS

Acts 19:24–41

Artemis was a Greco-Roman female deity whose worship during New Testament times largely centered in Ephesus in what is now the country of Turkey. One of the Seven Wonders of the World, the great temple of Diana, with its huge statue of the goddess, was located there. Artemis inspired not only worship in her devotees but also intense local pride. When Paul and his fellow missionaries introduced the worship of the invisible God, a riot erupted, fueled by angry silversmiths whose flourishing market for their small statues of Artemis was threatened by the new religion. A city official finally quieted the uproar, and Paul left for Macedonia.

Artemis of Ephesus.

Interpersonal struggles often begin as soon as we become self-aware.

Bible Women and Their Interactions with Men

IN THE BEGINNING

So God created man in his own image, in the image of God he created him; male and female he created them.

GENESIS 1:27 NIV

Male and female, we are created in God's image. From the very beginning of the Bible, God indicates that "man"—humankind—needs both genders to be complete. Together, males and females, we are the image of God. Our interactions as men and women are one way God's grace enters our world.

But we live in a fallen world, and what was intended to be a vehicle of God's blessing has often been twisted or broken. In the twenty-first century, we know all too well that women's relationships with men are not always healthy or positive. Interactions between the sexes can be filled with joy and love—but they can also be distorted by anger, selfishness, jealousy, and power struggles. Men hurt women, women hurt men, and God's perfect plan for the sexes fails to be fulfilled.

This is nothing new. Biblical men and women struggled with the same issues we do today. From the very beginning of Creation, women and men have sometimes allowed their relationships to be used for evil rather than good.

Consider the first man and woman who ever lived: Adam and Eve.

MAN AND WOMAN IN THE GARDEN OF EDEN

The LORD God caused the man to fall into a deep sleep; and while he was sleeping, he took one of the man's ribs and closed up the place with flesh. Then the LORD God made a woman from the rib he had taken out of the man, and he brought her to the man.

GENESIS 2:21–22 NIV

After God created the Earth with all its teeming plant and animal life, He still needed something more, a creature with whom He could

have a relationship. So He made a proposal, saying, "Let us make man in our image, in our likeness" (Genesis 1:26 NIV). (The word "our" here implies the Trinity—Father, Son, and Spirit.) Thus, "The LORD God formed the man from the dust of the ground and breathed into his nostrils the breath of life, and the man became a living being" (Genesis 2:7 NIV). (The Hebrew word for "man"—*adam*—is similar to the term for the red earth.)

God draws Eve from the side of a sleeping Adam.

At this point in the story, humanity is neither male nor female. But just as God longed for relationship with His Creation, He also knew "man" should not be alone. And so, God performed surgery on Adam: He took a piece out of man and made woman from it.

The word translated as "rib" in Genesis 2 is one that doesn't occur exactly the same again in the rest of the Hebrew Old Testament. Bible scholars have argued over its exact meaning and what that implies about the interactions between men and women. Does it mean that women are inferior to men, because women were created second from a relatively minor body part? Or does it mean something quite different—for instance, that Eve was the new-and-improved version of humanity?

Given what the rest of the Bible indicates about God's will for interactions between males and females, neither of those interpretations seems quite right! What is clear is that God intended for male and female to be deeply and intimately connected. As Adam says when he first sees Eve, "This is now bone of my bones and flesh of my flesh" (Genesis 2:23 NIV). Genesis continues: "For this reason a man will leave his father and mother and be united to his wife, and they will become one flesh" (Genesis 2:24 NIV). God intended that the interaction between men and women be one of unity, a deep intimacy that is both physical and spiritual. "The man and his wife were both naked, and they felt no shame" (Genesis 2:25 NIV); in other words, the first man and woman were completely vulnerable to each other, completely comfortable, completely secure. It is this kind of interaction—where both sides know they are safe from any kind of hurt or abuse—that God intended for all men and women.

Unfortunately, all too soon Satan corrupted the relationship between the first man and woman.

WOMEN WHO USED THEIR INFLUENCE FOR EVIL

The man said, "The woman you put here with me—she gave me some fruit from the tree, and I ate it." Then the LORD God said to the woman, "What is this you have done?"
GENESIS 3:12–13 NIV

Eve
In the garden, Adam and Eve have everything they need to be happy: direct fellowship with God, an abundant earth, a fulfilling relationship with each other, and the promise of children to come. What else could they possibly have wanted?

Satan, entering the scene, convinces Eve that in fact there is something else she wants: fruit from the Tree of Knowledge of Good and Evil. Our human nature is no different today; all too easily

Adam, shown with an iron shackle on his wrist, holds the forbidden fruit while his wife, Eve, looks on. The eighteenth-century painting is by the German Johann Michael Feuchtmayer.

we shift our attention from the many blessings we enjoy to some small thing we lack, letting our contentment and peace be erased by what is essentially greed. And this is exactly what happened to Eve. She believed Satan when he told her she would be happier if she could only have the one fruit God had not given her.

And as with any married couple, what affected Eve then easily infected Adam. Just as love and joy can be contagious, so can greed, discontent, and envy. Eve not only let Satan break her own union with God; she used her influence to break Adam's relationship with God as well: "When the woman saw that the fruit of the tree was good for food and pleasing to the eye, and also desirable for gaining wisdom, she took some and ate it. She also gave some to her husband, who was with her, and he ate it" (Genesis 3:6 NIV).

Immediately, "the eyes of both of them were opened, and they realized they were naked; so they sewed fig leaves together and made coverings for themselves" (Genesis 3:7 NIV). In other words, the intimacy and total security that had existed between them was gone; now they felt the need to hide their most vulnerable parts from one another.

Even worse, the relationship between the man and woman was not the only thing sin had damaged. Their relationship with God had also changed.

Then the man and his wife heard the sound of the LORD God as he was walking in the garden in the cool of the day, and they hid from the LORD God among the trees of the garden. But the LORD God called to the man, "Where are you?" He answered, "I heard you in the garden, and I was afraid because I was naked; so I hid."

GENESIS 3:8–10 NIV

Their sense of shame makes the man and woman not only hide from each other but from God as well.

Because humans are no longer united in intimacy with God, men and women from this time forward are also no longer united with the same security and closeness they experienced before the Fall. The break in the relationship between Eve and Adam is reenacted again and again.

Delilah

The Bible tells us the stories of other women who, like Eve, used their influence over men to bring about evil. These women misused their intimacy with the men in their lives to diminish the men, to draw them away from harmony with God. The story of Delilah and Samson is a good example.

Samson lived during the time when the children of Israel had no king to rule them. The Israelites had come out of Egypt hundreds of years earlier, and they were living now in the Promised Land. Unfortunately, the land was not uninhabited; the Philistines were among the people already when the Israelites arrived. By Samson's lifetime, his people had been at war with the Philistines on and off for hundreds of years.

During this time, the Israelites had also fallen into disobedience, allowed themselves to be turned away from their unique relation-ship with God, and were being ruled by the Philistines. This was the environment into which Sam-son was born.

An angel of the Lord had come to Samson's barren mother and told her she soon would have a son. "No razor may be used on his head, because the boy is to be a Nazirite, set apart to God from birth, and he will begin the deliverance of Israel from the hands of the Philistines" (Judges 13:5 NIV). Later the angel appeared to both parents. Afterward, Samson was born. He grew up to have amazing physical strength and the "Spirit of the LORD began to stir him" (Judges 13:25 NIV).

Samson falls in love with a beautiful Philistine woman. His parents try to persuade him to marry a nice Jewish girl instead, but an infatuated Samson tells his father, "Get her for me. She's the right one for me" (Judges 14:3 NIV).

Samson appears to be somewhat of a spoiled and arrogant young man accustomed to having his own way. He breaks the vows his parents made to God on his behalf and fails to dedicate himself totally to the Lord. But at least he doesn't cut his hair.

Turbulent for its beginning, the relationship Samson has with his wife is clearly not built on any sense of mature, self-sacrificing love. Instead, Samson refuses to explain a riddle to his wife, who then whines and pouts to get her way. Samson gives her the answer to his riddle, which she, in turn, tells her people. In anger, Samson kills thirty Philistine men. Samson and his wife are separated soon after their marriage and, though they are briefly reunited, the Philistines kill Samson's wife. Again enraged, he takes his revenge by killing still more Philistines.

Over the years, the Philistines learn that women are Samson's

Samson sleeps in Delilah's lap in this 1878 painting by Alexander Cabanel.

Samson gets her to leave him alone by telling her lies: "If anyone ties me with seven fresh thongs that have not been dried, I'll become as weak as any other man" (Judges 16:7 NIV). So the Philistines hide in the couple's bedroom, and when Samson falls asleep, Delilah ties him up with seven thongs. She shouts, "Samson, the Philistines are upon you!" (Judges 16:9 NIV). Samson wakes up, snaps himself free of the thongs, and easily fights off the Philistines.

She wheedles and plots, and he deceives her two more times but, unable to resist her charms, he never learns his lesson. Delilah finally says to Samson, "How can you say, 'I love you,' when you won't confide in me? This is the third time you have made a fool of me and haven't told me the secret of your great strength" (Judges 16:15 NIV). She seems oblivious to the fact

greatest weakness. When he falls in love with yet another Philistine woman, this time a woman named Delilah, they promise her an enormous pile of silver coins if she can discover the secret of his incredible strength. And so Delilah teases and flirts, begs and wheedles to learn Samson's secret.

that she's clearly tried to get him killed! Instead, she expects him to make himself vulnerable to her even when she has shown him she cannot be trusted. The Bible tells us that "with such nagging she prodded him day after day until he was tired to death" (Judges 16:16 NIV).

Delilah and Philistine soldiers shave a sleeping Samson, who awakens to find his supernatural strength gone. The painting is by sixteenth-century Italian artist Caravaggio.

And so he tells her everything: "No razor has ever been used on my head. . .because I have been a Nazirite set apart to God since birth. If my head were shaved, my strength would leave me, and I would become as weak as any other man" (Judges 16:17 NIV). Maybe Samson doesn't really believe he can lose his strength. He apparently has no real sense that it's his connection to God that makes him strong; he thinks his strength is his own, to use as he likes, and his relationship with Delilah is more important to him than his relationship with the Lord. He lies down with his head in Delilah's lap, a position of trust and vulnerability—and she betrays him. She calls a man to shave Samson's seven long braids from his head.

This time when Delilah shakes him, screaming, "Samson! The Philistines are upon you," he awakens to find his strength gone. The Bible says, "He did not know that the LORD had left him" (Judges 16:20 NIV). Clearly, Samson does not understand how Delilah has diminished him by coming between him and God.

The rest of Samson's story is a tragic one. The Philistines take him prisoner, gouge out his eyes, and chain him to a huge stone wheel used to grind grain. He spends the rest of his days doing the job an ox would do. In a culture that often saw women on the same level with cattle, Samson has ironically been forced into a similarly demeaning role. Delilah has stolen both his pride and his masculinity. In the end, Samson's hair grows back, he calls on the Lord, and gets his revenge on the Philistines, but he dies along with them.

OTHER BIBLICAL WOMEN WHO USED THEIR INFLUENCE FOR EVIL

- **Lot's daughters:** After Lot and his daughters escaped the destruction of Sodom and Gomorrah, the two women feared that they would find no husbands with which to have children. Out of that fear, they schemed to get their father drunk with wine on two successive nights. Each daughter committed incest with her father and became pregnant. Their two sons, Moab and Ben-Ammi, became the patriarchs of the Moabite and Ammonite people, who were two of Israel's most deadly enemies (see Genesis 19:30–38).
- **Solomon's wives and concubines:** Solomon's many foreign wives and concubines convinced him to worship other gods and build pagan temples, which led to his downfall (see 1 Kings 11).
- **Potiphar's wife:** Potiphar's wife tried to seduce Joseph. When Joseph resisted her charms, she told her husband Joseph had attempted to rape her. As a result, Potiphar had Joseph imprisoned (see Genesis 39:1–20).
- **Salome:** Herodias's beautiful daughter, Salome, used her seductive dance to persuade her stepfather, Herod, to have John the Baptist beheaded (see Matthew 14; Mark 6).

Much smaller than Solomon's harem, these women, photographed in the early twentieth century, feast with their husband.

The name Delilah in Hebrew means "languishing" and that was the effect Delilah had on Samson. Like Eve, she used her relationship with her man to come between him and God—and in the process, she caused him to become far less than what God had intended for him to be.

WOMEN WHO WERE USED BY MEN

The damage done to man-woman relationships at the Fall is a two-way street, of course. Perhaps, Delilah, like Eve, found she'd hurt herself as much as she hurt the man who loved her. And in the history of men and women, including the stories given to us in the Bible, it seems to be even more common that men take advantage of the women in their lives.

As [Abraham] was about to enter Egypt, he said to his wife Sarai, "I know what a beautiful woman you are. When the Egyptians see you, they will say, 'This is his wife.' Then they will kill me but will let you live. Say you are my sister, so that I will be treated well for your

sake and my life will be spared because of you."
GENESIS 12:11–13 NIV

Sarah

Genesis 12 tells us that because of a famine in the land, Abraham and his family travel to Egypt. As they near the land of the Pharaoh, Abraham is apparently worried about Sarah, who is not only his half sister but also his wife, and is thinking about how her beauty may get him in trouble. Because of his fears, he forbids her to let anyone know they're married. "Tell them you're my sister," he says to her. "That way they won't kill me—and they'll be nice to me."

Abram tells Sarai what he wants her to do when they get to Egypt, in James Jacques Tissot's late-nineteenth-century painting.

Abraham's protective measures work out well—for him, if not for

Sarah. Just as he predicted, Sarah's beauty attracts Pharaoh's attention. And just as Abraham also predicted, the Egyptian ruler treats Abraham well; he even pays Abraham a hefty sum for his "sister." With no regard for Sarah's feelings, Abraham allows his wife to be handed over to another man, as though she were merely an object. Sarah disappears into the royal harem.

Sarah has been betrayed—and yet she apparently still loves her husband enough to protect him by not revealing her true identity. Thinking of herself as chattel to be passed from man to man was probably nothing new for her.

During the era in which Sarah and Abraham lived, Middle East families rather than individuals owned wealth (in the form of farms or herds), and the husband or father was the manager of the household goods. A single woman had no access to resources; on her own, she would literally starve. When the time came for her to leave home, her father or brothers arranged a marriage. Her husband then assumed the role of governing her life and making decisions on her behalf. If her husband were to die, a woman could easily end up as a servant in her in-laws' household.

Both Sarah and Abraham regard women's role from within this historical context—but apparently God's perspective is different. God is not pleased with the half-truth Abraham told, so He intervenes on a woman's behalf. When the Egyptian royal house starts experiencing plagues, Pharaoh finds out the truth. He sends Sarah back to Abraham and banishes them both from Egypt.

Sometime after this event, we are given a picture of the man Abraham and the woman Sarah as equals before God. In Genesis 18, God speaks to them both directly, and He makes clear how much He values Sarah. But Abraham, the great patriarch of faith, is not above using his wife again when it becomes convenient for him to do so.

The same trick that worked so well in Egypt works equally well when Abraham and Sarah travel to Gerar in Genesis 20. There, Sarah catches the eye of Abimelech, the king of Gerar—and Abraham is still quite comfortable having her pretend to be his sister instead of his wife. During the time that Sarah lived under Abimelech's care, his wife and his servant girls were unable to bear children.

Once again, God steps in. In a dream, He reveals to Abimelech that Sarah is actually Abraham's wife, and that the king has no business sleeping with her. The king returns Sarah to her husband and gives Abraham land and silver to make amends. Then Abraham prays to God and the fertility of Abimelech's wife and maidservants is restored. Although Abimelech gave gifts to Abraham, Sarah is the one God rewards: "Now the LORD was gracious to Sarah as he had. . . promised" (Genesis 21:1 NIV), blessing her with the birth of Isaac.

Bathsheba

The story of Bath-sheba and David is yet another Bible account that reveals the contempt men all too often felt for women, even when they found them beautiful. Traditionally, Bathsheba has often been blamed for her adulterous relationship with the king of Israel, but a careful reading of 2 Samuel 11–12 makes clear that Bathsheba was the innocent and helpless recipient of David's lust.

The story begins: "In the spring, at the time when kings go off to war, David sent Joab out with the king's men and the whole Israelite army. . . . But David remained in Jerusalem" (2 Samuel 11:1 NIV). The implication is that David had no business staying in Jerusalem while he sent his men off to war. David is not where God wants him to be; he is out of alignment with God's will, and this puts him in a vulnerable place, a state of mind where he easily falls still farther away from God's grace.

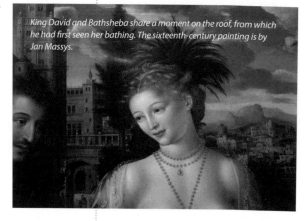

King David and Bathsheba share a moment on the roof, from which he had first seen her bathing. The sixteenth-century painting is by Jan Massys.

So as David is taking some time off from the serious business of war, he happens to be walking on his roof and sees a woman bathing on another rooftop. The story has been retold as though Bathsheba were displaying her charms on purpose, that she orchestrates the entire thing; but the picture that emerges from the scripture is that David has become a voyeur, a peeping tom. He spies on a woman taking a bath, and then he goes even further: He abuses the power he has as king, and he commands his men to bring the woman to him.

For David, Bathsheba is an object of desire, not another human being worthy of his respect. When he finds out she is married, he is not deterred. He sleeps with her, and then sends her back home. When Bathsheba discovers she is pregnant, she sends word to the king.

David responds by asking Joab to send Bathsheba's husband Uriah home from war, hoping Uriah will sleep with his wife and thus never know the king used his woman while he was away. The Bible makes clear that Uriah is far more honorable than David at this point. Although Uriah is a Hittite, a foreigner, he is a man of integrity determined to treat Israel with the

Uriah departs for the front line and his death. King David watches from behind, concealing his guilt, and the prophet Nathan looks on in despair. The 1665 painting is by Rembrandt.

respect David lacks; Uriah refuses to go home and sleep with his wife while his commander and the rest of the troops are still on the battlefield. When David's scheme fails, his sin becomes even uglier: He makes certain Uriah is killed in battle.

Bathsheba apparently loves her husband: "When Uriah's wife heard that her husband was dead, she mourned for him" (2 Samuel 11:26 NIV). With her husband gone, however, she has few options left to her. David sends for her to become his wife, and she goes. Like a cow or goat, she has been passed from man to man.

But God is not pleased, and He sends the prophet Nathan to David.

Nathan rebukes the king with the following story:

> *"There were two men in a certain town, one rich and the other poor. The rich man had a very large number of sheep and cattle, but the poor man had nothing except one little ewe lamb he had bought. He raised it, and it grew up with him and his children. It shared his food, drank from his cup and even slept in his arms. It was like a daughter to him.*
>
> *"Now a traveler came to the rich man, but the rich man refrained from taking one of his own sheep or cattle to prepare*

> *a meal for the traveler who had come to him. Instead, he took the ewe lamb that belonged to the poor man and prepared it for the one who had come to him."*
>
> 2 SAMUEL 12:1–4 NIV

Uriah, Nathan's story implies, rose above the cultural traditions of his surroundings; he treated Bathsheba with love and respect. David (the rich man in Nathan's story), however, not only treated Bathsheba as though she were cattle to be traded, but he handled the transaction deceitfully, stealing what was not his.

Nathan, speaking for God, continues: "I gave you the house of Israel and Judah. And if all this had been too little, I would have given you even more. Why did you despise the word of the LORD by doing what is evil in his eyes? You struck down Uriah the Hittite with the sword and took his wife to be your own" (2 Samuel 12:8–9 NIV). David's selfishness has not only destroyed Bathsheba's life with her husband; it has also come between him and God, breaking the close friendship they once had.

David repents (see Psalm 32; 51), and God does forgive him. David's relationship with God is restored, and he seems to become a gentle and loving husband to Bathsheba, doing his best to make up to her for what he did. They eventually become the parents of Solomon, the wise king who will one day inherit David's throne. Nevertheless, the consequences of David's sin cannot be undone, and they will affect the rest of his life—and surely Bathsheba's as well.

WOMEN WHO TRIUMPHED OVER MEN

Not all women are portrayed in the Bible as either chattel or as seductresses who abused their feminine beauty to control men. The Bible also tells us the stories of women who were able to triumph over men because of their strength, courage, and intelligence.

WOMEN'S POSITION IN ANCIENT TIMES

During the eras hundreds of years before Christ's birth, women faced the following restrictions:

- Unmarried women were not allowed to leave the home of their father.
- Married women were not allowed to leave the home of their husband.
- Women were normally restricted to roles of little or no authority.
- Women could not testify in court.
- Women could not appear unescorted in public venues.
- Women were not allowed to talk to strangers.

Despite these legal and cultural limits, the Bible makes clear that God's intervention brought about exceptions, instances where women were able to be seen as equals, individuals who played necessary roles in their own right.

A woman wears a black hijab, the traditional head covering of Middle Eastern women.

Deborah, a prophetess, the wife of Lappidoth, was leading Israel at that time.
    JUDGES 4:4 NIV

Deborah and Jael

Deborah, a strong and courageous woman, lived during the era when judges rather than a king ruled Israel. She is the only female judge whose story the Bible records and, given women's position in Old Testament cultures, her role is amazing. As a judge, she was also the leader of Israel's army, and clearly, her leadership was honored and respected.

During the centuries after God delivered the Israelites from Egypt, the Israelites went through seven apostasies, times when the Israelites fell away from God. During each apostasy, Israel suffers oppression and wars, after which

God, hearing the cry of His people, raises up a deliverer to rescue them. Deborah whose, story takes place during the third apostasy, is one of these deliverers.

For twenty years the Israelites have endured terrible atrocities under the Canaanite king Jabin and his commander, Sisera. Finally, Israel cries out to God for help. God answers by telling Deborah how to defeat the Canaanites.

Deborah gives her battle orders to her commander, Barak. The odds are terribly against Israel, and Barak, apparently nervous about following Deborah's command,

Deborah led the way: Female Israeli cadets march through the Old City of Jerusalem after a graduation ceremony.

tells her, "If you go with me, I will go; but if you don't go with me, I won't go" (Judges 4:8 NIV). The interaction between Deborah and Barak appears to be an uneasy one; as the judge, Deborah commands Barak's obedience, but as a man, Barak appears to doubt the judgment of a woman.

Deborah answers him, saying, "Very well...I will go with you. But because of the way you are going about this, the honor will not be yours, for the LORD will hand Sisera over to a woman" (Judges 4:9 NIV). Apparently, Deborah is not happy with Barak's unwillingness to put his complete trust in her.

Just as Deborah predicted, the Israelites defeat the Canaanites, killing them all except Sisera, their commander. Sisera flees and hides in the tent of Jael, the wife of Heber the Kenite. The commander believes he will be safe there, because the king of the Canaanites is at peace with Heber's clan. But as it turns out, Jael is no friend of the Canaanites or of Sisera, for she hammers a tent peg into the sleeping Sisera's skull, killing him. As Deborah predicted, it is a courageous woman who ultimately triumphs over the Canaanites' commander.

In Judges 5, Deborah's song of thanks to the Lord for delivering the Israelites from the Canaanites is the oldest poem found in the Bible, and throughout it, Deborah recounts the miracles God has done on Israel's behalf. She takes several entire stanzas to praise Jael (see Judges 5:24–27), whose bravery saved the Israelite women from rape and plunder.

Thanks to both Deborah and Jael, Israel enjoyed forty years of peace and prosperity after Canaan's defeat.

With God's help, these women were successful against all odds. The culture of Deborah's day did nothing to support her serving as the leader of the nation; and yet she did. What's more, Deborah not only led Israel, she led her nation's troops triumphantly against forces that vastly outnumbered them. And then, Jael, a solitary woman, all alone in her tent, brought down the powerful commander of the Canaanites' troops. The story of Deborah and Jael reveals a God who values women—a God who delights in using those who are considered weak and insignificant, those who are overlooked and dismissed, to accomplish His will on earth. As the apostle Paul wrote: "God chose the foolish things of the world to shame the wise; God chose the weak things of the world to shame the strong. He chose the lowly things of this world and the despised things—and the things that are not—to nullify the things that are" (1 Corinthians 1:27–28 NIV).

Esther

The story of Esther is another example where God saves the entire Jewish people through a woman's ability to triumph over a powerful man. Esther is a Jewish girl, an orphan who had been raised by her cousin Mordecai in Susa, the royal city of Persia. Her life as told in the book of Esther reads a little like a Cinderella story—except that the Bible doesn't end with the wedding and happily-ever-after. Instead, we learn what happened in the marriage after the wedding.

Xerxes, the king of Persia from about 486 to 465 BC, is already married at the beginning of the book of Esther, but his wife, Queen Vashti, refuses to obey his requests. Eventually, Vashti is banished from the king's presence for the rest of her life, and Xerxes seeks a new queen from among all the prettiest young women of his land. Esther is the one chosen, and she becomes queen.

Although the king does not know Esther is Jewish, she does not forget her people. She and her cousin Mordecai remain in contact. When Mordecai learns of an assassination plot against the king, he tells Esther, who then warns Xerxes, earning the king's gratitude.

But Mordecai also makes enemies within the kingdom. Haman, one of Xerxes' favorite officials, passes an edict that everyone must bow down before him, but Mordecai refuses. "When Haman saw that Mordecai would not kneel down or pay him honor, he was enraged. Yet having learned who Mordecai's people were, he scorned the idea of killing only Mordecai. Instead Haman looked for a way to destroy

Esther swoons before her husband, King Xerxes, in this 1865 photograph staged by English photographer Julia Margaret Cameron.

all Mordecai's people, the Jews, throughout the whole kingdom of Xerxes" (Esther 3:5–6 NIV).

Eleven months later, Haman has his plot in place. He goes to King Xerxes and says, "There is a certain people dispersed and scattered among the peoples in all the provinces of your kingdom whose customs are different from those of all other people and who do not obey the king's laws; it is not in the king's best interest to tolerate them. If it pleases the king, let a decree be issued to destroy them" (Esther 3:8–9 NIV). The king, trusting Haman, goes along with Haman's proposal.

When Mordecai learned of Haman's villainous actions, "he tore his clothes, put on sackcloth and ashes, and went out into the city, wailing loudly and bitterly" (Esther 4:1 NIV). Sheltered in the palace, Esther does not know initially what has happened, but when her servants tell her what Mordecai is doing, she sends someone to find out why he is so upset.

Mordecai sends back word to her that her people will be killed if she does not use her influence over the king to persuade him to revoke the edict. At first, Esther is reluctant. She may be the queen, but she still lives in a time and place where women have little power. According to the rules of the court, she is not allowed to enter the king's presence unless he sends for her first—and Xerxes has not sent for Esther in nearly a month. She is still new in her role as queen, and is apparently insecure in her relationship with Xerxes.

Esther sends this message back to Mordecai: "All the king's officials and the people of the royal provinces know that for any man or woman who approaches the king in the inner court without being summoned the king has but one law: that he be put to death. The only exception to this is for the king to extend the gold scepter to him and spare his life" (Esther 4:11 NIV).

Mordecai is impatient with Esther's fears; after all, he and all his people face certain death if the edict is carried out. His harsh and insistent reply to Esther ends with "Who knows but that you have come to royal position for such a time as this?" (Esther 4:14 NIV). At last, conquering her reluctance, Esther agrees to do whatever she can. She asks Mordecai to gather the Jews in Susa, to pray and fast for her for three days and nights, adding that she and her servants will do the same. Relying on God for her courage and strength, Esther tells him, "When this is done, I will go to the king, even though it is against the law. And if I perish, I perish" (Esther 4:16 NIV).

A swooning Esther approaches her husband unbidden in this anonymous eighteenth-century painting.

to join her again the following evening. Haman, assuming he is being honored, boasts to his family and friends that he'd been the only other invitee at the queen's banquet, and had been invited to return tomorrow. But Mordecai is still the fly in Haman's ointment. Haman tells his wife, Zeresh, and friends, "But all this gives me no satisfaction as long as I see that Jew Mordecai sitting at the king's gate" (Esther 5:13 NIV).

Haman's wife and friends respond, "Have a gallows built, seventy-five feet high, and ask the king in the morning to have Mordecai hanged on it. Then go with the king to the dinner and be happy" (Esther 5:14 NIV).

Haman, delighted with this advice, does as they suggest. Circumstances, however, will thwart his plan. Although God is never mentioned in the book of Esther, apparently He is at work behind the scenes, for:

When Esther goes into the king's presence, he is happy to see her. He holds out to her the gold scepter in his hand; Esther touches the scepter's tip, prompting the king to ask what she requests.

Esther does not get directly to the point. Instead, she invites the king and Haman to a banquet that evening, and there she invites them

That night the king could not sleep; so he ordered the book of the chronicles, the record of his reign, to be brought in and read to him. It was found recorded there that Mordecai had exposed. . .two of the king's officers who. . .had conspired to assassinate King Xerxes.

> *"What honor and recognition has Mordecai received for this?"* the king asked.
> *"Nothing has been done for him,"* his attendants answered.
>
> ESTHER 6:1–3 NIV

At this point, Haman happens to have just entered the court to speak to the king about having Mordecai hung on the gallows. But before Haman gets a chance to speak, Xerxes says to him: "What should be done for the man the king delights to honor?" (Esther 6:6 NIV).

Haman, smugly assuming he is planning his own award ceremony, answers that the man should wear the king's robes and ride his royal steed, with one of the king's top officers serving as herald. To his deep chagrin, Haman found himself parading Mordecai around Shushan, proclaiming his virtues.

That night as they sit eating and drinking together, the king again asks Esther, "What is your request? Even up to half the kingdom, it will be granted" (Esther 7:2 NIV).

And now, Queen Esther gathers her courage and asks the king to spare her life and those of her people, adding, "For I and my people have been sold for destruction and slaughter and annihilation" (Esther 7:4 NIV). She then adds that Haman is the one responsible for this disastrous situation.

King Xerxes does not appear to be in the least disturbed to discover Esther is a Jew. Instead, enraged at Haman, he withdraws to the palace garden, only to explode upon return when he sees Haman falling upon Esther's couch, begging for his life. Xerxes, seeing Haman pawing at his wife, determines to hang Haman on the gallows Haman himself had built for Mordecai. On the day of Haman's execution, Xerxes gives Esther Haman's estate, which she gives to Mordecai to manage. Then Xerxes issues a new edict that gives the Jews throughout his land the right to assemble, as well as the right to protect themselves against their enemies. Today, Jews celebrate Esther's victory, and the day they were given rest from their enemies, during the feast of Purim (see Esther 9:24–32).

The "Mausoleum of Esther and Mordechai" in Hamadan, in modern-day Iran.

OTHER COURAGEOUS WOMEN WHOSE STORIES ARE TOLD IN THE BIBLE

- **The Hebrew midwives:** Hebrew midwives outsmart the Egyptian Pharaoh and save the lives of Jewish newborn boys (see Exodus 1:17–21).
- **Jochebed and Miriam:** Jochebed circumvents Pharaoh's order to kill all the baby boys by hiding her newborn son Moses in the bulrushes, with his big sister Miriam watching over him. Miriam then influences Pharaoh's daughter to ensure that Moses is not permanently separated from his mother (see Exodus 2).
- **Rahab:** Rahab, a prostitute, hides two Israelite spies and saves their lives as well as the lives of her family (see Joshua 2:1–16; 6:17–25).
- **Michal:** David's first wife, Michal, tricks soldiers and engineers David's escape (see 1 Samuel 19:11–17).
- **Huldah:** The prophetess Huldah boldly spoke "as the voice of God," warning her people of pending disaster (see 2 Kings 22:14–19; 2 Chronicles 34:23–27).

Brave, quick-witted Michal helps David escape in this 1865 engraving by Gustave Doré.

The little orphan girl was transformed into a confident woman of authority who, using her power on behalf of others, triumphed over the male enemies of her people.

WOMEN WHO WERE LOVED AND RESPECTED BY MEN

Her husband. . .praises her: "Many women do noble things, but you surpass them all."
PROVERBS 31:28–29 NIV

Ruth
The book of Ruth takes place during the days of the judges. Because of a famine, an Israelite family from Bethlehem—Elimelech, his wife Naomi, and their sons Mahlon and Chilion—immigrate to the nearby country of Moab. There, the sons marry two Moabite women, Ruth and Orpah. Eventually, Elimelech dies, as do his sons, leaving the three women alone, without the protection of a man.

These are desperate circumstances for the women, and Naomi knows she needs to get back to her own family in Bethlehem. She tells her daughters-in-law to return to their own mothers and remarry. Orpah reluctantly obeys, but Ruth says her famous words of love and commitment: "Don't urge me to leave you or to turn back from you. Where you go I will go, and where you stay I will stay. Your people will be my people and your God my God. Where you die I will die, and there I will be buried. May the LORD deal with me, be it ever so severely, if anything but death separates you and me" (Ruth 1:16–17 NIV).

And so the two women, Naomi and Ruth, travel to Bethlehem where, to support her mother-in-law and herself, Ruth goes to the fields to glean, picking up the scattered grain left behind after the harvest. There she meets Boaz, a relative of her father-in-law.

Boaz seems impressed with Ruth as soon as he meets her, telling her, "Don't go and glean in another field and don't go away from here. Stay here with my servant girls. Watch the field where the men are harvesting, and follow along after the girls. I have told the men not to touch you. And whenever you are thirsty, go and get a drink from the water jars the men have filled" (Ruth 2:8–9 NIV).

Ruth replies modestly, expressing her surprise that he's treating her, a foreigner, so kindly. Boaz answers, "I've been told all about

what you have done for your mother-in-law since the death of your husband. . . . May the LORD repay you for what you have done. . . ." (Ruth 2:11–12 NIV).

Ruth expresses her gratitude and pleasure at his words, then later joins Boaz for lunch at his invitation.

Ruth encounters Boaz while gleaning in his fields, in this nineteenth-century children's Bible illustration.

As she gets up to go back to work, Boaz turns to his workers and says quietly, "Even if she gathers among the sheaves, don't embarrass her. Rather, pull out some stalks for her from the bundles and leave them for her to pick up, and don't rebuke her" (Ruth 2:15–16 NIV).

That night, Ruth tells her mother-in-law about Boaz's kindness, and she gleans in his field through the remainder of the harvest season. Naomi now plays the role of matchmaker. Since Boaz is a close relative of Naomi's husband's family, he is obliged by law to marry the widow of his kinsman in order to carry on his family line. Naomi sends Ruth to the threshing floor at night and tells her to "uncover the feet" of the sleeping Boaz. Ruth does so, Boaz awakes, and Ruth reminds him that he is a kinsman-redeemer. Boaz states he is willing to "redeem" Ruth by marrying her, but he tells Ruth that another male relative has the first right of redemption.

The next morning, Ruth goes back to Naomi, while Boaz discusses the issue with the other male relative before the town elders. The other man relinquishes his right of redemption, and Boaz and Ruth are married. Apparently, they live happily ever after. Ruth and Naomi are not separated, and Naomi soon has a grandson named Obed. Obed will grow up to become the grandfather of King David—and the ancestor of Mary, the mother of Christ.

Ruth kneels before Boaz in this sketch by the Dutch master Rembrandt.

A theme that runs through Ruth's story is that of *hesed*, a Hebrew word sometimes translated as "loving kindness," carrying with it the implication of commitment and loyalty. Naomi speaks of hesed when she blesses her two daughters-in-law. Ruth demonstrates hesed in her relationship with Naomi, and it is this quality that Boaz recognizes in Ruth and for which he praises her. Boaz then shows this same self-giving kindness in his interactions with Ruth.

Hesed, as revealed in the story of Ruth and Boaz, embodies the plan God intended for men and women who live together. It is an active, selfless commitment to the other's well-being that goes against the grain of our selfish natures. Through this kind of loyal, self-sacrificing love, the hesed of God is made real in our world. The relationship between Ruth and Boaz demonstrates a healthy man-woman interaction, one that conforms to what God intended. This sort of relationship blesses both the man and the woman, as well as the entire community (including the community that extends hundreds of years into the future).

BOAZ AS A CHRIST-FIGURE

Bible scholars sometimes speak of a "type of Christ." This term carries the meaning that Christ's shadow is cast backward in time across the lives of people who lived centuries before Him, Old Testament individuals who were like signposts pointing forward toward Jesus. According to this form of hermeneutics, Boaz is a type of Christ. Like Jesus, Boaz is of the tribe of Judah. Boaz marries Ruth (the Gentile bride), just as Christ is said to acquire for Himself a bride from among the Gentile nations. And like Christ, Boaz is given the title of Redeemer, one who saves and frees. This image of a healthy man-woman interaction acting as symbol for God's love for His people is repeated in both the Song of Solomon and the New Testament epistles.

In Nicolas Poussin's seventeenth-century painting, Boaz instructs his men to treat Ruth with respect.

Proverbs 31

Proverbs provides us with a snapshot image of a woman who, like Ruth, is respected and loved by her husband. The woman described in Proverbs 31 is a woman of "valor" (also translated as "virtue" in some Bible versions). Her relationship with her husband is built on trust: "Her husband has full confidence in her. . . . She brings him good, not harm, all the days of her life" (Proverbs 31:11–12 NIV).

The woman portrayed in this Bible passage is not meek and retiring; instead, the picture we have is that of a strong, independent, and confident woman. She is a hardworking businesswoman who thinks for herself: "She considers a field and buys it; out of her earnings she plants a vineyard. She sets about her work vigorously; her arms are strong for her tasks. She sees that her trading is profitable, and her lamp does not go out at night" (Proverbs 31:16–18 NIV).

The book of Proverbs, much of which was written by King Solomon, is a collection of godly wisdom that often presents viewpoints at odds with the culture of the day. In this case, we have a detailed image of an ideal woman who must have been unusual in her day, one who has nevertheless served as both a role model and an affirmation for generations of women down through the centuries. The description is presented as advice from a mother to her son King Lemuel, offering a collection of traits her son should look for in a woman.

This woman of noble character "is clothed with strength and

This woman—veiled in white for purity—is the personification of a woman of virtue. In the real world, though, it might be someone you work with, a woman down the street—or you!

dignity; she can laugh at the days to come. She speaks with wisdom, and faithful instruction is on her tongue. She watches over the affairs of her household and does not eat the bread of idleness" (Proverbs 31:25–27 NIV). This is a woman who is fully engaged in all of life; she interacts with her husband, her home, her family, and her business with strength, intelligence, and competence.

As a result, "Her children arise and call her blessed; her husband also, and he praises her: 'Many women do noble things, but you surpass them all.' Charm is deceptive, and beauty is fleeting; but a woman who fears the LORD is to be praised. Give her the reward she has earned, and let her works bring her praise at the city gate" (Proverbs 31:28–31 NIV).

This is a different image of the man-woman relationship from any we have yet seen portrayed in the Bible. There is no hint here that the woman is weak and dependent on the man for her livelihood, as was usually the case in Bible times. On the other hand, this is no Delilah, wielding her beauty like a weapon against her man. Instead, this woman's relationship with her husband is clearly one of mutual respect and gratitude, where man and woman trust and rely on one another.

ANOTHER WELL-LOVED BIBLICAL WOMAN

The Song of Solomon gives us yet another image of a man-woman relationship that is based on love and respect. While the woman portrayed in Proverbs 31 seems to be quite a practical and businesslike lady, the young woman in the Song of Solomon is simply in love. Much of this Old Testament book is written from the woman's point of view, expressing both the longing and the joy she feels in her relationship with her beloved. The rapturous desire she feels is completely mutual; her husband is as excited about her as she is about him.

The book has often been interpreted as an allegory for our relationship with God. This perspective foreshadows the instructions the apostle Paul offers in the New Testament for women and men's interactions.

Around the frame of The Beloved, a portait of a woman preparing for her wedding, the artist Rossetti wrote, "My Beloved is mine and I am his," a quote from the Song of Solomon.

CHRIST'S INTERACTIONS WITH WOMEN

Jesus turned and saw her. "Take heart, daughter," he said, "your faith has healed you." And the woman was healed from that moment.

MATTHEW 9:22 NIV

In Jesus' day, we find that women's cultural roles have changed very little from those described in the Old Testament. During Christ's lifetime, women and men were still engaged in unhealthy relationships: women used their influence over men for evil; women were still dependent on men for their safety and livelihood; and men still abused their power over women.

And yet, in Jesus Christ's interactions with women, He lived out the same attitude of honor and respect portrayed in Proverbs 31. The Gospels tell us several stories about His interactions with women, and one of the most famous is that of the woman at the well.

The Woman at the Well

The story begins with Jesus and His disciples traveling from Judea to Galilee. On the way, they pass through Samaria and stop outside the village of Sychar. Jews normally avoided contact with their Samaritan neighbors by traveling other, longer routes, for Jews and Samaritans were ethnic enemies in these days, with a long history of prejudice, discrimination, and violence. Nevertheless, Jesus and the disciples are here in Samaria where Jesus seems almost intentionally seeking out an encounter with one special individual.

While the disciples go into town to buy food, Jesus stays behind and rests by Jacob's well. When a Samaritan woman comes to draw water, He initiates a conversation with her. By doing so, He is breaking the cultural norms of His day, and He clearly takes her by surprise.

According to Jewish tradition, men did not speak in public to women, even their own wives. A rabbi (teacher), which is what Jesus was considered, would never think of teaching a woman of ill repute. But here, as in all cases within the Gospel accounts, Jesus does not treat women according to cultural expectations. Instead, He talks with them, teaches them, and trusts them to proclaim His Good News. As He encounters the woman at the well, He reaches out to her and draws her into a relationship with Him.

Clues from the scripture allow us to imagine this woman. She is an

Jesus and the Samaritan woman have an in-depth conversation while others look on in wonder and confusion. Stefano Erardi painted the picture around the late seventeenth century.

ordinary woman, lacking money and influence (a well-to-do woman would not be drawing her own water from a well in those days); she has had a hard life and has been involved with at least six different men (see John 4:18).

Jesus starts the conversation by asking her for a drink of water, putting Himself in the more vulnerable position of someone needing a favor. As the conversation continues, He shifts ground, changing the topic from physical water to spiritual water.

He seems to have little use for small talk and moves quickly to some very personal and intimate observations about both the woman's life and Himself:

Jesus said to her, "You are right when you say you have no husband. The fact is, you have had five husbands, and the man you now have is not your husband. . . ."

"Sir," the woman said, "I can see that you are a prophet. Our fathers worshiped on this moun-

tain, but you Jews claim that the place where we must worship is in Jerusalem."

Jesus declared, "Believe me, woman, a time. . .is coming and has now come when the true worshipers will worship the Father in spirit and truth, for they are the kind of worshipers the Father seeks. God is spirit, and his worshipers must worship in spirit and in truth."

The woman said, "I know that Messiah" (called Christ) "is coming. When he comes, he will explain everything to us."
Then Jesus declared, "I who speak to you am he."

JOHN 4:17–21, 23–26 NIV

The woman then carries the news back to her village, making her one of the first missionaries to carry the Gospel to those who had not heard it. If a modern-day church was choosing the appropriate person to evangelize a new group, it's unlikely they would choose someone like the woman at the well—but Jesus looked past His culture and saw this woman as the ideal person to relay the Good News. His interaction with her is based on respect, and He reveals His true Self to her even as He insists that she be equally honest with Him.

Mary and Martha

Jesus' interactions with Mary and Martha reveal a similar respectful intimacy. In Luke 10:38–42, we have a clear picture of Mary's and Martha's personalities. We can tell that as overwhelmed and irritated as Martha clearly is, she still feels completely comfortable bringing her frustration to Jesus. And He is able to confront her annoyance with both honesty and compassion. Meanwhile, He is encouraging both sisters to step out of their traditional feminine roles of waiting on the men and instead become students of His teaching. (Again, studies and learning were important in Jewish tradition, but only for males, never for women.)

We hear more about Jesus' relationship with these two sisters in John 11, after the death of their brother Lazarus. This time, it is Martha who leaves her household duties in order to be with Jesus: "When Martha heard that Jesus was coming, she went out to meet him, but Mary stayed at home" (John 11:20 NIV).

Martha's first words reveal her absolute trust in Jesus, but they also tell us once again that she felt completely comfortable reproaching Him for something she did not understand. She says to Him, "Lord. . .if you had been here, my brother would not have died. But I know that even now God will give you whatever you ask" (John 11:21–22 NIV).

Jesus' next words make Martha think He is giving her the sort of comfort we all have to offer at a funeral, telling her Lazarus will rise again. She answers, "I know he will rise again in the resurrection at the last day" (John 11:24 NIV). Jesus then makes clear to Martha that He's offering her no vague, spiritual comfort; what He has to say is an immediate reality related to His very identity: "I am the resurrection and the life. He who believes in me will live, even though he dies; and whoever lives and believes in me will never die. Do you believe this?" (John 11:25–26 NIV).

Martha then expresses her belief in Jesus' identity. Thus, not only does Jesus know Martha, but Martha knows Jesus. Their relationship is a mutual one.

Now Mary gets her turn to talk with Jesus and express her grief. Like her sister, Mary seems to reproach Jesus for not coming sooner.

Jesus cares about these two women friends so much that their sorrow moves Him to tears. He must know He is about to bring Lazarus back to life, and yet He is with Mary and Martha in the present moment, the here-and-now where they know nothing of what is to come. He does not dismiss their grief by saying to Himself that once they know the whole picture and see what's

Mary meets Jesus at the door of the house she shares with Martha. The 1864 painting is by Nikolaj Ge.

going to happen, they won't be sad anymore. Instead, He respects their feelings; He acknowledges the reality of their sadness before He commands them to roll away the stone from Lazarus' grave.

In response to Jesus' request, Martha tells Him, "By this time there is a bad odor, for he has been there four days" (John 11:39 NIV). Obviously, Martha is a no-nonsense sort of woman.

Jesus reminds her to take into consideration the full context of His relationship with her, this relationship of respectful intimacy and love: "Did I not tell you that if you believed, you would see the glory of God?" (John 11:40 NIV).

We know the end of the story: Mary and Martha's brother comes back to life. Rumors of this amazing event travel to the Pharisees and contribute to the circumstances that eventually lead to Jesus' execution. Jesus must have known what would happen, and yet His actions seem to have been completely deliberate. He loved Mary and Martha enough to make Himself vulnerable.

NEW TESTAMENT PERSPECTIVES ON WOMEN'S INTERACTIONS WITH MEN

Submit to one another out of reverence for Christ.
EPHESIANS 5:21 NIV

This mutual vulnerability and respect in male-female interactions is spelled out clearly in the New Testament's epistles. Often Christians

SOME OTHER WOMEN WITH WHOM JESUS INTERACTED

- The woman with an issue of blood: This woman trusted Jesus enough that she knew if she could just touch His robe, she would be healed. Jesus did not disappoint her! (See Matthew 9:20–22.)
- The woman who anointed Jesus' feet with perfume: This woman loved Jesus so much she poured expensive perfume on His feet to express her deep feelings. When the disciples complained about the impracticality of her actions, Jesus reproved them and commended her (see Matthew 26:6–13).
- The woman caught in adultery: John 8:3–11 tells of a woman about to be stoned to death by a group of self-righteous men. As the men disappeared guiltily, one at a time, Jesus made clear that the men were as blameworthy as the woman, then told her to leave her life of sin.

have paid attention only to the New Testament's exhortations to women, without reading them in their full context of a mutual man-woman relationship. As a result, ultraconservative groups have sometimes used these verses to support women having few rights at all, while liberal feminist groups have often reacted with anger and resentment. But reading the New Testament epistles in their entirety reveals a model for man-woman relationships that is in direct contrast to some of the interactions we saw in the Old Testament.

For example, in First Peter 3, women are expressly instructed not to use their physical beauty to manipulate their husbands, as Delilah did in the Old Testament.

Wives, in the same way be submissive to your husbands so that, if any of them do not believe the word, they may be won over without words by the behavior of their wives, when they see the purity and reverence of your lives. Your beauty should not come from outward adornment, such as braided hair and the wearing of gold jewelry and fine clothes. Instead, it should be that of your inner self, the unfading beauty of a gentle and quiet spirit, which is of great worth in

God's sight. For this is the way the holy women of the past who put their hope in God used to make themselves beautiful. They were submissive to their own husbands, like Sarah, who obeyed Abraham and called him her master. You are her daughters if you do what is right and do not give way to fear.

1 PETER 3:1–6 NIV

Note that the author acknowledges that fear is likely to play a major part in women's consciousness, particularly in a time when men still have all the legal and cultural power; a woman could very well feel that her physical charms are the only weapon she has in any struggle between the sexes. Despite this reality, Peter indicates that women who dare to be vulnerable to their men, finding their security in God, will ultimately have greater strength and beauty.

And lest Peter's readers think he is talking only to women, the next verse in this scripture passage is directed to the men: "Husbands, in the same way be considerate as you live with your wives, and treat them with respect" (1 Peter 3:7 NIV). The disrespect Abraham and David showed to the women they supposedly loved, treating them as though they were objects to be used for their convenience, is clearly far outside the boundaries of this verse.

We see this perfect man-woman relationship spelled out most clearly in Ephesians 5:22–24, when Paul writes: "Wives, submit to your husbands as to the Lord. For the husband is the head of the wife as Christ is the head of the church, his body, of which he is the Savior. Now as the church submits to Christ, so also wives should submit to their husbands in everything" (NIV).

That word—submit—is a difficult one to swallow sometimes; we often connect it with an image of obedience to a harsh master, but that is not the reality being described throughout the New Testament. Instead, "submit" means here to yield oneself in utter trust to another (just as Ruth did to Boaz, just as Martha and Mary did to Jesus), utterly confident that one is safe and loved and respected.

Paul makes the mutuality of this submission very evident in the next verses:

Husbands, love your wives, just as Christ loved the church and gave himself up for her to make her holy... In this same way, husbands ought to love their wives as their own bodies. He who loves his wife loves himself. After all, no one ever hated his own body, but he feeds and cares for it, just as Christ does the church—for we are members of his body.

EPHESIANS 5:25–26, 28–30 NIV

Yes, wives are to yield themselves to their husbands—but husbands are given even more demanding terms for their relationships with their wives: They are to lay down their lives, as Christ did for the Church; they are to love their wives in the same way they look out for the interests of their own bodies. These are high standards to live up to!

Within this relationship of mutual vulnerability and mutual respect, both men and women can know they are secure. Women have no more need to manipulate men or misuse their trust, as Eve and Delilah did; men do not need to control or abuse women, as Abraham and David did. Both sides of the man-woman equation can become what God intended them to be.

Paul concludes Ephesians 5 with this quotation from Genesis 2:24: "For this reason a man will leave his father and mother and be united to his wife, and the two

Royal marriages have often been a uniting of powers. The marriage of a man and woman is nonetheless a combining of different but complementary powers and attributes. This painting by Jacopo di Chimenti da Empoli shows the marriage of Maria de Medici and Henry IV of France.

will become one flesh" (Ephesians 5:31 NIV). We have come full circle now, back to where we began this chapter, with the Genesis story of the beginning of man-woman interactions. Here in the New Testament, God again makes clear that He wants husbands and wives to be as intimately concerned for one another as they are for their own selves. This deep connection exists on both the physical and spiritual levels.

There's a clear lesson to be learned from these biblical accounts of women's interactions

Ideally, the tradition of serving each other the first bite of wedding cake is only the beginning of many years of mutual service to come.

for encouraging and uplifting our spouses, helping them to draw closer to God as well. This is what Eve and Delilah and Abraham and David failed to do. And just like these individuals from the Bible, when we fail at the first, we also fail at the second. When Adam and Eve damaged their relationship, they damaged their relationship with God; when David sinned against Bathsheba, he also sinned against God. We cannot be right with God if we are not also right in our sexual relationships! These two aspects of our lives (our relationship with God and our sexual relationships) are meant to support one another; when one goes awry, the other does as well.

Paul writes: "Be imitators of God, therefore, as dearly loved children and live a life of love, just as Christ loved us and gave himself up for us as a fragrant offering and sacrifice to God" (Ephesians 5:1–2 NIV). This relationship based on mutual yielding and submission, where we imitate God in our efforts to outdo each other in our expressions of self-sacrificing love (or hesed), is

with men: Not only are we intended individually to be in a close relationship with God, one where we yield our selfish needs to Him, but we are also called to be in equally unselfish relationships with the opposite sex.

And when we interact with the opposite sex within the boundaries of a marriage, we are responsible what God wants for the human race. When women and men achieve this, then they can also know they are both safe from hurt or abuse, for "perfect love casts out fear" (1 John 4:18 NKJV).

The biblical accounts of male-female interactions also indicate that when these go off course and become abusive or exploitive, the entire community suffers. The implication is that we cannot say these are private sins between the injured party, God, and ourselves. When man-woman relationships are unhealthy, the entire community is affected, and sometimes this negative effect can have an impact on the future as well as the present. (Think of Adam and Eve!) By the same token, however, the Bible stories tell us that healthy man-woman relationships bless the entire community, as did the woman portrayed in Proverbs 31, and this blessing can also extend down through the generations (as it did with Ruth and Boaz).

God designed us for relationships with each other, and men and women's interactions can lead to one of the most powerfully intimate of all human relationships. Like the Song of Solomon's portrayal of intimate joy, the New Testament indicates that male-female interactions can also reveal to us the loving self-sacrifice of Christ's relationship with the Church. Through healthy, respectful relationships with the opposite sex, we can come to understand more deeply our relationship with God.

Ultimately, however, the Bible indicates that our gender is not what is most important in God's eyes, for in Christ, "There is neither . . .male nor female; for you are all one in Christ Jesus" (Galatians 3:28 NIV). This relationship we share in Jesus should be the foundation of our interactions as men and women. It is this relationship with Christ that makes us equals in God's eyes.

PAUL'S INTERACTIONS WITH EARLY CHRISTIAN WOMEN

In his epistles, the apostle Paul indicates that he thinks of women as his equals in the Lord's work, and he speaks of many of these women by name:

- Tryphena, Tryphosa, and Persis (see Romans 16:12)
- Euodias and Syntyche (see Philippians 4:2–3)
- Phoebe (see Romans 16:1)
- Eunice and Lois (see 2 Timothy 1:5)

WOMEN IN THE GOSPELS AND THEIR INTERACTIONS WITH MEN

- **Elizabeth:** In Luke 1, we read the story of Elizabeth and Zechariah, who will become the parents of John the Baptist. When the angel comes to Zechariah with word that they will become parents in their old age, Zechariah lags behind Elizabeth in his belief, and as a result he loses his ability to speak. Meanwhile, the strong voice of Elizabeth has been recorded so that generations have been inspired by her faith.

- **Mary:** Like Elizabeth, Mary's faith in God is stronger, at least at first, than her husband Joseph's, who doubts that Mary's pregnancy is of God. In Luke 1:38, Mary's words to the angel express the state of yielding submission to which God calls us all: "I am the Lord's servant. . . . May it be to me as you have said" (NIV).

- **Salome, the mother of James and John:** In Matthew 20, this woman tried to persuade Jesus to give her sons a higher rank in His kingdom. Jesus explains to her that she doesn't know what she's asking. She rises above her disappointment and remains faithful to Jesus; later, Salome is at the foot of the cross, still following Jesus, ready "to care for his needs" (Matthew 27:55 NIV).

- **Joanna, Susanna, Mary Magdalene:** Luke 8:2–3 reveals that these women traveled with Jesus and His disciples, "helping to support them out of their own means" (Luke 8:3 NIV).

- **Pilate's wife:** This woman does what she can to persuade her husband not to go through with the crucifixion of Jesus. She sends word to Pilate that Jesus is innocent, explaining that she has had bad dreams about Him (see Matthew 27:19). Pilate is apparently influenced by his wife to the point that he washes his hands of responsibility for Christ's death.

Church tradition calls Pilate's wife Claudia Procula. She dreamed about Christ and tried to persuade her husband to have nothing to do with the trial.

Mary looks over baby Jesus and his relative John the Baptist in this detail from a charcoal sketch by Leonardo da Vinci.

The Named Women of the Bible

This list includes the name of every woman mentioned in scripture, followed by the total number of mentions and number of women by that name in parentheses. The meaning of the name is then given, followed by a brief biography of each woman. The scripture reference or references that complete each entry constitute either the only mention in scripture, or the reference(s) that is most important.

1. Abi (1/1).
"Fatherly." Daughter of Zachariah and mother of Judah's good king Hezekiah. 2 Kings 18:2.

2. Abiah (1/1).
"Worshipper of God." Wife of Hezron, a descendant of Abraham through Jacob's son Judah. 1 Chronicles 2:24.

3. Abigail (17/2).
"Source of joy."
1) A wife of King David. See Section 3—Women's Roles and Jobs. 2) Mother of Amasa, whom Absalom made captain of his army, and aunt of David's commander Joab. 2 Samuel 17:25; 1 Chronicles 2:16–17.

4. Abihail (2/2).
"Possessor of might." 1) Wife of Abishur, a descendant of Abraham through Jacob's son Judah. 1 Chronicles 2:29. 2) One of the wives of King Rehoboam of Judah. 2 Chronicles 11:18.

5. Abijah (1/1).
"Worshipper of God." Mother of Judah's good king Hezekiah. 2 Chronicles 29:1.

6. Abishag (5/1).
"Blundering." A beautiful young woman called to serve the dying King David by lying with him to keep him warm. After David died, his son Adonijah wanted to marry Abishag, but he was put to death by his half brother Solomon, who feared Adonijah was trying to usurp the kingship. 1 Kings 1:3, 15; 2:17, 2:21–22.

7. Abital (2/1).
"Fresh." One of several wives of King David; mother of David's son Shephatiah. 2 Samuel 3:4; 1 Chronicles 3:3.

8. Achsa (1/1).
"Anklet." Daughter of Caleb, descendant of Abraham through Jacob's son Judah. Same as *Ashsah*. 1 Chronicles 2:49.

9. Achsah (4/1).
"Anklet." Caleb's daughter, whom he promised in marriage to the man who could capture the city of Kirjath-sepher. His brother Othniel captured the city and won Achsah as his wife. Afterward Caleb gave her land that held springs, since the lands of her dowry were dry. Same as *Achsa*. Joshua 15:16–17; Judges 1:12–13.

10. Adah (8/2).
"Ornament." 1) A wife of Lamech, the first man in scripture to have two wives. Her son was named Jabal. Genesis 4:19–20, 23. 2) A wife of Esau, "of the daughters of Canaan." Same as *Bashemath* (2). Genesis 36:2, 4, 10, 12, 16.

11. Agar (2/1).
"Flight." Greek form of the name *Hagar,* used in the New Testament. Galatians 4:24–25.

12. Ahinoam (7/2).
"Brother of pleasantness." 1) Wife of Saul, Israel's first king. 1 Samuel 14:50. 2) Woman from Jezreel who became David's wife. 1 Samuel 25:43; 27:3; 30:5; 2 Samuel 2:2, 3:2; 1 Chronicles 3:1.

13. Ahlai (1/1).
"Wishful." Descendant of Abraham through Jacob's son Judah. 1 Chronicles 2:31.

14. Aholibamah (5/1).
"Tent of the height." A wife of Esau, "of the daughters of Canaan." Genesis 36:2, 5, 14, 18, 25.

15. Anah (4/1).
"Answer." Mother of Aholibamah and mother-in-law of Esau. Genesis 36:2, 14, 18, 25.

16. Anna (1/1).
"Favored." Widowed prophetess. See Section 3— Women's Roles and Jobs.

17. Apphia (1/1).
"Increasing." Christian woman of Colosse called "beloved" by the apostle Paul. Philemon 1:2.

18. Asenath (3/1).
"She belongs to her father." Daughter of an Egyptian priest and given

as wife to Joseph by the Pharaoh. Asenath bore two sons to Joseph: Manasseh and Ephraim. Genesis 41:45, 50; 46:20.

19. **Atarah** (1/1).
"Crown." Second wife of Jerahmeel, a descendant of Abraham through Jacob's son Judah. 1 Chronicles 2:26.

20. **Athaliah** (15/1).
"God has constrained." Wife of Jehoram and mother of Ahaziah, two kings of Judah. See Section 3—Women's Roles and Jobs.

21. **Azubah** (4/2).
"Desertion." 1) Mother of King Jehoshaphat of Judah and daughter of Shilhi. 1 Kings 22:42; 2 Chronicles 20:31. 2) Wife of Caleb. 1 Chronicles 2:18–19.

22. **Baara** (1/1).
"Brutish." One of two wives of a Benjamite named Shaharaim. He divorced her in favor of other wives in Moab. 1 Chronicles 8:8.

23. **Bashemath** (6/2).
"Fragrance." 1) Hittite wife of Esau. Same as *Adah*. Genesis 26:34. 2) Ishmael's daughter and another wife of Esau. Mother of Reuel, Nahath, Zerah, Shammah, and Mizzah. Genesis 36:3–4, 10, 13, 17.

24. **Basmath** (1/1).
"Fragrance." A daughter of King Solomon who married Ahimaaz, a royal official over the king's provisions. 1 Kings 4:15.

25. **Bath-sheba** (11/1).
Genealogy of Jesus: Yes (Matthew 1:6). "Daughter of an oath." Wife first of Uriah the Hittite, then King David; mother of Solomon. When David's son Adonijah tried to take the throne just before the king's death, Bath-sheba intervened, asking David to remember his promise. Later she intervened with Solomon when Adonijah sought to marry Abishag, David's concubine. (See 1 Kings 1). See Section 4—Bible Women and Their Interactions with Men.

26. **Bath-shua** (1/1).
Yes (Matthew 1:6). "Daughter of wealth." A form of the name *Bathsheba*, a wife of King David. 1 Chronicles 3:5.

27. **Bernice** (3/1).
"Victorious." Daughter of Herod Agrippa and sister of Agrippa II. With her brother, she heard Paul's testimony before Festus. Acts 25:13, 23; 26:30.

28. Bilhah (10/1).
"Timid." Rachel's handmaid, whom she gave to Jacob to bear children for her. As Jacob's concubine, Bilhah had two sons, Dan and Naphtali. Jacob's son Reuben also slept with her. Genesis 29:29; 30:3–5, 7; 35:22, 25; 37:2; 46:25; 1 Chronicles 7:13.

29. Bithiah (1/1).
"Daughter of God." A daughter of an Egyptian pharaoh and the wife of Mered, a descendant of Judah. 1 Chronicles 4:18.

30. Candace (1/1).
Queen of Ethiopia whose treasurer was converted to Christianity by Philip the evangelist. Acts 8:27.

31. Chloe (1/1).
"Green herb." Corinthian Christian and acquaintance of Paul. Her family informed the apostle of divisions within the church. 1 Corinthians 1:11.

32. Claudia (1/1).
"Lame." Roman Christian who sent greetings to Timothy in Paul's second letter to his "dearly beloved son." 2 Timothy 4:21.

33. Cozbi (2/1).
"False." Daughter of a Midian prince, she was killed for consorting with an Israelite. Numbers 25:15, 18.

34. Damaris (1/1).
"Gentle." A woman of Athens converted under the ministry of the apostle Paul. Acts 17:34.

35. Deborah (10/2).
"Bee." 1) Rebekah's nurse. See Section 3—Women's Roles and Jobs. 2) Prophetess and Israel's only female judge. See Section 3—Women's Roles and Jobs and Section 4—Bible Women and Their Interactions with Men.

36. Delilah (6/1).
"Languishing." Samson's lover. See Section 4—Bible Women and Their Interactions with Men.

37. Dinah (8/1).
"Justice." Daughter of Jacob and Leah, who was sexually assaulted by the prince Shechem. Her brothers retaliated, killing the men of his city. Genesis 30:21; 34:1, 3–5, 13, 25–26; 46:15.

38. Dorcas (2/1).
"Gazelle." A Christian of Joppa. Same as *Tabitha*. See "Tabitha or Dorcas" in Section 3—Women's Roles and Jobs.

39. Drusilla (1/1). "Strong one." Wife of Felix, the Roman governor of Judea in Paul's time. Acts 24:24.

40. Eglah (2/1). "Calf." One of several wives of King David and mother of David's son Ithream. 2 Samuel 3:5; 1 Chronicles 3:3.

41. Elisabeth (9/1). "God is my oath." Wife of Zacharias and mother of John the Baptist. See Section 3—Women's Roles and Jobs.

42. Elisheba (1/1). "God is my oath." Aaron's wife, who bore him four sons. Exodus 6:23.

43. Ephah (1/1). "Obscurity." Concubine of Caleb. 1 Chronicles 2:46.

44. Ephratah (2/1). "Fruitfulness." Wife of Hur; mother of Caleb, the son of Hur. Same as *Ephrath*. 1 Chronicles 2:50; 4:4.

45. Ephrath (1/1). "Fruitfulness." An alternative form of the name *Ephratah*. 1 Chronicles 2:19.

46. Esther (56/1). "Star." Jewish wife of the Persian king Ahasuerus. See Section 4—Bible Women and Their Interactions with Men.

47. Eunice (1/1). "Victorious." Jewish mother of Timothy. See "Paul's Other Sisters in Christ" in Section 3—Women's Roles and Jobs.

48. Euodias (1/1). "Prosperous journey." A Christian woman of Philippi. See "Paul's Other Sisters in Christ" in Section 3—Women's Roles and Jobs.

49. Eve (4/1). "Life-giver." Adam's wife, "the mother of all living." See Section 3—Women's Roles and Jobs.

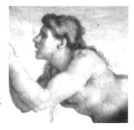

50. Gomer (1/1). "Completion." Unfaithful wife of the prophet Hosea. She represented the unfaithfulness of God's people. God told Hosea to redeem her from her lover and live with her again. Hosea 1:3.

51. Hadassah (1/1). "Myrtle." Alternative name for *Esther*, the Jewish woman who became queen of Persia. Esther 2:7.

52. Hagar (12/1).
"Flight." Sarai's Egyptian maid; surrogate wife to Abram; mother of Ishmael. See Section 3—Women's Roles and Jobs.

53. Haggith (5/1).
"Festive." One of several wives of King David and mother of David's son Adonijah. 2 Samuel 3:4; 1 Kings 1:5, 11; 2:13; 1 Chronicles 3:2.

54. Hammoleketh (1/1).
"Queen." Sister of Gilead and a descendant of Abraham through Joseph's son Manasseh. 1 Chronicles 7:18.

55. Hamutal (3/1).
"Father-in-law of dew." Mother of kings Jehoahaz and Zedekiah of Judah. 2 Kings 23:31; 24:18; Jeremiah 52:1.

56. Hannah (13/1).
"Favored." Wife of Elkanah; mother of Samuel. See Section 3—Women's Roles and Jobs.

57. Hazelelponi (1/1).
"Shade-facing." Descendant of Abraham through Jacob's son Judah. 1 Chronicles 4:3.

58. Helah (2/1).
"Rust." Wife of Ashur, a descendant of Abraham through Jacob's son Judah. 1 Chronicles 4:5, 7.

59. Hephzibah (1/1).
"My delight is in her." Wife of Judah's good king Hezekiah and the mother of the evil king Manasseh. 2 Kings 21:1.

60. Herodias (6/1).
"Heroic." Granddaughter of Herod the Great whose second marriage was opposed by John the Baptist. When Herodias's daughter asked what she should request from Herod Antipas, she pushed her to ask for John the Baptist's head on a plate. Matthew 14:3, 6; Mark 6:17, 19, 22; Luke 3:19.

61. Hodesh (1/1).
"A month." Third wife of Shaharaim, with whom she had children in Moab. 1 Chronicles 8:9.

62. Hodiah (1/1).
"Celebrated." Wife of Mered, a descendant of Abraham through Jacob's son Judah. 1 Chronicles 4:19.

63. Hoglah (4/1). "Partridge." One of five daughters of Zelophehad. See "Daughters of Zelophehad" in Section 3—Women's Roles and Jobs.

64. Huldah (2/1). "Weasel." Prophetess. See Section 3—Women's Roles and Jobs.

65. Hushim (2/1). "Hasters." One of two wives of a Benjamite named Shaharaim. He divorced her in favor of other wives in Moab. 1 Chronicles 8:8, 11.

66. Iscah (1/1). "Observant." Niece of Abraham, daughter of Abraham's brother Haran. Genesis 11:29.

67. Jael (6/1). "Wild goat." Wife of Heber the Kenite; she killed the Canaanite commander Sisera. See Section 3—Women's Roles and Jobs; also Section 4—Bible Women and Their Interactions with Men

68. Jecholiah (1/1). "Jehovah will enable." Mother of Judah's good king Azariah, also known as Uzziah. Same as *Jecoliah*. 2 Kings 15:2.

69. Jecoliah (1/1). "God will enable." Mother of Judah's good king Uzziah, also known as Azariah. Same as *Jecholiah*. 2 Chronicles 26:3.

70. Jedidah (1/1). "Beloved." Mother of Judah's good king Josiah. 2 Kings 22:1.

71. Jehoaddan (2/1). "Jehovah pleased." Mother of Amaziah, king of Judah. 2 Kings 14:2; 2 Chronicles 25:1.

72. Jehoshabeath (2/1). "Jehovah is her oath." Daughter of Judah's king Jehoram and sister of Judah's king Ahaziah. See Section 3—Women's Roles and Jobs.

73. Jehosheba (1/1). "Jehovah is her oath." King Joash's aunt. Same as *Jehoshabeath*. See Section 3—Women's Roles and Jobs.

74. Jehudijah (1/1). "Female descendant of Jehudah." Wife of Ezra, a descendant of Abraham by way of Judah. 1 Chronicles 4:18.

75. Jemima (1/1).
"Dove." Oldest of three daughters born to Job after God restored his fortunes. Jemima and her two sisters, Kezia and Keren-happuch, were more beautiful than any other woman "in all the land" (Job 42:15). Job 42:14.

76. Jerioth (1/1).
"Curtains." Descendant of Abraham through Jacob's son Judah. 1 Chronicles 2:18.

77. Jerusha (1/1).
"Possessed (married)." Mother of Jotham, king of Judah. 2 Kings 15:33.

78. Jerushah (1/1).
"Possessed (married)." Another spelling for *Jerusha,* mother of King Jotham of Judah. 2 Chronicles 27:1.

79. Jezebel (22/1).
"Chaste." Sidonian princess who married King Ahab of Israel. See Section 3—Women's Roles and Jobs.

80. Joanna (2/1).
"God is gracious ." Wife of Chuza. See Section 3—Women's Roles and Jobs.

81. Jochebed (2/1).
"Jehovah gloried." Wife of Amram and mother of Moses, Aaron, and Miriam. See Section 3—Women's Roles and Jobs.

82. Judith (1/1).
"Jew, descendant of Judah." One of Esau's Hittite wives, the daughter of Beeri. Genesis 26:34.

83. Julia (1/1).
"Youthful." A Christian in Rome. See "Paul's Other Sisters in Christ" in Section 3—Women's Roles and Jobs.

84. Junia (1/1).
"Youthful." Roman Christian who spent time in jail. See Section 3—Women's Roles and Jobs.

85. Keren-happuch (1/1).
"Horn of cosmetic." Youngest of three daughters born to Job when God restored his fortunes. Keren-happuch and her two sisters, Jemima and Kezia, were more beautiful than any other women "in all the land" (Job 42:15). Job 42:14.

86. Keturah (4/1).
"Perfumed." Abraham's concubine and wife. He may have married her following Sarah's death, but her children were not part of God's promised line. Genesis 25:1, 4; 1 Chronicles 1:32–33.

87. Kezia (1/1).
"Cassia." Second of three daughters born to Job when God restored his fortunes. Kezia and her two sisters,

Jemima and Keren-happuch, were more beautiful than any other women "in all the land" (Job 42:15). Job 42:14.

88. Leah (34/1). "Weary." Laban's daughter; Rachel's sister; wife of Jacob. See Section 3—Women's Roles and Jobs.

89. Lois (1/1). "Superior." Grandmother of Timothy. See "Paul's Other Sisters in Christ" in Section 3—Women's Roles and Jobs.

90. Lo-ruhamah (2/1). "Not pitied." Second child of the prophet Hosea's adulterous wife, Gomer. God gave the girl the prophetic name Lo-ruhamah to indicate that "I will no more have mercy upon the house of Israel" (Hosea 1:6 KJV). Hosea 1:6, 8.

91. Lydia (2/1). "Bending." Woman of Thyatira. See Section 3—Women's Roles and Jobs.

92. Maacah (1/1). "Depression." One of David's wives who was daughter of Talmai, the king of Geshur, and mother of Absalom. Same as *Maachah* (4). 2 Samuel 3:3.

93. Maachah (13/6). "Depression." 1) Daughter of David's son Absalom and the favorite among King Rehoboam's eighteen wives and sixty concubines. 1 Kings 15:2; 2 Chronicles 11:20–22. 2) Mother of King Asa of Judah. 1 Kings 15:10, 13; 2 Chronicles 15:16. 3) Concubine of Caleb, the brother of Jerahmeel. 1 Chronicles 2:48. 4) One of David's wives who was daughter of Talmai, the king of Geshur, and mother of Absalom. Same as *Maacah*. 1 Chronicles 3:2. 5) Wife of a descendant of Manasseh named Machir. 1 Chronicles 7:15–16. 6) Wife of Jehiel, the leader of Gibeon. 1 Chronicles 8:29; 9:35.

94. Magdalene (12/1). "Woman of Magdala." Surname of Mary (2). See Section 3—Women's Roles and Jobs.

95. Mahalath (2/2). "Sickness." 1) Daughter of Ishmael who married Esau. Genesis 28:9. 2) Granddaughter of David and wife of Rehoboam, king of Judah. 2 Chronicles 11:18.

96. Mahlah (4/1).
"Sickness." One of Zelophehad's
five daughters. See "Daughters of
Zelophehad" in Section 3—Women's
Roles and Jobs.

97. Mara (1/1).
"Bitter." Name Naomi gave herself
after the men of her family died, and
she felt that God had dealt bitterly
with her. Ruth 1:20.

98. Martha (13/1).
"Mistress." Sister of
Lazarus and Mary (5).
See "Martha of Bethany"
in Section 3—Women's
Roles and Jobs.

99. Mary (54/7).
"Bitterness." 1)
Jesus' mother. Yes
(Matthew 1:16).
See Section 3—
Women's Roles
and Jobs. 2) Called
Mary Magdelene.
See Section
3—Women's
Roles and Jobs. 3)
Mary, the mother
of James and
Joses. See Section
3—Women's
Roles and Jobs. 4)
Wife of Cleophas.
Possibly the same

as *Mary* (3). John 19:25. 5) Sister of
Lazarus and Martha. See "Mary of
Bethany" in Section 3—Women's
Roles and Jobs. 6) Mother of John
Mark (4). See "Mary, John Mark's
Mother" in Section 3—Women's
Roles and Jobs. 7) Christian at Rome.
See "Paul's Other Sisters in Christ" in
Section 3— Women's Roles and Jobs.

100. Matred (2/1).
"Propulsive." Mother-in-law of a
king of Edom, "before there reigned
any king over the children of Israel"
(Genesis 36:31 KJV). Genesis 36:39;
1 Chronicles 1:50.

101. Mehetabel (2/1).
"Bettered of God." Wife of a king of
Edom, "before there reigned any
king over the children of Israel"
(Genesis 36:31 KJV). Genesis 36:39;
1 Chronicles 1:50.

102. Merab (3/1).
"Increase." King Saul's firstborn
daughter who was promised to
David but married another man.
1 Samuel 14:49; 18:17, 19.

103. Meshullemeth (1/1).
"A mission or a favorable release."
Mother of King Amon of Judah.
2 Kings 21:19.

104. Mezahab (2/1).
"Water of gold." Grandmother of a

wife of a king of Edom, "before there reigned any king over the children of Israel" (Genesis 36:31 KJV). Genesis 36:39; 1 Chronicles 1:50.

105. Michaiah (1/1).
"Who is like God?" Mother of King Abijah of Judah. 2 Chronicles 13:2.

106. Michal (18/1).

"Rivulet." Daughter of King Saul and wife of David. To win her, David had to give Saul a hundred Philistine foreskins; he killed two hundred of the enemy, fulfilling the king's request twice over. When Saul sought to kill David, Michal warned her husband and let him out a window. She told Saul's men that David was sick. Discovered, she claimed David threatened to kill her. Saul married Michal to Phalti. When David sent for her, after he became king, she was returned to him. But David danced before the ark, and Michal despised and berated him. She had no children. 1 Samuel 14:49; 18:20, 27–28; 19:11–13, 17; 25:44; 2 Samuel 3:13, 14; 6:16, 20–21, 23; 21:8; 1 Chronicles 15:29.

107. Milcah (11/2).
"Queen." 1) Wife of Nahor, Abraham's brother. The couple had eight children together. Milcah was

Rebekah's grandmother. Genesis 11:29; 22:20, 23; 24:15, 24, 47. 2) One of Zelophehad's five daughters. See "Daughters of Zelophehad" in Section 3—Women's Roles and Jobs.

108. Miriam (15/2).

"Rebelliously." 1) Sister of Moses and Aaron and a prophetess of Israel. See Section 3—Women's Roles and Jobs. 2) Descendant of Jacob through his son Judah. 1 Chronicles 4:17.

109. Naamah (4/2).
"Pleasantness." 1) Descendant of Cain and sister of Tubal-cain. Genesis 4:22. 2) Mother of King Rehoboam, she was an Ammonite. 1 Kings 14:21, 31; 2 Chronicles 12:13.

110. Naarah (3/1).
"Girl." Wife of Ashur, who was a descendant of Abraham through Jacob's son Judah. 1 Chronicles 4:5–6.

111. Naomi (21/1).

"Pleasant." Elimelech's wife; mother-in-law of Ruth; nurse to Obed, who was considered her grandson. See "Ruth" in Section 4—Bible Women and Their Interactions with Men.

112. Nehushta (1/1).
"Copper." Mother of King Jehoiachin of Judah. 2 Kings 24:8.

113. Noadiah (2/2).
"Convened of God." 1) Levite who weighed the temple vessels after the Babylonian Exile. Ezra 8:33. 2) Prophetess who opposed Nehemiah. See Section 3—Women's Roles and Jobs.

114. Noah (4/1).
"Rest." One of Zelophehad's five daughters. See "Daughters of Zelophehad" in Section 3—Women's Roles and Jobs.

115. Nymphas (1/1).
"Nymph; bride." Colossian Christian who had a house church in her home. Colossians 4:15.

116. Orpah (2/1).
"Mane." Naomi's daughter-in-law who did not follow her to Bethlehem. Ruth 1:4, 14.

117. Peninnah (3/1).
"A pearl, round." Elkanah's wife who had children and provoked his wife Hannah, who was barren. 1 Samuel 1:2, 4.

118. Persis (1/1).
"Persian woman." Christian at Rome. See "Paul's Other Sisters in Christ" in Section 3—Women's Roles and Jobs.

119. Phoebe (1/1).
"Bright." Hosted a church in Cenchrea. See Section 3—Women's Roles and Jobs.

120. Prisca (1/1).
"Ancient." Wife of Aquila. Same as *Priscilla*. See Section 3—Women's Roles and Jobs.

121. Priscilla (5/1).
"Ancient." Wife of Aquila. Same as *Prisca*. See Section 3—Women's Roles and Jobs.

122. Puah (1/1).
"Splendid." Hebrew midwife. See Section 3—Women's Roles and Jobs.

123. Rachab (1/1).
Yes (Matthew 1:5). "Proud." Greek form of the name *Rahab*, used in the New Testament. Matthew 1:5.

124. Rachel (47/1).
"Ewe." Daughter of Laban; sister of Leah; wife of Jacob; mother of Joseph and Benjamin.

Same as *Rahel*. See "Sisters" and "Fertility (and the Lack Thereof)" in Section 1—Women in Bible Times; also "Leah" in Section 3—Women's Roles and Jobs.

125. Rahab (7/1).
Yes (Matthew 1:5). "Proud." Prostitute of Jericho who hid Joshua's spies. Same as *Rachab*. See Section 3— Women's Roles and Jobs.

126. Rahel (1/1).
"Ewe." Variant spelling of the name of Jacob's wife *Rachel*. Jeremiah 31:15.

127. Rebecca (1/1).
"Fettering by beauty." Greek form of the name *Rebekah*, used in the New Testament. Romans 9:10.

128. Rebekah (30/1).
"Fettering by beauty." When Abraham's servant came to Nahor, seeking a wife for Abraham's son Isaac, Rebekah watered his camels, proving she was God's choice as the  bride. She agreed to marry Isaac and traveled to her new home, where Isaac loved and married her. At first barren, when Rebekah conceived, she had the twins Esau and Jacob. Because she loved her second son best, she conspired with Jacob to get him the eldest son's blessing from his father. When Esau discovered what Jacob had done, he became so angry that Rebekah arranged for Jacob to leave before his brother killed him. Same as *Rebecca*. Genesis 22:23; 24:15, 29–30, 45, 51, 53, 58–61, 64, 67; 25:20-21, 28; 26:7-8, 35; 27:5-6, 11, 15, 42, 46; 28:5; 29:12; 35:8; 49:31.

129. Reumah (1/1).
"Raised." Concubine of Abraham's brother Nahor. Genesis 22:24.

130. Rhoda (1/1).
"Rose." Young woman serving in the Jerusalem home of Mary, mother of John Mark. Responding to a knock at the gate, Rhoda heard the voice of Peter, who had just been miraculously freed from prison while Christians in Mary's home prayed for him. In her excitement, she forgot to let Peter in—and had a hard time convincing those praying that their request had been answered. Acts 12:13.

131. Rizpah (4/1).
"Hot stone." Concubine of Saul. See Section 3—Women's Roles and Jobs.

132. Ruth (13/1).
Yes (Matthew 1:5). "Friend." Moabite

daughter-in-law of Naomi; widow of Mahlon; wife of Boaz. See Section 3—Women's Roles and Jobs; also Section 4—Bible Women and Their Interactions with Men.

133. Salome (2/1).
"Welfare." Follower of Jesus. See Section 3—Women's Roles and Jobs.

134. Sapphira (1/1).
"Sapphire." Wife of Ananias. The couple agreed to sell property and give only a portion of their gains to the church, while claiming they gave the whole price. When she lied to the apostle Peter, Sapphira died. Acts 5:1.

135. Sara (2/1).
"Female noble." Greek form of the name *Sarah,* used in the New Testament. Hebrews 11:11; 1 Peter 3:6.

136. Sarah (41/2).
"Female noble." 1) Name God gave Sarai, wife of Abram (Abraham). See Section 3—Women's Roles and Jobs; also Section 4—Bible Women and Their Interactions with Men. 2) Daughter of Asher and granddaughter of Jacob. Numbers 26:46.

137. Sarai (17/1).
"Controlling." Wife of Abram. Same as *Sarah.* See Section 3—Women's Roles and Jobs; also Section 4—Bible Women and Their Interactions with Men.

138. Serah (2/1).
"Superfluity." Daughter of Asher, a descendant of Abraham through Jacob. Genesis 46:17; 1 Chronicles 7:30.

139. Shelomith (2/2).
"Peaceableness, pacification."
1) Mother of a man who was stoned for blaspheming the Lord. Leviticus 24:11. 2) Daughter of Zerubbabel and a descendant of Abraham through Jacob's son Judah, in the line of the nation of Judah's third-to-last king, Jeconiah (also known as Jehoiachin). 1 Chronicles 3:19.

140. Sherah (1/1).
"Kindred." Descendant of Abraham through Joseph's son Ephraim. She built the city of Beth-horon. 1 Chronicles 7:24.

141. Shimeath (2/1).
"Annunciation." Mother of Zabad, a royal official who conspired to kill Judah's king Joash. 2 Kings 12:21; 2 Chronicles 24:26.

142. Shimrith (1/1). "Female guard." Mother of Jehozabad, a royal official who conspired to kill Judah's king Joash. Same as *Shomer*. 2 Chronicles 24:26.

143. Shiphrah (1/1). "Brightness." Hebrew midwife. See Section 3—Women's Roles and Jobs.

144. Shomer (1/1). "Keeper." Mother of one of two royal officials who conspired to kill Judah's king Joash. Same as *Shimrith*. 2 Kings 12:21.

145. Shua (?/2). "A cry." 1 Daughter of Heber and a descendant of Abraham through Jacob's son Asher. 1 Chronicles 7:32.

146. Susanna (1/1). "Lily." Follower of Jesus. See Section 3—Women's Roles and Jobs.

147. Syntyche (1/1). "Common fate." Christian woman of Philippi. See "Paul's Other Sisters in Christ" in Section 3—Women's Roles and Jobs.

148. Tabitha (2/1). "Gazelle." Christian of Joppa. Same as *Dorcas*. See "Tabitha or Dorcas" in Section 3— Women's Roles and Jobs.

149. Tahpenes (3/1). Queen of Egypt during the rule of Solomon and sister-in-law of Solomon's adversary Hadad the Edomite. 1 Kings 11:19–20.

150. Tamar (22/3). "Palm tree." 1) Daughter-in-law of Jacob's son Judah. She married Judah's eldest two sons, whom God killed for wickedness. Judah refused to marry her to his third son, so she pretended to be a harlot, lay with Judah, and had twins by him. Same as *Thamar*. Genesis 38:6, 11, 13, 24; Ruth 4:12; 1 Chronicles 2:4. 2) Daughter of King David and the half sister of Amnon. Amnon fell in love with her and pretended to be sick so David would send Tamar to him. He raped Tamar and threw her out of his house. Her full brother Absalom heard of this and later had his servants kill Amnon. 2 Samuel 13:1-2, 4-8, 10, 19-20, 22, 32; 1 Chronicles 3:9. 3) Beautiful only daughter of the very hand-some Absalom, son of King David. 2 Samuel 14:27.

151. **Taphath** (1/1).
"Drop of ointment." Daughter of Solomon and the wife of one of the king's commissary officers. 1 Kings 4:11.

152. **Thamar** (1/1).
Yes (Matthew 1:3). "Palm tree." Greek form of the name *Tamar,* used in the New Testament. Same as *Tamar* (1). Matthew 1:3.

153. **Timna** (3/2).
"Restraint." 1) Concubine of Esau's son Eliphaz. Genesis 36:12. 2) Daughter of Seir, who lived in Esau's "land of Edom." Genesis 36:22; 1 Chronicles 1:39.

154. **Tirzah** (4/1).
"Delightsomeness." One of five daughters of Zelophehad. See "Daughters of Zelophehad" in Section 3—Women's Roles and Jobs.

155. **Tryphena** (1/1).
"Luxurious." Christian woman in Rome. See "Paul's Other Sisters in Christ" in Section 3—Women's Roles and Jobs.

156. **Tryphosa** (1/1).
"Luxuriating." Christian woman in Rome. See "Paul's Other Sisters in Christ" in Section 3—Women's Roles and Jobs.

157. **Vashti** (10/1).
"Beautiful." Queen of the Persian king Ahasuerus, Vashti refused to appear at his banquet. The king revoked her position and had no more to do with her. Esther 1:9, 11–12, 15–17, 19; 2:1, 4, 17.

158. **Zebudah** (1/1).
"Gainfulness." Mother of the evil Jehoiakim, the third-to-last king of Judah. 2 Kings 23:36.

159. **Zeresh** (4/1).
"Misery." Wife of Haman. See "Esther" in Section 4—Bible Women and Their Interactions with Men.

160. **Zeruah** (1/1).
"Leprous." Widow and the mother of Jeroboam, who became the first king of the northern Jewish nation of Israel. 1 Kings 11:26.

161. **Zeruiah** (26/1).
"Wounded." Sister of King David and mother of David's battle commander, Joab, and his brothers, Abishai and Asahel. 1 Samuel 26:6; 2 Samuel 2:13, 18; 3:39; 8:16; 14:1; 16:9–10; 17:25; 18:2; 19:21–22; 21:17; 23:18, 37; 1 Kings 1:7; 2:5, 22; 1 Chronicles 2:16; 11:6, 39; 18:12, 15; 26:28; 27:24.

162. Zibiah (2/1).
"Gazelle." Mother of Joash, one of the good kings of Judah. 2 Kings 12:1; 2 Chronicles 24:1.

163. Zillah (3/1).
"Shade." Second wife of Lamech, a descendant of Cain. Her son was Tubal-cain. Genesis 4:19, 22–23.

164. Zilpah (7/1).
"Trickle." Servant of Leah. Leah gave Zilpah to her husband, Jacob, as a wife because she thought her own childbearing days were ended. Zilpah had two sons, Gad and Asher. Genesis 29:24; 30:9-10, 12; 35:26; 37:2; 46:18.

165. Zipporah (3/1).
"Bird." Daughter of the Midianite priest Reuel (also known as Jethro) and wife of Moses. She had a disagreement with her husband over the circumcision of their firstborn son. Exodus 2:21; 4:25; 18:2.

166. Zobebah (1/1).
"Canopy." Daughter of Coz, a descendant of Abraham through Jacob's son Judah. 1 Chronicles 4:8.

The Unnamed Women of the Bible

OLD TESTAMENT

Cain's Wife
While the Bible clearly states that Cain had a wife who gave birth to their son Enoch, it gives us no specifics about who Cain's wife was or where they met. Genesis 4:17.

Daughters of Men
These beautiful women were chosen as wives by the "sons of God," a phrase that has engendered much discussion. The sons born to these women became heroes and men of renown. Genesis 6:1–4.

Noah's Wife
See Section 3—Women's Roles and Jobs. Genesis 6:18–7:13; 8:15–18.

Noah's Sons' Wives
Genesis 7:7, 13; 8:18. See Section 3—Women's Roles and Jobs.

Lot's Wife
Lot's wife is best remembered for her hesitation when leaving Sodom and Gomorrah as the cities were destroyed. Although Lot's family had been instructed not to look back as they left, his wife did, and was turned into a pillar of salt. Jesus refers to Lot's wife as a warning about not turning back on the day of His return. Genesis 19:15–26; Luke 17:32.

Lot's Daughters
Genesis 19:30–38. See "Other Biblical Women Who Used Their Influence for Evil" in Section 4—Bible Women and Their Interactions with Men.

Abimelech's Wife
Genesis 20:1–18. See "Sarah" in Section 4—Bible Women and Their Interactions with Men.

Potiphar's Wife
Genesis 39:1–20. See Section 3—Women's Roles and Jobs.

Pharaoh's Daughter

Exodus 2:1–10; Acts 7:21; Hebrews 11:24. See Section 3—Women's Roles and Jobs.

Daughters of Reuel, a Midian Priest

These seven daughters met Moses at a well as they went to water their father's flock. Because Moses helped them, he was invited into their home and even married Zipporah, one of the sisters. Exodus 2:16–22.

Ethiopian Wife of Moses

Moses married an Ethiopian, sometimes called Cushite, woman. This marriage caused dissension between Moses and his coleaders, his brother Aaron and his sister Miriam, to the point that his siblings revolted against Moses' leadership. Numbers 12:1–16.

Sisera's Mother

This woman's grief when her son did not return home from battle is recorded in a song sung by Deborah, a leader of Israel, and Barak, one of her generals. Sisera was a military commander who oppressed Israel for twenty years. The song recounted his death at the hands of the tent-dwelling woman named Jael, and the Israelites' victory over his army. Judges 5:28–30.

Woman Who Dropped a Millstone on Abimelech's Head

Judges 9:50–57; 2 Samuel 11:21. See "Woman of Thebez" in Section 3—Women's Roles and Jobs.

Jephthah's Daughter

Because of an oath her father made to God in the hopes of gaining a military victory, this virgin, an only child, was offered as a sacrifice. After that, young Israelite women spent four days each year commemorating her plight. Judges 11:30–40.

Manoah's Wife/ Samson's Mother

Judges 13:1–25; 14:1–6. See Section 3—Women's Roles and Jobs.

Samson's Wife

Judges 14:1–15:6. See "Delilah" in Section 4—Bible Women and Their Interactions with Men.

Gaza Prostitute

This prostitute was visited by Samson, the judge of Israel famous for his long hair and great strength. It was while Samson was with this woman that the people of Gaza plotted to kill him the next morning. Samson not only escaped but prevailed against the city. Judges 16:1–3.

Micah's Mother

Micah and his mother lived during the time of the judges when Israel cycled through periods of faith then idolatry. Micah had taken silver from his mother, but then returned it. She gave the pieces of silver to a silversmith, who used them to make a carved image and a cast idol. While these items were clearly not a part of the Mosaic Law, in this case they seem to have been incorporated into the worship of Jehovah, perhaps an apt picture of the state of religion in Israel at this time, when "everyone did as he saw fit" (Judges 17:6 NIV). Judges 17:1–6.

Levite's Concubine

This woman came to a disastrous end. After first being unfaithful to her Levite husband, she returned to her father's house. After he persuaded her to return home with him, the couple traveled through the land of Benjamin, stopping for the night in the city of Gibeah. While they were there, wicked men of the area came to the home of their host, threatening the safety of her husband. In an effort to assuage these wicked men, this woman (as well as the host's virgin daughter) was offered to them. During the night the Levite's concubine was raped and although she made her way back to the house where her husband was staying, by morning she was dead. In an attempt to reveal the evil that had been done and to rally some retribution, the Levite cut up the woman's corpse and sent the pieces out to the tribes of Israel, which led to a war between Israel and the Benjamites. Judges 19:1–30.

Four Hundred Young Virgins

These women from Jabesh-Gilead were the survivors of a massacre that occurred because the tribe of Jabesh-Gilead had not been represented at a gathering in Mizpah. The women were left with no prospects for husbands from their own tribe and thus became prime candidates to become wives of the men of the tribe of Benjamin, a tribe that would die out unless enough wives could be found. Judges 21:12–23.

Eli's Daughter-in-Law

This woman was the pregnant wife of Phinehas, son of the priest Eli. After a devastating battle in which her husband and his brother were killed and the holy ark of the covenant was stolen, her father-in-law also died. Having lost so much, this woman went into a difficult labor and birthed a son. Immediately afterward, as she was dying, she named the boy Ichabod, which means "the glory of God has departed." 1 Samuel 4:16–22.

Women Celebrating David's Deeds

After David killed Goliath and the Israelites conquered the Philistines, these women greeted the returning warriors, dancing and singing. Unfortunately, their song attributed more deaths to David than to King Saul. This began Saul's jealousy toward David, which grew to murderous contempt. 1 Samuel 18:6–9.

Sorceress of Endor

King Saul himself had exiled all mediums and spiritualists from his land. Nevertheless, in disguise, he traveled to Endor to consult with this woman. He asked her to contact the deceased prophet Samuel, who had served as Saul's advisor, so that Saul could speak with him. The woman was successful in contacting Samuel beyond the grave, but in doing so she recognized King Saul, the gravity of his request, and the risk it brought upon her. 1 Samuel 28:7–25.

Nurse Who Let Jonathan's Son Fall

Though mentioned only once, and within parentheses at that, this woman took part in a key event in the Israelite monarchy. She was caring for a five-year-old named Mephibosheth, who was the son of Jonathan and grandson of King Saul. When Jonathan and Saul were killed in battle, it was necessary to hide Mephibosheth, the heir to the throne. As the nurse was making her escape with the young boy, he fell (some translations say she dropped him) and became lame in both feet. 2 Samuel 4:4.

Wise Woman of Tekoa

Joab persuaded this wise woman of Tekoa to play a role in reconciling David to his son Absalom. The woman told King David a tale about a son who had killed his brother, a story that paralleled David's experience with Absalom. Because of her story, David allowed Absalom to return to Jerusalem. 2 Samuel 14:1–21.

Woman Who Hid Jonathan and Ahimaaz

2 Samuel 17:17–20. See "Woman of Bahurim" in Section 3— Women's Roles and Jobs.

Woman Who Saved a City

2 Samuel 20:16–22. See "Wise Woman of Abel" in Section 3—Women's Roles and Jobs.

Pharaoh's Daughter (Solomon's Wife)

As part of an alliance with Egypt, Solomon married an Egyptian princess. Although this princess was not Solomon's only wife, she is mentioned several times within the account of Solomon's reign. Because the Egyptian princess came from a land of other religions, after a time Solomon moved her away from King David's palace, a place where the Ark of God had been honored. 1 Kings 3:1–2; 9:16–24; 11:1; 2 Chronicles 8:11.

Two Prostitute Mothers Who Visited King Solomon

1 Kings 3:16–28. See Section 3—Women's Roles and Jobs.

Queen of Sheba

1 Kings 10:1–10, 13; 2 Chronicles 9:1–9, 12; Matthew 12:42. See Section 3—Women's Roles and Jobs.

Jeroboam's Wife

King Jeroboam asked his wife to disguise herself and go to the prophet Ahijah to find out the fate of their sick child. Before the queen arrived, however, God had revealed her identity to the prophet. Rather than simply glean news of her son, she received bad news about the entire kingdom. Then, as Ahijah had predicted, her son died as she returned home. 1 Kings 14:1–18.

Widow at Zarephath

The prophet Elijah approached this woman, asking her for a piece of bread and some water. She revealed to the prophet that

she had only a handful of flour and a little oil. When those supplies were gone, she expected that she and her son would die from starvation due to a drought that had caused a famine. Elijah assured the widow that if she would make him some bread first, then some for her and her son, the flour and oil would not run out until rain came and the famine was over. Jesus referred to this widow in comparing Elijah's ministry to His own. 1 Kings 17:1–16; Luke 4:25, 26.

Widow Whose Oil Was Multiplied

This widow's deceased husband was a member of a group of prophets who worked with Elisha. She approached Elisha because a creditor was about to take her two sons as slaves. Her only asset was a little oil. Elisha instructed her to gather as many jars as she could and begin to fill them from that bit of oil. What had been a little continued to flow until the woman had filled all the jars. She was able to sell the multiplied oil and pay her debts. 2 Kings 4:1–7.

Wealthy Woman of Shunem

2 Kings 4:8–37; 8:1–6. See Section 3—Women's Roles and Jobs.

Maid of Naaman's Wife

2 Kings 5:1–14. See Section 3—Women's Roles and Jobs.

Naaman's Wife

While Naaman's wife's servant girl is more of a focus of the account of his illness and healing, it seems that it was his wife who passed along the information about Elisha, the prophet who could heal Naaman of his leprosy. 2 Kings 5:2–4.

Two Women Who Agreed to Eat their Sons

During a famine, these women made a bargain to eat their own sons to survive. After they sacrificed the first woman's infant for food, however, the second woman refused to do the same with her son. When the woman brought the situation to the king, it revealed to him the severity of the national food crisis, moving him to action. 2 Kings 6:26–30.

Shallum's Daughters

Nehemiah 3:12. See Section 3—Women's Roles and Jobs.

Job's Wife

While Job is remembered for his righteousness in the face of great adversity, his wife is remembered for her lack of hope. It was she who told the stricken Job to go ahead and curse God and die. Job responded by asking whether they were to accept the good from God but not the bad. Job 2:9–10.

King Lemuel's Mother

Proverbs 31:1. See Section 3—Women's Roles and Jobs.

Shulammite Sweetheart

"Shulammite" was the name by which the female lover in Song of Songs, an Old Testament book of love poems, was identified. There are theories to the woman's actual identity, but her name is never revealed. Song of Solomon 6:13.

Canaanite Goddess

The worship of this Canaanite goddess, referred to as the Queen of Heaven, infiltrated the Israelite nation of the prophet Jeremiah's day. Jeremiah renounced the practice. Some associate this goddess with Ishtar, a Babylonian deity. Jeremiah 7:18; 44:17–19.

Ezekiel's Wife

The prophet Ezekiel lived out several lessons that became teaching opportunities. In one case, it was the death of his wife. God describes Ezekiel's wife as precious, the delight of his eyes. Yet, when she died, Ezekiel was to not mourn publicly. When the people questioned Ezekiel regarding this unusual behavior, he told them that his wife's death was a kind of foreshadowing to the eventual loss of the temple, which was the delight of the Jewish culture of Ezekiel's day. Ezekiel 24:16–27.

Belshazzar's Mother

After King Belshazzar witnessed a hand writing on the wall, the message of which neither he nor his wise men could understand, it was the queen mother who suggested that he call on Daniel, an Israelite who had been exiled to the kingdom, for an interpretation. Daniel 5:1–12.

NEW TESTAMENT

Peter's Wife's Mother

The mother of Peter's wife was in bed sick with a fever when Jesus visited. When He touched her hand, the fever left her, and she got up and tended to Jesus. Matthew 8:14–15; Mark 1:30–31; Luke 4:38–39.

Jairus' Daughter

This daughter of Jairus, a synagogue leader, had just died. Her father came to Jesus, claiming in faith that his daughter would live again if Jesus touched her. After healing another woman on the way, Jesus entered Jairus's house, took the girl by the hand, and she rose. Matthew 9:18–25; Mark 5:21–24, 35–43; Luke 8:41–56.

Woman Who Suffered from Bleeding

This woman, who had suffered from bleeding for twelve years, came up behind Jesus and touched the hem of his clothes, believing she would be healed. Jesus told her that her faith had made her well. She was immediately healed. Matthew 9:20–22; Mark 5:25–34; Luke 8:43–48.

Herodias's Daughter

This daughter of Herodias (once the wife of King Herod's half brother Philip, she was now married to Herod), danced for her uncle Herod and his dinner guests on his birthday. Greatly pleased by her performance, Herod rashly promised to give her anything she asked. After consulting with her mother, she requested the head of John the Baptist. Herod honored his promise and John was beheaded. Matthew 14:6–10; Mark 6:22–28.

Canaanite Woman

This Canaanite woman, sometimes referred to as a Syrophenician, begged Jesus to drive out an evil spirit that possessed her daughter. In His conversation with the woman, Jesus had a notable exchange with her about whether His miracles were only for His own people, the Jews. Later, when the woman returned home, she found her daughter lying on the bed with the demon gone. Matthew 15:21–28; Mark 7:25–30.

Two Servants Who Heard Peter Deny Jesus

These servant girls, after the arrest of Jesus, identified Peter as one of the men who had been with Jesus. Each time they did so, Peter angrily denied the truth, saying he did not know Jesus. Matthew 26:69–72; Mark 14:66–70; Luke 22:56–60.

Pilate's Wife

Matthew 27:19. See section 4—Bible Women and Their Interactions with Men.

Women Who Followed Jesus from Galilee

While we hear more about the men who followed Jesus, many women followed Him as well, taking care of His needs. These women also witnessed His crucifixion and death, though from a distance. Matthew 27:54–56.

Widow with Two Small Coins

This poor widow offered two small coins as an offering at the temple.

Although many rich people offered large amounts, Jesus said the widow's offering was greater than all—for she gave everything she had. Mark 12:41–44; Luke 21:1–4.

Widow of Nain, Whose Son Jesus Raised From the Dead

This widowed woman, who was preparing to bury her only son, aroused pity in Jesus, and He told her not to cry. Touching the coffin, He told the young man to get up. Not only did the young man sit up, he began to talk, and Jesus returned him to his mother. Luke 7:11–17.

Sinful Woman Who Anointed Jesus' Feet

Luke 7:36–50. See Section 3 —Women's Roles and Jobs.

Woman Who Blessed Jesus' Mother

While listening to Jesus preach with a crowd of other people, this woman cried out a blessing on the mother who gave birth to Jesus. Jesus responded to her with a clarification—it is the people who hear the word of God and obey it who are blessed. Luke 11:27–28.

Crippled Woman Healed by Jesus

This Jewish woman, a "daughter of Abraham," had been crippled for eighteen years. She was bent over and unable to straighten her back. In the synagogue where Jesus was teaching, He called her forward and set her free from her illness. She immediately stood up straight and began praising God. The synagogue ruler took offense to Jesus performing such a miracle on the Sabbath, which prompted Jesus to criticize the hypocrites who would tend to their animals on the Sabbath but not help a neighbor in need. Luke 13:10–16.

Women Mourning as Jesus Is Led to Be Crucified

Among the crowd of people who followed Jesus as Simon from Cyrene carried His cross to Calvary were women who mourned for Him. Jesus called the women "daughters of Jerusalem." He told them to weep for themselves and their children, rather than for Him. Luke 23:27–28.

Samaritan Woman at the Well

John 4:5–42. See "The Woman at the Well" in Section 4—Bible Women and Their Interactions with Men.

Woman Caught in Adultery

Caught in the act of adultery, this woman was brought before Jesus by the scribes and Pharisees. They claimed, according to the Law of Moses, that she should be stoned to death. They hoped to trick Jesus into saying something that would give them grounds to bring a charge against Him. Jesus, however, simply responded that whoever was without sin could cast the first stone at the woman. One by one, the woman's accusers departed, leaving the woman alone with Jesus. He then told her to change her ways. John 8:3–11.

Women Who Prayed with the Disciples

These women prayed with the disciples in the Upper Room after the crucifixion of Jesus. Acts 1:13–14.

Greek Widows

It was because of the neglect that these New Testament widows experienced that the early church chose seven servant leaders who could care for the daily needs of the community of faith. This enabled the apostles to dedicate themselves to teaching. Acts 6:1–4.

Devout Women of Antioch

These women of Antioch were known as influential religious leaders. Along with their male counterparts, they were incited by Jews, who were threatened by Paul and Barnabas's popularity, to drive the two traveling preachers out of their area. Acts 13:44–52.

Slave Girl Possessed by Fortune-Telling Spirit

Inhabited by a spirit that allowed her to tell fortunes, this slave girl was exploited by her owners for profit. She followed Paul, Silas, and Luke, praising the men as servants of God. After days of this, Paul became annoyed and commanded the spirit to leave the girl. With the spirit gone, the girl's owners lost their ability to make money from her. Angrily, they seized Paul and Silas and took them before the authorities. Acts 16:16–19.

Sister Prophetesses (Four Daughters of Philip)

Acts 21:9. See Section 3—Women's Roles and Jobs.

Rufus's Mother

Rufus's mother was important in the life of Paul, who mentioned her in his letter to the Romans. He not only sent his greeting but also said she had been a mother to him. Romans 16:13.

Wives of the Apostles

Paul's letter to the Corinthian church reveals the fact that some of the disciples, including Jesus' brothers, were married. While we often read the stories of Jesus and his followers from a simple perspective of men who serve in isolation, this reveals a new texture—wives who observed and were affected by Jesus' band of followers. 1 Corinthians 9:1–6.

Holy Women

These holy women of the past, including Abraham's wife, Sarah, were used by Peter to illustrate how women should exhibit pure and reverent behavior, with a focus on inner beauty rather than outward appearances. This kind of behavior,

Peter wrote, would win over non-believing husbands to the Lord. 1 Peter 3:1–6.

Chosen Lady

The chosen lady and her children were the recipients of John's second epistle, or letter. John urged the lady to walk in love for other people and to beware of false teachers. It is unclear whether this letter is directed to a specific lady or to a church spoken of figuratively as a woman. 2 John 1:1–13.

PARABLES

Woman Mixing Leaven

Matthew 13:33; Luke 13:20–21. See "Women Making Bread: Mixing Leaven" in Section 3—Women's Roles and Jobs.

Wife Who Was to Be Sold For Debt

In a parable about an unforgiving servant, the master of a man in debt ordered that he, along with his wife and children, be sold to repay what he owed. Matthew 18:25.

Woman Who Married Seven Brothers

This woman who married seven brothers in succession, each after the death of the previous one according to the Law of Moses, was the subject of a question posed to Jesus by the Sadducees. Though this religious group did not believe in the resurrection, these Sadducees asked Jesus which of the seven brothers would be considered this woman's husband at the resurrection. Jesus responded that they did not know the scriptures or the power of God—that at the resurrection people would not be considered married or unmarried but would rather be like the angels in heaven. Matthew 22:23–32; Mark 12:18–25; Luke 20:27–40.

Two Women Grinding Meal

Matthew 24:41; Luke 17:35. See "Women Making Bread: Grinding Meal" in Section 3—Women's Roles and Jobs.

Ten Virgins

Matthew 25:1–13. See Section 3—Women's Roles and Jobs.

Woman Who Found Lost Coin

Luke 15:8–10. See Section 3—Women's Roles and Jobs.

Persistent Widow

Luke 18:1–8. See Section 3—Women's Roles and Jobs.

Woman in Labor

Jesus described a woman who endured the pain of labor only to forget that pain in the joy of the arrival of her baby. In the same way, there is sorrow in this world, but when Jesus comes again, His children will forget that sorrow in light of their everlasting joy. John 16:20–22.

PROVERBS

The Loose Woman

Proverbs 2:16; 5:3, 20; 7:5; 20:16; 23:27, 33; 30:20.

The Wife of Your Youth

Proverbs 5:18.

Another Man's Wife

Proverbs 6:29.

The Prostitute

Proverbs 7:10–12; 29:3.

The Foolish Woman

Proverbs 9:13; 14:1.

The Gracious Woman
Proverbs 11:16.

The Woman without Discretion
Proverbs 11:22.

The Wise Woman
Proverbs 14:1.

The Wife (whoever finds her finds a good thing)
Proverbs 18:22.

The Quarrelsome Wife
Proverbs 19:13; 27:15.

The Prudent Wife
Proverbs 19:14.

The Angry Woman
Proverbs 21:19.

The Brawling Woman
Proverbs 21:9; 25.24.

The Contentious Woman
Proverbs 27:15.

The Bitter Woman
Proverbs 30:21-23.

Scripture Index

Genesis

2:12–13—172
3:7—172
4–5—78, 94, 138
4:4—212
4:8—213
4:9—213
4:17–24—153
5—213
5:24–27—153, 213
5:28–30—256
6:25–30—172
9:50–57—155, 256
10:6–7—172
11:30–40—256
13—167
13:1–25—256
13:3—167
13:5—167, 202
13:25—202
14:1–6—256
14:1–9—167
14:1–15:6—256
14:3—202
16:1–3—256
16:7—203
16:9—203
16:15—203
16:16—204
16:17—204
16:20—204
17:1–6—257
17:6—257
19:1–30—257
21:12–23—257

Ruth
1:4, 14—248
1:16–17—219
1:20—246
1–4—154
2:8–9—14, 219
2:11–12—219
2:15–16—219–220
3:3—19

4:11—162
4:12—251

1 Samuel
1—82, 164
1:2, 4—248
2:1–11, 18–21—164
2:22–25—143
4—88
4:16–22—258
7:3–4—172
8:13—19
12:10—172
14:49—246, 247
14:50—238
18:6—142
18:6–9—258
18:17, 19—246
18:20, 27–28—247
19:11–13, 17—247
19:11–17—218
21:4–5—40
25—78
25:2–43—145
25:43—238
25:44—247
26:6—252
27:3—145, 238
28:7–25—258
30:5—145, 238
31:10—172

2 Samuel
2:1–3—145
2:2—238
2:13, 18—252
3:1–14—247
3:2—238
3:2–3—145
3:3—245
3:4—238, 242
3:5—241
3:7—165
3:13–14—247

3:39—252
4:4—258
6:16, 20–21, 23—247
8:16—252
11:1—208
11:21—155, 256
11:26—210
11–12—208
12:1–4—210
12:8–9—210
13—69
13:1–2, 4–8, 10, 19–20, 22, 32—251
14:1—252
14:1–21—258
14:27—252
16:9–10—252
17:17–20—259
17:17–21—155
17:25—237, 252
18:2—252
19:21–22—252
20:14–22—156
20:16–22—259
20:19—156
21—103
21:1–14—165
21:8—247
21:17—252
23:18, 37—252

1 Kings
1—239
1:3, 15—237
1:5, 11—242
1:7—252
2:5, 22—252
2:13—242
2:17—237
2:18–20—15–16
2:21–22—237
3:1–2—259
3:16–28—168, 259
4:1–18—259

Index of Proper Names

Regular type=mention   **Bold type=feature**   Gold type=image

Bibliography

Section 1—Women in Bible Times
(please note: the bibliographic records for this section are mixed with those of Section 2, Daily
  Experiences of Bible Women)
Baker, James R. *Women's Rights in Old Testament Times.* Salt Lake City: Signature Books, 1992.
Banks, Amanda Carson. *Birth Chairs, Midwives, and Medicine.* Jackson, MS: University Press of
  Mississippi, 1999.
Bickel, Bruce, and Stan Jantz. *Bruce and Stan's Guide to the Bible.* Eugene, OR: Harvest House
  Publishers, 1998.
Bimson, J.J.; J.P. Kane; J.H. Paterson; D.J. Wiseman; and D.R.W. Wood, ed. *New Bible Atlas.* 1985,
  Inter-Varsity Press, Leicester, England, and Lion Publishing, Oxford, England.
Bottero, Jean; Elena Cassin; and Jean Vercoutter, ed. *The Near East: The Early Civilizations.* New York:
  Delacorte Press, 1967.
Clements, R.E., ed. *The World of Ancient Israel.* Cambridge, England: Cambridge University Press,
  1989.
Connolly, Peter. *The Holy Land.* New York: Oxford University Press, 1998.
Deen, Edith. *All the Women of the Bible.* New York: Harper & Row, 1993.
—*The Bible's Legacy for Womanhood.* Garden City, NY: Doubleday and Co., 1969.
Douglas, J.D., and Merrill C. Tenney, ed. *The New International Dictionary of the Bible.* Grand Rapids:
  Zondervan, 1987.
Dué, Andrea. *The Atlas of the Bible Lands: History, Daily Life and Traditions.* Florence, Italy: McRae
  Books, 1998.
Elwell, Walter A., and Philip Wesley Comfort. *Tyndale Bible Dictionary.* Carol Stream, IL: Tyndale House
  Publishers, Inc., 2001.
Hart, George. *Eyewitness Books: Ancient Egypt.* New York: DK Publishing, 2008.
Higgs, Liz Curtis. *Slightly Bad Girls of the Bible.* Colorado Springs, CO: WaterBrook Press, 2007.
King, Philip J., and Lawrence E. Stager. *Life in Biblical Israel.* Louisville, KY: Westminster John Knox
  Press, 2001.
Kraemer, Ross Shepard, and Mary Rose D'Angelo. *Women & Christian Origins.* New York: Oxford
  University Press, 1999.
Kroeger, Catherine Clark, and Mary J. Evans. *IVP Women's Bible Commentary.* Downers Grove, IL:
  InterVarsity Press, 2002.
Landau, Elaine. *The Sumerians.* Brookfield, CT: The Millbrook Press, Inc., 1997.

—*Life and Times Historical Reference Bible Nelson, The.* Nashville: Thomas Nelson, Inc., 1997.

—*Life Application Study Bible,* New International Version. Carol Stream, IL: Tyndale House Publishers, Inc., 1997.

—*Lion Concise Bible Encyclopedia, The.* Oxford: Lion Publishing, 1980.

—*Living in Ancient Mesopotamia.* Living in the Ancient World Series. New York: Chelsea House, 2009.

Lockyer, Herbert. *All the Women of the Bible.* Grand Rapids: Zondervan, 1967.

Malam, John. *Mesopotamia and the Fertile Crescent: 10,000 to 539 BC.* Austin, TX: Steck-Vaughn Company, 1999.

Mastro, M. L. del. *All the Women of the Bible.* Edison, NJ: Castle Books, 2006.

Meyers, Carol. *Discovering Eve: Ancient Israelite Women in Context.* New York: Oxford University Press, 1988.

Miller, Kathy Collard, and Larry Richards. *Women of the Bible: The Smart Guide to the Bible Series.* Nashville: Nelson Reference, 2006.

Miller, Stephen M. *Who's Who and Where's Where in the Bible.* Uhrichsville, OH: Barbour Publishing, 1984.

Mohney, Nell W. *From Eve to Esther: Letting Old Testament Women Speak to Us.* Nashville: Dimensions for Living, 2001.

Murphy, Cullen. *The World According to Eve: Women and the Bible in Ancient Times and Our Own.* New York: Houghton Mifflin Company, 1998.

Newsom, Carol, and Sharon H. Ringe. *Women's Bible Commentary.* Louisville, KY: Westminster John Knox Press, 1998.

Osiek, Carolyn, and Margaret Y. MacDonald with Janet H. Tulloch. *A Woman's Place: House Churches in Earliest Christianity.* Minneapolis: Fortress Press, 2006.

Owens, Virginia Stem. *Daughters of Eve: Women of the Bible Speak to Women of Today.* Colorado Springs, CO: NavPress Publishing Group, 1995.

Pemberton, Delia. *The Atlas of Ancient Egypt.* New York: Harry N. Abrams, Inc., 2005.

Richards, Sue, and Larry Richards. *Every Woman in the Bible.* Nashville: Thomas Nelson, Inc., 1999.

Richards, Sue Poorman, and Lawrence O. Richards. *Women of the Bible: The Life and Times of Every Woman in the Bible.* Nashville: Thomas Nelson, Inc., 2003.

Roaf, Michael. *Cultural Atlas of Mesopotamia and the Ancient Near East.* Oxfordshire, England: Facts On File, Andromeda Oxford Limited, 1999.

Snell, Daniel C. *Life in the Ancient Near East.* New Haven, CT: Yale University Press, 1997.

Steele, Philip, and John Farndon. *Eyewitness Books: Mesopotamia.* New York: DK Publishing, 2007.

Tagholm, Sally. *Everyday Life in the Ancient World: A Guide to Travel in Ancient Times.* New York: Kingfisher, 2002.

Torstrick, Rebecca L. *Culture and Customs of Israel.* Westport, CT: Greenwood Press, 2004.

Triglio Jr., Rev. John, and Rev. Kenneth Brighenti. *Women in the Bible for Dummies.* Hoboken, NJ: Wiley Publishing Inc., 2005.

Trimiew, Anna. *Bible Almanac.* Lincolnwood, IL: Publications International Ltd., 1997.

Weiss, Sonia, with Lorna Biddle Rinear, M.A. *The Complete Idiot's Guide to Women's History.*

Indianapolis: BookEnds LLC, Alpha Books, 2002.
http://sabbathmeals.typepad.com/
http://soniclight.org
www.bible-history.com
www.bibleplus.org
www.christianodyssey.com
www.jesusfamilytomb.com
www.jewfaq.org
www.jewishencyclopedia.com
www.myjewishlearning.com
www.opendoorministrieswv.org/ancientjewishwedding.html
www.thetruthconnection.com
www.wikipedia.org

Section 2—Daily Experiences of Bible Women
(sources for this section are included in Section 1, "Women in Bible Times")

Section 3—Women's Roles and Jobs

Gardner, Paul D., ed. *New International Encyclopedia of Bible Characters: The Complete Who's Who in the Bible.* Grand Rapids: Zondervan Publishing House, 2001.

Kroeger, Catherine Clark, and Mary J. Evans, eds. *The InterVarsity Press Women's Bible Commentary.* Downers Grove, IL: InterVarsity Press, 2002.

Lockyer, Herbert. *All the Men of the Bible. All the Women of the Bible.* Grand Rapids: Zondervan Publishing House, 1996.

—*Life Application Bible.* New International Version. Grand Rapids: Zondervan Publishing House, 1991.

Meyers, Carol, ed. *Women in Scripture: A Dictionary of Named and Unnamed Women in the Hebrew Bible, the Apocryphal/Deuterocanonical Books, and the New Testament.* Boston: Houghton Mifflin Company, 2000.

Newsom, Carol A., and Sharon H. Ringe, eds. *Women's Bible Commentary with Apocrypha.* Expanded edition. Louisville, KY: Westminster John Knox Press, 1998.

Peloubet, F. N., ed. *Peloubet's Bible Dictionary.* Grand Rapids: Zondervan Publishing House, 1971.

Webber, Robert E., ed. *The Biblical Foundations of Christian Worship.* Nashville, TN: Star Song Publishers, 1993.

Section 4—Bible Women and Their Interactions with Men

Davis, Dale Ralph. *Judges: Such a Great Salvation.* CF4: Ross-Shire UK, 2007.

Hoerth, Alfred and John McRay. *Bible Archeology: An Explanation of the History and Culture of Early Civilizations.* Grand Rapids: Baker, 2006.

MacArthur, John. *Ruth & Esther: Women of Faith, Bravery & Hope.* Nashville: Thomas Nelson, 2000.

Rana, Fazale, and Hugh Ross. *Who Was Adam: A Creation Model Approach to the Origin of Man.* Colorado Springs, CO: NavPress, 2005.

Art Credits

Alinari / Art Resource, NY: 11

Bildarchiv Preussischer Kulturbesitz / Art Resource, NY: 17

Cameraphoto Arte, Venice / Art Resource, NY: 179, 216

Erich Lessing / Art Resource, NY: 66, 149, 176

Fotolia: 84, 88, 142, 151, 222

HIP / Art Resource, NY: 90

iStockphoto: vii, viii, 30, 33, 36, 40, 49, 51, 109, 110, 115, 124, 137, 150 (left), 191, 197, 211, 212, 219, 232

The Jewish Museum / Art Resource, NY: 67, 206

Library of Congress: 75, 81, 205

National Gallery, London / Art Resource, NY: 61, 64, 125

National Trust Photo Library / Art Resource, NY: 45

Nimatallah / Art Resource, NY: 165

Réunion des Musées Nationaux / Art Resource, NY: 34

Scala / Art Resource, NY: 12, 37, 120, 189, 204

Schoyen Collection: ix

The Trustees of the British Museum / Art Resource, NY: 192

UNICEF Iran, Mojgan Parssa-Magham: 13

U. S. Department of Defense: 112

Werner Forman / Art Resource, NY: 58

Whitehouse.gov / Eric Draper: 42

Whitehouse.gov / Shealah Craighead: 15

Wikimedia: 14, 29, 32, 41, 46, 48, 55, 60, 62, 68, 70, 71 (top), 72, 73, 77, 80, 85, 86, 87, 91, 92, 93, 95, 96, 98, 101, 102, 103, 111, 116, 117, 119, 128, 133, 138, 139, 141, 143, 145, 146, 147, 148, 150 (right), 152, 153, 154, 155, 156 (both), 157, 159, 161, 163, 166, 167 (left), 168, 172, 174, 175, 177, 178, 180, 184, 185, 186, 187, 188, 193, 194, 198, 203, 208, 214, 218, 220, 221, 223, 227, 231, 234, 235

Wikimedia / Andreas Praefcke: 200

Wikimedia / Andwhatsnext aka Nancy J. Price: 118

Wikimedia / Rita Banerji: 127

Wikimedia / Canwest News Service: 82

Wikimedia / Philippe Chavin: 217

Wikimedia / Delart: 170

Wikimedia / Steve Evans, Citizen of the World: 71 (bottom)

Wikimedia / Eric Gaba: 21

Wikimedia / Gryffindor: 169

Wikimedia / Yair Haklai: 162

Wikimedia / Matthewsharris: 225

Wikimedia / Jastrow: 69, 195

Wikimedia: Ji-Elle: 114

Wikimedia / Juan R. Cuadra: 31

Wikimedia / Kit36: 79

Wikimedia / Louis le Grand: 57

Wikimedia / Matthew Trump: 78

Wikimedia / Matthias Kabel: 121, 123

Wikimedia/ Milkbreath: 100

Wikimedia / Ian W. Scott: 190

Wikimedia / Shooting Brooklyn: 132

Wikimedia / Sir Kiss: 122

Wikimedia / Steerpike: 94

Wikimedia / Steve Evans: 71 (bottom)

Wikimedia / Xenon 77: 26

Wikimedia / Yoninah: 129

Wikimedia / The Yorck Project: 23, 56, 63, 104, 107, 167 (right), 171, 182, 209

Zev Radovan: 18, 20, 24, 28, 43, 53